Folklore of Highland County, Ohio

Folklore of Highland County, Ohio

VIOLET MORGAN

Commonwealth Book Company
St. Martin, Ohio
2019

Copyright © 1946 by Violet Morgan
Copyright © 2019 by Commonwealth Book Company, Inc.
All Rights Reserved
Printed in the United States of America

ISBN: 978-1-948986-14-4

Cover Photograph: View of Hillsboro from the College Building
Title Page Illustration: Hillsboro in 1846 by Henry Howe

This book is for the soldiers of Highland county, for those who gave their lives and for those who offered their lives "for God and country"; and especially, too, for all the children of Highland county.

Acknowledgment

WITHOUT the help of kind friends everywhere, some of whom are now dead, this book could never have been written.

Some loaned old scrap books, diaries, and church records; some wrote letters telling of incidents in their family history; some loaned pictures; some gave personal interviews and advice. Each and every one gave courage and inspiration; so the flavor of Highland County as an Ohio scene must surely be in the pages of this book, because of these contributing factors.

To all these Highland County people, to Milton Caniff who drew the cover picture and to Dr. Willis H. Hall, Professor of History, of Wilmington College, go my sincere thanks and my deep appreciation.

Table of Contents

CHAPTER ONE: INTRODUCTION TO HIGHLAND COUNTY
                              BEFORE THE BEGINNING OF LOCAL HISTORY   1
                              THE BEGINNING........................   2

CHAPTER TWO: GENERAL PICTURE
                              GEOGRAPHY AND TOPOGRAPHY............   3
                              BIRD AND PLANT LIFE..................   7
                              THE CLIMATE.........................   9

CHAPTER THREE: THE HIGHLAND COUNTY WILDERNESS
                              THE STORY OF THE MOUNDBUILDER....... 12
                              THE STORY OF THE INDIANS.............. 17
                              SOME INDIAN TALES................... 23

CHAPTER FOUR: THE WHITE MEN CAME
                              WHO THEY WERE...................... 31
                              WHAT THEY DID...................... 33

CHAPTER FIVE: THE COUNTY GREW
                              WHAT THE LAND HAS GIVEN US......... 54
                              OUR HOMES.......................... 59
                              OUR SCHOOLS........................ 64
                              OUR CHURCHES...................... 73
                              OUR ROADS.......................... 82

CHAPTER SIX: TRUTH-IS-STRANGER-THAN-FICTION
                     STORIES
    1. MOTHER THOMPSON..................... 89
    2. CASPAR COLLINS...................... 94
    3. JOHN WOOD GOES TO THE GOLD
         DIGGINGS.......................... 99
    4. HILLSBORO'S MYSTERY CHILD........... 114
    5. THE COMING OF THE FRENCH........... 116
    6. THE GIST SETTLEMENT................. 123
    7. ROBERT McKIMIE..................... 126
    8. THREE HILLSBORO BOYS "GO WEST"..... 136
    9. AMELIA'S GRANDFATHER GOES TO
         AFRICA............................ 138
   10. UNDERGROUND RAILROAD STATIONS....... 143
       GHOST TOWNS........................ 145

CHAPTER SEVEN: HIGHLAND COUNTY'S TOWNS AND
                 VILLAGES........................ ..

CHAPTER EIGHT: SOME INTERESTING PEOPLE............. 203
               CONGRESSMEN AND SENATORS 229
               TABLE OF POPULATION 229

BIBLIOGRAPHY 231

INDEX 235

Foreword

WHEN THE REVEREND SAMUEL HIBBEN, who became a chaplain in the United States Army during the Civil War, wrote, in 1859, to his brother, Joseph M. Hibben, owner of the Hibben Dry Goods Store in Hillsboro, the oldest store of its kind west of the Alleghenies, his letter was one of many letters typical of those written by cultured men and women in those days.

"I regret," he said, "the duties of life that have caused us to separate. I hope that the pursuit of happiness will not cause you to forget God, the Creator."

This, then, must be the reason for the urge that has been upon me to bring to print, "Folklore of Highland County." Not an attempt to improve upon nor ape past local histories, this book, rather, is merely another contribution to the history of Highland county, with additional historical facts not heretofore published, in the sincere hope that the history of this county as distinguished from the other 87 counties of Ohio may never be forgotten and may be retained for this and all the future generations.

CHAPTER ONE

BEFORE THE BEGINNING OF LOCAL HISTORY:

HERE, in southern Ohio, the trails linking us with the past grow dim and dimmer as they recede through Indian history, through the Moundbuilder Era, and vanish altogether in what scientists call the Ice Man Age. Beyond this we know nothing of the history of this section of the State, nor are we concerned. Our beginnings lie not here, but in some far distant land, generations and generations before our forefathers crossed the rolling waters, bound for America.

We are all of us familiar with the Indian history of Ohio. We know that French missionaries and traders were the first white men to discover Ohio's fertile land. We know that when Celeron floated down the beautiful Ohio in 1749, marking his course as he came by burying leaden, engraved plates at the mouths of all the rivers from the Muskingum to the Miami as he took possession for his king, the Shawnee and Miami Indians had already named these streams and claimed the land drained by them for their own.

We know that England disputed possession of this land because of charters granted Virginia by James the First, and that war between France and England was the inevitable result; that the sound of the gun broke the strange quiet of the wilderness that had been the kingdom of the Indian, the Moundbuilder, and the Ice Man. Historians have recorded this for us.

Interesting to us because we are a result of it, is the story of the flow of immigration that began about 1771 toward what is now Ohio, following the exploration of Kentucky by Daniel Boone and his companions. During the Indian hostilities in Kentucky, white men crossed at intervals through the Ohio forests to recover prisoners taken by the Indians, to make treaties with the red men, and to protect their trading posts. The beauty of this wild, virgin country was as a siren beckoning the adventurer and the explorer on to "greener pastures."

Virginia, who had laid further claim to this territory because of the conquests of General George Rogers Clark, 1778-1779, ceded to the United States her territory northwest of the Ohio River in 1784, but reserved the land lying between the Miami and Scioto Rivers. This land was called the Virginia Military District and was portioned to Revolutionary War soldiers as the Government's method of paying them for their services in the war.

Many of the soldiers did not want their lands and sold them to prospective settlers for about a dollar an acre. Free religion, Habeas

Corpus, property rights, just taxation, and no slavery were other special inducements held out as possible in the land beyond the Ohio River. A general rush began for the Ohio country.

Over the Alleghenies they came, English, Irish, Scotch, French, and Dutch, with their different religions and their different customs, all searching for illusive peace. By way of the national turnpike they poured in steady streams, the national turnpike that once had been merely an Indian trail.

Soon their log cabins dotted the forests. They were usually made square with a clapboard roof, one door, a puncheon floor and a cat-and-clay chimney. The logs were chinked with a plaster of mud and straw called daubing and fastened to it by wooden pegs. Windows, when there were any, were greased with bear's oil and were translucent. The baby's cradle was a hollowed, rockerless gum log.

The men wore leather hunting shirts, buckskin breeches, moccasins, and coonskin caps. After the importation of sheep and the raising of flax, the wool hat, linsey shirt, and cowhide shoe or brogan, took their places. Women wore linsey garments and went barefoot except on Sunday when they put on their woolen stockings and heavy shoes before reaching the meeting house. Little boys wore blue linsey shirts fringed with red and yellow. They wore tow-linen pants supported by galluses made of deer skin and secured with large waist band buttons at both front and back. Girls were dressed like their mothers.

THE BEGINNING:

WHEN that part of the Northwest Territory known as the Virginia Military District was being carved into states, it was in the year 1803 that Ohio came into being and was admitted into the Union. At first Ohio had but four counties, a small number compared to the 88 of today. Highland county was the 21st county organized and was created by an act passed by the general assembly February 18, 1805. It was cut out of Ross, Adams, and Clermont counties and lay in the southwestern part of Ohio, in a particularly fine section. The location of its high land between the Little Miami and Scioto Rivers gave it its name. When organized, there were four townships, Brushcreek, Fairfield, Liberty, and New Market.

The first county seat was New Market, 1805. A more centrally located site was sought by the legislature and Hillsboro was chosen for this honor in 1807.

The area of the county was made smaller in 1810 when Fayette and Clinton counties were formed and again in 1813 when more land was given Clinton. Highland county contains 549 square miles, or 346,307 acres. The population was 27,099 in 1940, dropping to an estimated 25,018 in November, 1944.

CHAPTER TWO

GEOGRAPHY AND TOPOGRAPHY:

HIGHLAND COUNTY is bounded on the north by Clinton and Fayette counties, on the east by Ross and Pike counties, on the south by Adams and Brown counties, and on the west by Brown and Clinton counties.

There are 17 townships: Brushcreek; Clay; Concord; Dodson; Fairfield; Hamer; Jackson; Liberty; Madison; Marshall; New Market; Paint; Penn; Salem; Union; Washington; White Oak.

The shapes and sizes of the townships are irregular because a soldier could locate his land wherever he pleased and because the Virginia Military District was not surveyed into townships until it was done in the different counties by order of the commissioners for civil purposes or organization.

After receiving his certificate of service, a soldier obtained a printed warrant from the land office. He then was allowed to select his own land. After surveying it, he returned to the officials and they gave him a deed for the chosen land from the Government.

It is claimed by some sources that the grapevine method of measuring was used in surveying the land by many soldiers, and that they naturally ran the lines to where there were springs and other supplies of water. Hence arose an old saying that "everything is crooked in Highland county but the people."

Seven incorporated towns, Greenfield, Highland, Hillsboro, Leesburg, Lynchburg, Mowrystown, and Sinking Spring, are surrounded by a number of smaller villages and hamlets. Hillsboro and Greenfield are the largest towns.

Limestone makes up the soil of Highland county except for deposits of phosphate rock in Brushcreek Township, asphalt rock in Willettville, some zinc north of Samantha, impure iron ore in the bed of Rocky Fork, and Clinton ore near Sinking Spring.

Good building stone is general throughout the county, but unsurpassed crops are found at Greenfield and south of Highland. Nodules of zinc-blend, silica, and asphaltum·are characteristic of the Greenfield stone. According to authorities, Highland county has the most even-bedded and best building stone in the state. Quarrying has become an important industry and lime is a product of the waste. Greenfield, Leesburg, and Highland regions lie in a superior lime belt.

Highland county rocks include some of the lowest and oldest in Ohio and all the divisions of rocks are represented here, with the greatest rock formation in Ohio lying in the southeastern part of the county and the northern and eastern parts of Adams county.

Hillsboro is in the sandstone region which terminates at Hillsboro, and is noted for its dominant corals, the honey-comb and the chain. Interesting, too, is the junction of slate and limestone at Sinking Spring and the various limestones, slates, and sandstones. Crumbling limestone in and around Sinking Spring is used there in farming lands and in road making.

Many fossils were found in Highland county, especially in the deep valleys of the western and southern parts; and are found today as covering on stone. Jacob Saylor, born in Hillsboro in 1837, collected some of the finest and most valuable fossils ever found in Ohio. Once, wading in Clear Creek, he found a chunk of crystallized carbon that was pronounced a diamond at first. Had it not been for some defect in the crystallization, it is believed that it would have been worth a fortune. Mr. Saylor's collection, which was purchased by the Ohio Archaeological and Historical Society in 1912, contained brachiopods, corals, chrysoprases, and tourmalines.

The part rolling, part level surface of the county lies in the southern limit of the great glacial formation that once came to rest here and its movement and its disintegration wrought miraculous changes. The strata dipping consistently west and north discloses not only fertile valleys but barren land. Blue clay is the oldest drift deposit and forms the base of the rock deposits. The first trees were cedar, beech, and sycamore.

Geologists have divided the surface of Highland county into five well-defined sections: hilly parts; low-lying and poor lands; low lands varying in fertility; plateaus; highlands.

The highest altitudes are on the eastern border of Brushcreek Township where the hills are mountainous. Next to Richland and Logan counties this is the highest land in the state. Chestnut and oak trees predominate. Some of the highest elevations are:

    Washburn Hill ....1334 feet
    Stults Mountain ....1325 feet
    Long Lick Mountain ....1323 feet
    Reed's Hill ....1321 feet
    McCoppin's Hill ....1314 feet
    Fisher's Knob ....1300 feet
    Bald Mountain or Slate Knob.............1250 feet
    Fort Hill ....1232 feet
    Rapid's Forge ....1160 feet
Other elevations in the county are:
Cemetery Hill (*Quaker Hill*),
    near Samantha ....1214 feet
High School hill, Hillsboro................1140 feet
Court House, Hillsboro.....................1132 feet
Samantha...................................1124 feet

Children's Home, Hillsboro ....1095 feet
Haggerty's hill, U. S. Route 50, east........1047 feet

The low-lying, poor lands are in Dodson, Salem, Clay, Hamer, and White Oak Townships, where there is a general level of from 930 to 1030 feet above the sea and where the land is covered heavily with clays.

Low lands varying in fertility are in the townships of Marshall, western half of Brushcreek, eastern half of Jackson, and the northern half of Paint. This section descends to an elevation of less than 1000 feet above sea level, and has almost barren land as well as fine farm land.

Hillsboro is on a summit of one of the plateaus in the plateau region which includes Union, Liberty, New Market, Washington, Concord, and Jackson Townships. There are rich soils and barren uplands here; valuable farm land and cliff-limestone soils on slopes and hills suitable to fruit growing.

The highlands lie in the northern part of the county and some of this land is higher than that of the plateau section. Penn, Fairfield, Madison, and the northern part of Paint Township compose this high, level land. Here are found the best farm lands and the best quarries; and such picturesque features as the Seven Caves.

The Seven Caves were formed, geologists say, by the combined force of erosion of underground streams and a chemical action of carbonic acid gas exerted upon the Niagara limestone. There are 34 openings all told in the rocks, and the passages have a range from 10 feet to 1000 feet.

Forming a natural scenic park, this region has been a favorite place for swimming, fishing, picnicking, and summering, from earliest days. Once settlers went there on horseback and on foot; later they went in buggy and "hack"; now they go in automobiles, in no time at all.

Two thousand feet of subterranean passages lie along three trails: The Cave-Canyon Trail; The Palisades Trail; The Indian Trail. The time it takes to follow them is about three hours.

There are five closely-grouped caves on the Cave-Canyon Trail. These are: Witches' Cave; Cave of the Springs (Wet Cave); Phantom Cave; Dancing Cave; Bear Cave.

The entrance of the largest cave, The Cave of the Springs, is 175 feet long, 65 feet wide, and 28 feet high. A miniature lake called Jade Spring, lies 600 feet in from the entrance. Pioneers believed that this spring was bottomless. Branching off to the right is a narrow, twisting passage 500 feet long, which terminates in *"the crystal room."*

The Dancing Cave received its name from the first settlers who were said to have held dances there and to have used the stalagmite along the walls as seats.

The Palisades Trail, which begins at Echo Point, borders, as the name implies, along the palisades that sentinel Rocky Fork creek. From this lofty point, the creek needles its graceful way through the limestone, below, as it flows towards Paint creek. Revealed from this point is the Rocky Fork gorge, largest gorge in Ohio, bordered by majestic, centuries-old trees and cliffs. There are grottoes, glens, gulches, and small *"caves"*; and beyond Camel's Back rock is the McKimie Cave where Robert McKimie, notorious outlaw, hid years ago among the creeping cave spiders and the rare cave-camel crickets, and where sympathizers came to smuggle food to him.

The Marble Cave on this trail is regarded by some as the most beautiful cave of all. It receives its name from its resemblance to marble and to the small stalagmite formations resembling marbles found here that small boys always have loved to collect.

The Indian Trail meanders softly through spreading trees and wild flowers, leading us through leafy Gypsy Glenn in the cup of a cliff, and over a quaint, rustic bridge. Farther on, at Hemlock Point, we look down on the rapids and the big gorge. Far above us, we look up at Etnah woods, where so many years ago, wigwams and camp fires captured the scene. An Indian ford is at the riffle above a pool in which are interesting rock formations.

This park contains 100 acres filled with miracles wrought by the hands of time and nature. In a botanical survey of the grounds made by William Bridge Cooke, naturalist, in 1934, over 250 kinds of plants and 60 kinds of trees, were identified. Many rare specimens are among these. Birds find havens here.

Four streams and their tributaries drain Highland county; the East Fork, draining to the Miami River; White Oak, draining to the Ohio River; Brush Creek, draining to the Ohio; and Rocky Fork, draining to the Scioto. These water systems form the main watershed and natural drainage trends southeasterly. The water break is through the central part.

Rattlesnake Creek, a large tributary of Paint Creek, drains the northeastern part of the county and also forms the northeastern border of the county. This stream with its tributaries, Lees and Hardin, is an important part of the geography of the northern section. At East Monroe, the waters of Rattlesnake rush over rapids, drop 21 feet into a deep basin and ripple over a rough bed through a narrow, rocky gorge. Miniature Rocky Fork gorges are found elsewhere throughout Highland county, adding to the county's natural beauty.

The first settlements were made along these streams because the soil was productive and rich. Fishing was good, and grist and wool-carding mills flourished. The settlers were attracted by the abundant springs and by salt licks where springs spread their salty deposits upon the surfaces and offered supplies of needed salt to pioneers and animals.

Good fishing waters abounding in small-mouthed bass, rock bass, catfish, and crappies, are Lees, Rocky Fork, Rattlesnake, and Paint creeks.

BIRD AND PLANT LIFE
OF HIGHLAND COUNTY

MISS KATIE ROADS, one of the 11 persons in the State of Ohio, whose migration records are filed with the department of agriculture and whose reports and bird migration records are also sent in to the Ohio State University, has gained an enviable reputation for her knowledge of birds and findings concerning birds found in this part of the state.

When a young girl it was my privilege to take a nature study trip with Miss Roads along the creek on the Belfast pike. Hidden in the bushes, we listened to the music of the birds and watched them all the warm, bright summer afternoon. I had never known before that there are so many different kinds of birds and plant life.

In 1940, Miss Roads was interviewed by a reporter for the local papers. She wrote two brief reports on her findings which were published in the News-Herald and Press-Gazette, which are herewith reprinted:

HIGHLAND COUNTY FLORA IS LISTED

Three Plant Areas Here, Local Writer Avers —
46 Plants Recorded Here

by KATIE M. ROADS

HIGHLAND COUNTY, unlike any other county in the state, is divided into three distinct and separate plant areas. The southeastern one-fourth of the county occupies the area in the eastern unglaciated area of the Allegheny plateau, which probably owes much of its peculiar floristic composition to past physiographic conditions and changes produced by the glaciers to the northwest, reversing much of the drainage." This condition accounts for a large number of southeastern and southern Appalachian species. The western half of the county is in the Illinois glaciated area. Here are found the Sweet Gum and Lyre-leaf Sage. One-fourth of the area, in the north, belongs to the area known as the Miami region. This region occupies about two-thirds of the western area of the state. It is mostly composed of beech forests, some oak forest, and in some parts prairies prevail.

Thus far 2488 species have been collected in the state. Of these

576 are of general distribution. 566 have been reported from less than five counties. Of the 455 native rare plants of the state, thus far 46 have been collected in Highland County.

The Darlington Spurge grows on a steep hillside on the Henry Dunlap farm, Liberty Township, and thus far this is the only place in the state where it has been observed. The False Aloe, a close relative of the Century Plant, grows in a cliff wood lot in New Market Township. Thousands of these plants occur in all stages of growth, a small transplanted part of the southland.

Among the native plants that would ornament any garden might be mentioned Turk's Cap Lily, Purple Cone Flower, the Illinois.

Acuans, a member of the sensitive family, with dense white flowering balls followed by a ball of twisted pods and two common plants, Virginia Cowslip and large flower Trillium might also be mentioned.

An interesting group of native plants are the parasites including the coral-roots, a member of the orchid family by three species; the broom-rape, with three; the naked Broomrape; Squawroot and Beech-drops, all of beech woods; the dodders, masses of low twining vines with dense masses of small flowers.

When the collector finds a new or a rare plant, he can't but ask the question from whence it came and how it was transported. One of the most prolific sources of distribution is along the railroad tracks. New species occurring are Rough Rush-grass, Mealy Lambsquarter, Red Hempnettle Garlic, small flowered Hawk and rare Erect Hedge Parsley, Perfoliate Penny Cress, Cylindric Blazingstar and Hoary Berteroa.

Our earliest flower is the Harbinger of Spring, a small lacy plant with small white flowers. The brown tipped flower to which is given the name of Pepper and Salt appears in mid-February or the first of March and there is a succession of bloom throughout the season only ended by the autumn frosts which kill the Golden Rods, fall Asters, and late Sunflowers.

SUMMARY ON LOCAL BIRDS

THE BIRD population depends upon suitable nesting places. With the disappearance of the woods, the shrub pastures and the tangled fence rows, the frequenters of these places will go elsewhere. And add to this another factor, the indiscriminate destruction of our hawks and owls. Only the eastern Sparrow Hawk and eastern Screech Owl are here in any numbers. Formerly the Red-tailed and Red-shouldered Hawks were common.

Today they are seen as rare migrants. Our migration records are always variable as we are on the outer edge of the great Mississippi flyway. One year one specie may be common and the next entirely wanting. Some migrants pass directly through while others tarry awhile.

The residents are our best known and most common birds.

They are: Hawks, Eastern Bobwhite, Eastern Mourning Dove, Owl family, Woodpecker family, Prairie Horned Lark, Northern Blue Jay, Eastern Crown, Blackcapped Chickadee, Tufted Titmice, Bewick Wren, Carolina Wren, Eastern Mocking Bird, Eastern Cardinal and Mississippi Song Sparrow.

Introduced residents: Ringnecked Pheasants, European Partridge, English Sparrow and Starling.

In a mild winter may be added the less hardy birds such as Bluebird, Meadowlarks and Mourning Doves. During any warm spell in winter there is a marked increase in the number of these birds, showing that some of them winter only a few hundred miles to the south.

Milton B. Trautman in a revised list of the birds of Ohio in 1932 lists 336 birds as occurring in the state. Of these 181 are known to breed.

Thus far only 100 have been found in Highland county. One of these is extinct, the Passenger Pigeon. We all know the Pigeon Roost Road. During migrations at one time the millions obscured the sun. They roosted in a woods on the late D. S. Roads farm. The numbers in a tree were so great as to bend the limbs to the ground or break them off. The Wild Turkey was formerly plentiful in the county but is not found in Ohio. The Ruffed Grouse and the Greater Prairie Chicken were also earlier residents.

Two very interesting birds are the Black Vulture nesting in the cliffs of Washington Township and the Bachman Sparrow, nesting in Washington Township and Liberty Township.

The sunny south has lent us two of her gaily colored birds, the Baltimore Oriole and Summer Tanager. The birds range in size from the Gt. Blue Heron to the Ruby-throated Humming bird.

Soon it will be migration time and I will vie with 340 others of America for a new species or an earlier migration record. Migration is a full year's work.

THE CLIMATE:

HIGHLAND COUNTY has a variable and temperate climate, its seasons often marked by extremes of heat and cold, and favorable for the raising of farm crops and fruit.

Often the spring comes late and is followed by a short, hot summer, a long, colorful autumn, and late winter. In the summer and spring seasons, hills and valleys rival any of the loveliest mountain regions in the United States.

Severe wind and hail storms and killing frosts are the exception but there are often late and early frosts. Frosts usually come later here than in the surrounding country because of the county's high elevation and this factor, too, affects the changing seasons.

The hardest winds usually come from the southwest and the east. A wind storm in 1933 did considerable damage in and around Hillsboro. A few years previous, a destructive wind storm struck Hamer and Salem Townships. Careytown experienced a bad hail storm in 1934. A cyclonic wind storm in 1942 wrought havoc in and around New Petersburg.

There have been extremes of temperatures at intervals throughout the county's history. In 1856, according to the town weatherman, Rev. J. McDowell Matthews, who for over 40 years had taken daily observations of the weather for the Smithsonian Institute, and who was conceded to have *"the most correct instruments in town,"* announced that January 9 of that year was the coldest it had been since 1833. The temperature, he said, was 18 degrees below.

Twenty-three years later, in 1879, local newspapers stated that it was the coldest it had been for 81 years. Thermometers fell to from 20 to 24 degrees below zero. *"We hear of a great many cases of frosted feet, hands and ears, and there is a rumor that two horses were frozen to death a short distance west of town on Friday."*

Then, a year later, almost to the day, comes this announcement: January 8, 1880: *"Last Saturday was a remarkable day for January. The grass in the yards looked as bright and green almost as in spring. The sun shone warm and pleasant, and doors and windows were thrown open in the afternoon to let in a breath of the balmy air. Then, as Rev. Kendall said in his Thanksgiving sermon, that if you wanted to live in a climate where you couldn't tell what the weather would be from one day to the next, you would find it in Highland county, — on the Sunday night following this remarkable Saturday, after another balmy day, "presto change!" down went the mercury to 18 above zero, or 14 below freezing point! A change of 42 degrees in 24 hours!"*

Another record claims that in 1833, thermometers dipped to 22 degrees below zero. Then, in close parallel to these previous records of cold weather, are the bitter, snowy winter of 1917 and the cold spells of December, 1935, and January, 1936. The sub-zero weather was continuous for days, causing suffering and sickness, and a cessation of county activities.

It is interesting to recall that coasting, ice skating, sleighing, and sled parties, once leading winter sports in this county, seem to have been consigned to past history, due to climatic conditions.

The hottest summer of recent years was that of **1936**. The county, at the eastern edge of the worst damaged region in Ohio, suffered a terrible drought when gardens and crops were completely lost.

The summer of 1944 found the county sweltering in another such drought, with June 17 and 18 a record two-day heat wave of high temperature and humidity. Sunday, June 18, was believed to have been the hottest June 18 ever on record, with the mercury climbing to 100 degrees. Late Sunday night cooling breezes brought relief to sleepless citizens, but the drought continued. Rain clouds passed over the town intermittently. On July 9, about seven o'clock in the evening, a gentle rain fell softly for a few seconds as though it were being shaken from a noiseless, giant sifter in the heavens. The rain stopped as suddenly as it had begun. The water supply became serious, grass browned and died, gardens dried up, and leaves hung yellowing and lifeless on the trees. The old saying, *"People don't pay their preachers,"* went the rounds, but it did not seem much of a joke, the situation had become so critical. Residents claimed that the thermometers on their porches registered as high now and then, as 104 degrees. At last, on July 12, in the afternoon, after mild threats of rain during the day, a healing rain fell lightly upon the thirsty soil.

According to Frank Brouse, local official weather man, the average yearly rainfall is 40.37", with few exceptions. During the rainy seasons, which we often experience, the streams are swollen, but only small surfaces are inundated.

Mr. Brouse says that the normal yearly snow fall is 27.9" and that the least snow fall he has ever recorded was that of February, 1934, when the average was less than 1".

CHAPTER THREE

THE STORY OF THE MOUND BUILDERS:

VEILED in mystery is the story of the strange race of men called Mound Builders who once dwelled in Highland county, so-called because of the burial mounds they left behind them. The mounds, earthworks, and sites of ancient villages, were the first human remains discovered in the county.

Edwin H. Davis, born in Hillsboro in 1811, became intrigued by the wealth of these remains and commenced the exploration, drawing, and mapping of them. Although when he was grown he studied medicine and became a physician, he continued his hobby. Daniel Webster, in 1833, had heard the youth deliver an address on archaeology, at Kenyon College, and encouraged him in his work. Davis later was to become one of the most noted archaeologists of all time.

Mr. Davis practiced medicine in Chillicothe from 1838 until 1850. Together, with another archaeologist, E. G. Squier, he continued exploring and recording mounds. Then, as Squier and Davis, they produced a valuable record of the ancient mounds in Ohio, which made both famous.

A more complete picture of the Mound Builder period would have been preserved for us had settlers recognized the historical value of these relics, like Squier and Davis. Mound Builder relics were everywhere, proving that these people loved our hills and valleys. No effort was made by settlers to preserve the relics on their farm lands and thus, today, in all, there are only about 35 mounds and remains of potteries and 61 earthworks remaining in the county, most of these in Salem and Clay Townships. One of the largest mounds existing is the one near Belfast which has not been completely explored. It is the scene of the last Indian-White skirmish in the county.

One of the leading archaeologists of the United States is Dr. Frank C. Hibben, son of Fred and Lucy West Hibben, natives of Hillsboro. Dr. Hibben, who is a professor in the University of New Mexico at Albuquerque, started his archaeological work in Ohio, his early work including excavations of the Seip Mound near Bainbridge, Ohio and excavations in northern counties along the shores of Lake Erie.

He wrote, *"A Preliminary Study of the Mountain Lion," "Excavation of Riana Ruin and Chama Valley Survey," "Excavation of*

Tse Tso," "*Early Evidences of Occupation in Sandia Cavern, New Mexico,*" and "*The Lost Americans.*"

Dr. Henry Shetrone, Director of the Museum of the Ohio Archaeological and Historical Society, and a famous Ohio archaeologist and historian said that "*scientists agreed that the first inhabitants of North America came after the last glacial drift but disagreed as to when it was; that some place it 15,000 years ago and some 30,000 years ago. It is believed that they came from Asia by way of the Bering Strait and were Mongoloids; that these were the ancestors of what we know as American Indians and all of the inhabitants of North America were Indians until the white man came.*"

Dr. Shetrone says that it is vain to attempt to differentiate between the various tribes because the Toltecs, Aztecs, and Incas all sprang from the same racial source.

He says, moreover, that there were Mound Builders in all of the States east of the Mississippi, except the New England States, and that excavations of the mounds and earthworks have disclosed three groups: Hopewell; Adena; Fort Ancient. Of these groups, the Hopewell Mound Builders were the most civilized and the most advanced in aesthetics, knowing something of exact science for their towns and mounds were laid off geometrically. The Adenas came second. After them came the Fort Ancient Mound Builders who comprised the lowest group. However, they are believed to have been the hardiest. To this last group belong the Indians who built Highland county's Fort Hill and the surrounding mounds. Authorities have called them the "*first Ohioans.*"

When the mounds were excavated and corn and tobacco both were disclosed, we knew to whom we are indebted for these gifts to mankind.

Of the mounds found in Highland county, the Cooper mound near Leesburg was probably the most interesting ever explored. Jeptha and Daniel Johnson and George Upp, of Charlestown, Clarke county, were the first to open it and bring to light a woven fabric which was like that unearthed a short time before in Ross county. The mound was reopened in 1879. In Williams Brothers "*History of Ross and Highland counties,*" the findings were recorded:

"*It was originally a symmetrical and beautiful mound, probably from 100 to 120 feet in diameter and 25 to 30 feet high. It was found to have regularly stratified composition. The first layer was three feet of loam. Next came 10 to 12 feet of hard, compact clay showing in some places the effect of intense heat. Then came three or four feet of ashes, charcoal, calcined bones and fragments of wood, which, when removed, disclosed a thin layer of a plaster-like substance containing skeletons of five humans, stone tools, ornaments, etc. These skeletons lay with the skulls together and the feet wide* apart which suggested the form of a star or spokes in a wheel. At the feet of the tall skeleton of a woman about seven feet long, were found awl or needle-shaped bone or horn implements and close by three copper bracelets. It was claimed that pearl-like necklaces were also found around her neck.

"To the east of this group a few feet away was another skeleton shrouded in a plaited rough fabric made in three plaits each a half inch in diameter and gathered at the edges with a large cord. It was in a wooden case and all was highly carbonized. Under this outer covering was another which was similar to our ordinary coffee sacking except that the warp was about one half inch apart. There were 15 more layers graduating in fineness until the last layer which was the finest of all. It bound the body. It appeared that the folds of the cloth started from the chin downward until the body was shrouded."

Several ancient camps or sites of villages were located when plowed land brought to light discolored soil, ashes, and cinders. Some of these camps were found in Washington Township and one a short distance south of Fort Hill.

Among the relics plowed up on farms and placed in museums were: bits of charcoal; remains of a brick kiln; a kiln for burning pottery; bits of coarse pottery; a stone spool covered with hieroglyphics; axes; javelin heads; mastodon teeth; arrow heads; fleshers; pestles; human bones; tomahawks; stone cairns used in religious ceremonies.

An earthwork known as Fort Salem because of its location in Salem Township, has a large mound in the center about nine feet high and on its southeast edge, a small mound. It is believed that a double mound had been planned or that the mounds were a part of the fort.

No more eloquent remains of the Mound Builder may be found anywhere than Fort Hill, the best preserved stone fort in Ohio, located 17 miles southeast of Hillsboro and three miles north of Sinking Spring.

Rising 500 feet above the bed of the East Fork of Brush Creek which washes its base north and west as it cuts its meandering way through a deep gorge of Niagara limestone, this 1232-foot long mountain known as Fort Hill, stands. It is crowned with cathedrals of trees and can be picked out easily from a distance, from the surrounding peaks, by its flat top. It overlooks one of the wildest sections in Ohio, where Highland, Pike, and Adams counties meet. The Fort Hill area contains, approximately, 1000 acres.

Fort Hill is in an excellent state of preservation and has remained virtually untouched by civilization. Inside the fortification is the site of the village in which these first Ohioans lived, and a stone quarry from which it is believed the earth used in constructing Serpent Mound was taken.

Timber covers the great hill and there is a tract of land enclosed by the fort on which is the largest and finest stand of virgin timber left in Ohio. There is Ohio's finest stand of chestnuts. There are hickory groves, oaks, beeches, and tulip poplars centuries old.

South of the hill, where there are important earthworks, circle, mounds, and burials, and just beyond the Mechlin homestead, a settlement named Lincoln sprang up, in the fore part of the 1800's. Attracted by the trees, settlers came to establish a thriving tanning industry.

Chestnut oaks were numerous and the bark from these trees was stripped or peeled in the spring and seasoned. After the bark was dried, it was crushed and then mixed with water in large vats, ready for the tanning process. Business was so good that hides were shipped in from other places.

The top of Fort Hill is an almost level plateau of 35 acres. It has a sharp descent and is excavated around the brink. The ditch formed by the excavation is nearly 50 feet thick at the base and from 10 to 20 feet high. It is 8582 feet long, and contains 50,000 cubic yards of material. Thirty-three gateways range in width from 10 to 15 feet and are irregularly arranged; the inside ditches of 11 of them are filled up.

Our own Hugh Fullerton vividly describes Fort Hill and boyhood experiences, in a story published in the Columbus Dispatch:

"*Brush creek carves its way around the base of the hill, and cuts a gorge hundreds of feet deep, for more than five miles of scenic grandeur. The hill itself is roughly a figure eight, with one loop much smaller than the other. The sides of the hill are extremely steep, and show evidence of having been scraped down to add to the steepness. There are more than 30 entrances to the fort, and eight curving roadways may be traced up its sides to eight main gates. The main gates were, at the time the fort was built, formed after the manner of Roman gateways, entering the enclosure in a right angle turn — the only gateways found that were so built that an enemy, striving to rush a gateway, would have to turn a sharp corner without knowing what force defended it.*

"*The fort itself is built of weathered limestone, in blocks and sheets, stones piled one on another. At places the stone work is 35 feet high and conforms with the slant of the hill. At others, the masonry is only a few feet high.*

"*The interior of the fort is on two levels, the main plateau being almost flat, as if graded. A break separates the two sections of the fort, and when I was a boy, the remains of a spare stone citadel stood in the center, on the line of this cliff, which is 10 to 12 feet high.*

"*Inside the walls is a wide ditch, following the outline of the stonework, and back of that a second level, or bench, narrow and evidently used by the archers or spear throwers, shooting or throw-*

ing over the heads of the rock rollers, in the ditch. Evidently the main defense consisted of rolling huge boulders down the steep sides of the hill.

"There was a storage basin for water inside the fort, traces of which remain.

"When I was a kid of twelve or thereabouts, Harvard University was interested in preservation of the ancient monuments in Ohio, and especially in the Serpent Mound and Fort Hill. Harvard really saved the Serpent which was being destroyed by plowing as was the great circle a few miles from it in Adams county. Nathaniel Massie (son of the pioneer Nathaniel) who was 80 years old, hired me and his grandson to carry chain and rod, while he surveyed the fort. We spent weeks on the hilltop, cutting brush and running lines — and nothing was done about saving it until the Ohio Archaeological Society and Representative Albert Daniels got busy and have now succeeded in buying a large part of the fort and are proceeding to condemn the other holdings to save it from being exploited commercially.

"In the gorge still exist evidences of cliff dwelling, and cave dwelling, and out in the valley, are two untouched mounds, one a "chocolate drop," the other one of the mysterious circles which abound in Ohio. The country is wide, and scarcely touched by civilization. Long ago, there was a tradition that an early settler found an "idol" made of solid copper in his fields and beat it to pieces with an ax, rather than have a "heathen image" on the farm."

Dr. Shetrone states that Fort Hill is second only to Fort Ancient as the greatest example of the work of this group of Mound Builders. He says that this people selected high hills with flat tops and steep sides for their homes, places practically impregnable against attack by their enemies; also that the earthworks on Fort Hill when inhabited, had large poles close together, with sharp points to prevent the entrance of their enemies.

Almost all of the land has been purchased now by the State.

A CCC camp was located here, a few years ago, and two projects were successfully completed. One project was for the purpose of the arrangement of the state park and reforestation. Trails were marked, wells of good drinking water drilled, outdoor furnaces built, and a shelter house constructed of native sandstone from the top of nearby Butler Hill. Grouse was released in the forested sections. The second project was soil conservation. Gullies were filled, a driveway made, and trees were posted. Many other improvements added to, without spoiling or disturbing in any way, the natural beauty of this wildwood park.

A sign at the entrance of the park reads:

THIS AREA INCLUDES 800 ACRES UPON WHICH IS LOCATED FORT HILL, A PREHISTORIC HILLTOP DEFENSIVE EARTHWORK ENCLOSING ABOUT 55

ACRES. THE EARTHWORK OF THIS FORT WHICH FOLLOWS THE EDGES OF THE HILLTOP IS MORE THAN ONE MILE LONG. BAKER'S FORK OF BRUSH CREEK SKIRTS THE NORTH AND WEST EDGES OF THE HILL AND HAS CARVED A DEEP GORGE WHICH CONTAINS TWENTY PLANT AND ROCK FORMATIONS.

"These counties," Clark B. Firestone says, in an article, "*Into the Ohio Wilderness*," published in the Times Star, in 1938, and referring to this section of Ohio, "*are sui generis. They continue, and conclude, the long sweep of the Kentucky knobs, also known throughout their oxbow stretch into three states as Muldraugh's Hill, after a legendary eighteenth century Irishman who may never have existed. In this area, bordering the Serpent Mound, is a district of township size, where some strange upthrust and subsidence has made a record of geological changes, which is a pocket edition of the entire story of the Appalachians. In this area, also, is a genuine prairie, and flowers to match; a region in which northern and southern plants grow together; one of the last surviving stands of virgin forest; the ancient watering place of Mineral Springs; the great aboriginal monuments of Serpent Mound and Fort Hill; a Southern hill-billy population, hill-billy place names, squirrel hunters who can hit things with muzzle-loading rifles. . . . . .*

"*Also, there are old mills and covered bridges. We halted at one place where there were both. This was Beaver Mills on the Rocky Fork of Paint Creek. We were beyond the divide, for Paint, a small river which gets its name from colored clays on its banks out of which the Indians made pigments, enters the Scioto at Chillicothe.*

"*I did not know that there was anything so romantic and quite so wild this side of the Great Smokies or the heart of Kentucky's deepest Cumberlands. . . . . . .*"

A. THE STORY OF THE INDIANS

ALTHOUGH bands of Shawnee Indians dwelled along the streams of Highland county, there are conflicting beliefs as to where they originated. A general consensus of opinion is that they formerly belonged to nomadic tribes which roved from Florida to Kentucky and that they claimed foreign origin. They composed one of the five tribes occupying and struggling for possession of, early Ohio soil, — the Shawnees, Wyandots, Delawares, Mingoes, and Miamis.

The trails that the Indians made radiated to salt licks, springs, camping, and hunting grounds. They made a fascinating pattern of embryo roads for the white settlers to choose from when they appeared upon the scene. Many of these trails became the traces for our roads.

Because of Indian outrages against the encroaching whites in Kentucky, the Governor of Kentucky employed brave scouts and spies known as "border soldiers" to traverse the frontier country for the purpose of protecting the lives and property of the settlers.

Historians tell us that the Highland county Shawnees were continually moving up and down country between Lake Erie and the Ohio River, driven by bitter cold, or hunger, or in pursuit of the invading white or red foe. Our county was one of their favorite hunting grounds and a large encampment on the site of Lynchburg was not abandoned until 1806. Other encampments were near Greenfield and Leesburg. The Indians were for the most part friendly and peaceful. There were but two battles between them and the white newcomers. The trouble arose over horses, so valuable to both Indians and whites, and which the latter claimed had been stolen from them.

Historians differ as to the exact scene of the first conflict, and to other details as well, some placing the scene near Williamsburg, in Clermont county, near a salt lick, but Indians, authorities say, do not as a rule, settle near salt licks. Evidence proves the fact that it occurred on the southeast bank of the East Fork of the Little Miami River, on the Donald Prickett farm, ¼ mile south of Lynchburg on State Route 134, *"around a little prairie."*

On this farm, once owned by William Gibler, human remains were unearthed, "bullet-scarred trees and bullets or musket balls deep-bedded in the trees, an Indian tomahawk lying in the path of the retreating whites, marks of camp fires; all were mute evidences of a battle. What were claimed to have been the bones of McIntyre, one of the white men killed by the Indians, were found months later, and buried. The figure of an Indian in war dress, holding a tomahawk, was carved on the bark of a beech tree, and under it deep notches thought to have represented the number killed in the battle, and short notches the ones wounded.

A Revolutionary Trail marker placed on US 62, near Samantha, northeast of Lynchburg, asserts:

"NINE MI. W., KENTON AND A PARTY OF KENTUCKIANS OVERTOOK A MARAUDING BAND OF INDIANS, UNDER TECUMSEH, AND ENGAGED THEM IN BATTLE WITH INDECISIVE RESULTS, IN MARCH, 1792."

Benjamin Drake, in his *"Life of Tecumseh,"* says: *"It seems that some horses had been stolen by the Indians from the settlers in Mason county, Kentucky, and a party of whites, consisting of 36 men, and including Simon Kenton, Whiteman, McIntyre, Downing, Washburn, Calvin, Ward, Barr, and a number of thoroughly-experienced woodsmen, immediately set out in pursuit of the depredators. The trail of the Indians being taken, it was found that they had crossed the Ohio, just below the mouth of Lees Creek, which was reached by the whites toward evening. The river was crossed by the pursuing party at night, and in the morning, they again took the trail. Twelve of the men gave out, and on the succeeding morning were permitted to return."*

Late that day, the remaining 24 men neared the Indian camp, guided by bells they heard on grazing Indian horses. Kenton and three others went ahead to spy. A lone Indian, riding towards them, was shot and killed. Knowing that other Indians must be near, one of the scouts who preceded Kenton a short distance, returned to tell him that they were close now to the camp.

The men stealthily crept back to their party where Kenton stationed them in a breastwork of leaves and branches against the rainy weather and in preparation for an emergency attack.

Then Kenton and a scout proceeded back through the drizzling rain towards the Indian encampment which, they discerned, was made up of tents and marquees. They saw, too, that they were greatly outnumbered by the enemy, perhaps as many as four Indians to one white. The Indians from all appearances, were awaiting the return of the Indian who had been killed by one of Kenton's men a short time before.

The two men turned back and rejoined their company and all prepared to move against the Indians.

Some accounts claim that the men were grouped into three detachments, each group composed of four men, with Kenton commanding the right detachment, McIntyre the center, and Downing the left. Other accounts claim that there were two divisions and that Calvin led the upper division and Kenton the lower. But it is agreed that the plan was to move forward simultaneously and to attack when they heard firing from Kenton's detachment, also that the hour for attack should be midnight.

In plain sight of the camp now, an Indian dog, spying them, sprang in their direction, baying. Then an Indian appeared. He spoke to the dog and came cautiously toward the spot where the hidden watchers had their rifles ready to fire. Then Calvin, Scott's History relates, raised his own rifle and shot the Indian as he was silhouetted against the camp fire.

"*A heavy fire now commenced from the Indian camp, which was returned with equal spirit by the whites, but without much effect on either side. Trees were barked very plentifully, dogs bayed, the Indians yelled, the whites shouted, the squaws screamed, and a prodigious uproar was maintained for about 15 minutes, when it was reported to Calvin that Kenton's party had been overpowered, and was in full retreat.*

"*It seems that both sides were equally frightened by the other, with the outnumbered whites fleeing in panic. Some fled upon their own horses, others mounted those of their friends. A sad confusion of property took place, and to their great terror, a few were compelled to return on foot.*"

McIntyre's heroic but rash act of turning aside from the main route of retreat and returning to the breastwork for flour and venison left behind, met with tragedy. He was followed by Indians who overtook, tomahawked and scalped him. McIntyre was the second white killed, Barr having been killed in action. Fourteen Indians were killed and 17 wounded.

Until late the next day, the Indians continued their pursuit of the whites but finally gave up the chase. Kenton and his men were three days getting back to Limestone (Maysville) and for two days they were without food.

White prisoners released and returned to Kentucky following the peace treaty of 1795, told that the Indians at Lynchburg had formed together to attack settlements in Kentucky and keelboats upon the Ohio River. They said that 100 warriors were included in the Lynchburg encampment and that there were several Shawnee chiefs among them, Tecumseh, Battise, Black Snake, Wolf, and Chinskau.

One of the most dramatic moments in the Battle of Lynchburg was recounted afterwards by Whiteman, one of the participants. Ward, one of his comrades, had had a brother who, in 1758 when he was three years old, had been captured by Tecumseh's Indians and had been adopted into their tribe. He remained with them and when grown, married an Indian woman. They were the parents of several children. Just before the battle began, Ward saw an Indian figure standing before a tent, and discovered that it was that of an Indian girl of about 15 years. He was struck by her light complexion, and fearing that she might be a white captive, instinctively did not fire. He afterwards learned and it was proved that this girl was his lost brother's child.

The Battle of Belfast took place within a year or two after the Battle of Lynchburg, on what is now the John G. West farm, two miles northwest of Belfast. John McNary, an Indian spy of Kentucky, was sent out with a company of 40 men, on a mission to collect and bury the bones of McIntyre and Barr who had fallen at Lynchburg. Scott's History of Highland County describes the battle thus:

"Owing to the determined hostility and characteristic vigilance of the Indians in the vicinity, they were unable to accomplish the desired object. After they discovered the impossibility of the undertaking, they commenced a retreat. Several of the party had already been picked off by the wily enemy, and an effort was made to elude them, and if possible, baffle pursuit.

"But they had not proceeded far on their homeward route before they became aware that the Indians were dogging them. A hurried march was resolved upon, and as they doubted not but the Indians were much stronger than their party, all their skill was employed to prevent an attack. The forced march continued until the party of Kentuckians were within a day's march of Manchester.

"The morning of that day was dark and rather misty. The party of whites were still on the lookout for their pursuers, although they

had succeeded in baffling them the preceding night and afternoon, and had therefore ventured to stop and take such repose as they could during the night, taking care to make as little noise as possible, and kindle no fires. They passed the night in security, free from interruption.

"Early in the morning they moved some four or five miles farther south, when they concluded to halt and take a hasty breakfast. The point at which they stopped for this purpose, as remembered by McNary later, was at the first fork of Brush Creek, immediately above the town of Belfast, and south of a mound which stands in a meadow in the forks of the creek.

"The Indians came on them whilst they were eating, unexpectedly and apparently unintentionally. It seemed, from their actions, that they were themselves surprised, for before they could fire the whites were able to give them a well-directed broadside, and fled. They saw several of the Indians fall after their fire, but as the enemy numbered at least four to one, they did not feel like risking a battle while escape was possible. The party of whites ran for several miles. The Indians fired on them just as they started, but fortunately without killing or wounding any of them.

"After a pursuit of several hours the Indians, finding the whites gaining on them, abandoned the chase, and the party arrived safely at Manchester in the evening."

The most conspicuous and colorful figure of all Indian history of Highland county is that of Waw-wil-a-way, peace-loving Shawnee chieftain who lived near the mouth of Hardin's Creek with his wife and two sons, and who was deliberately murdered by three white men.

Many virtues have been attributed to him. He was said to have been well-known and beloved throughout this region because of his courage, intelligence, manliness, and generosity. He had been on surveying tours with General Nathaniel Massie as his faithful hunter and guide, and was an admirer and true friend of the white man.

The story is, that a report had been circulated by some white men that the Indians, who had been adhering to the terms of the peace treaty of 1795, were rising to make a terrible surprise attack upon the settlers in this part of the country. When a messenger on horseback rode through from Chillicothe, bringing the word, settlers everywhere collected and fortified themselves.

Shortly after this, the tomahawked and scalped body of Captain Herrod, a prominent settler living a few miles west of Chillicothe, was found by some hunters in the woods near the clearing of his home. Indians were blamed for the deed and feeling was bad. Investigation by Governor Tiffin revealed that the Indians had only peaceful intentions and the story of the intended uprising had been a hoax. Some thought that it had all been part of an unscrupulous plan by a white man who might have wished to supersede Captain

Herrod in office in the State militia. At any rate, even today, Herrod's murder is as much a mystery as ever.

While on his way, in 1803, to Old Town (Frankfort) on foot, where he and his sons were accustomed to exchange their peltries for powder, lead, and other supplies, Waw-wil-a-way was met by three white men on horseback, Wolfe, Williams, and Ferguson.

The meeting was casual and friendly, Waw-wil-a-way shook hands with them cordially and asked about their health and their families.

Wolf asked the chief if he would trade guns with him and the unsuspecting Indian, assenting, turned over his gun to him for examination. After stealthily removing the priming from the pan of Waw-wil-a-way's gun, Wolfe handed it back stating that he did not wish to trade.

"Have the Indians commenced war?" Wolfe and Williams made inquiry as they dismounted from their horses.

"No, no! the Indians and the white men are now all one, all brothers," Waw-wil-a-way replied.

"Have you heard that the Indians killed Captain Herrod?" Wolfe asked the surprised chief.

The Indian, doubting the truth of the story, suggested, "Maybe whiskey, too much drink was the cause of the quarrel."

"But Herrod had no quarrel with the Indians."

"Then maybe some bad white man killed Captain Herrod," said Waw-wil-a-way.

The conversation ended in the friendly manner in which it began. Waw-wil-a-way again shook hands with the white men and they resumed their ways.

The chief had gone only a few steps when Wolfe, raising his rifle, took aim at his back and fired. The ball passed through his body, but he did not fall.

Although mortally wounded, Waw-wil-a-way turned upon his murderers. He raised his rifle and aimed it at Wolfe for the smoking gun revealed who had shot him. Wolfe jumped behind his horse.

Then the chief shot Williams, who fell dead from his frightened and plunging horse. The scheme to remove the priming from Waw-wil-a-way's gun and render it useless had failed, for the cushion had been left on the tube.

Making a club of his gun, the Indian rushed upon Wolfe, and with one blow sent him prostrate to the earth. Wolfe regained his feet and attempted to seize Waw-wil-a-way by the tuft of hair on the top of his head. Instead he got hold of the shawl wound around Waw-wil-a-way's head. When he jerked the shawl to bring Waw-wil-a-way to the ground the shawl gave way, and Wolfe fell backwards.

"At this," Scott's History of Highland County says, "*the Indian drew his scalping knife and made a thrust at his antagonist, who,* seeing his danger, and throwing up his feet to ward it off, received the blade of the knife in his thigh. In the scuffle the handle broke off and left the entire blade in the wound.

"Wolfe at the same time made a blow at the Indian with his knife, which entered his breast bone. Just at this critical juncture, Ferguson ran to Wolfe's assistance. The Indian then seized Wolfe's fallen gun and struck Ferguson a most fearful blow on the head and brought him to the earth, laying bare his skull from the crown to the ear. Here the sanguine conflict ended.

"During the entire encounter, Waw-wil-a-way never uttered a word. When the strife was over, his strength failed him rapidly from loss of blood, and his sight became dim. He cast one glance on his fallen foe, ... turning, walked a short distance out into the grass, and sank upon his face amid the wild flowers."

B. SOME INDIAN TALES

WAW-WIL-A-WAY's death was the climax of a number of incidents that led to the last Indian alarm in southern Ohio.

His body was found where he fell, legend claims, and was taken to an Indian cemetery in Deer Park, the John McMullen land now owned by his son, Attorney Robert McMullen. The grave has never been identified. This land lies near the Seven Caves, and a trail near it is said to have been the place where the Indians attacked a band of travelers on their way to a crossing on Paint creek, and massacred them.

Wolfe and Ferguson survived the fray to find the countryside in a turmoil, Indians and whites not knowing what to do or what to expect. General McArthur and a detachment of men rode away to hold council with the great chief, Tecumseh, near Fort Greenville, where the peace treaty of 1795 had been enacted between the Indians and whites. Here the white men were assured that the Indians held the terms of the treaty sacred. The chief himself went with the men to Chillicothe where he addressed the people there through an interpreter and allayed their fears.

In the meantime, several hundred Indians had collected at the forks of Lees creek in Highland county, near Leesburg. Some of the chiefs went to the home of a Quaker settler, Nathaniel Pope, asking that a council be held. Pope sent for his Quaker neighbors, and they met with the chiefs *under a spreading elm* which stood by a spring on Pope's farm.

It was not an unfriendly meeting. The Indians suggested that they make a property settlement and agreed to maintain friendly relations with the white settlers should actual hostilities break out. They asked for half of the settlers' provisions and salt, all of their blankets, and demanded that the men should seek out the murderers of Waw-wil-a-way.

Mrs. Pope objected to parting with her blankets and it looked as though the treaty had been made only to be broken. An Indian picked up her youngest son, a lad of about 12 years. This boy in later years became General J. W. Pope. Standing him up against a tree, the Indian pretended to tomahawk and scalp him as a threat as to what would happen to her family should she continue to refuse to give up her blankets. When she did not instantly agree, he stepped back and began throwing his tomahawk and sticking it into the tree just above the boy's head. This was too much for Mrs. Pope. She relinquished the blankets and the Indians went away, taking with them William Pope and other young men to hunt down Waw-wil-a-way's murderers.

It was an Indian law that the nearest relatives of the murdered man had a right to kill the murderer whenever and wherever he could find him. Knowing this, Wolfe had fled to Kentucky. Here he employed an agent to act for him and a negotiation was entered into with the sons of Waw-wil-a-way. The agent, acting for Wolfe, agreed to give each son a horse, a new saddle and bridle, and a new rifle. Thereupon peace was made between Waw-wil-a-way's family and Wolfe.

A great ceremony was made of this truce. In the presence of a large gathering of Indians and whites at Old Town (Frankfort) the two sons of Waw-wil-a-way and Wolfe occupied the center of a hollow square. The horses, the new saddles and bridles, and the new rifles, were there too, ready to change hands.

Solemnly raising their hands toward heaven, Waw-wil-a-way's sons relinquished their claim to the life of the murderer when they called upon the Great Spirit to accept the blood and life of Wolfe.

The scene was so impressive that *many were moved to tears*. Waw-wil-a-way's sons took Wolfe by the hand, called him brother, lighted the pipe of peace, and smoked with him.

At the conclusion of the meeting the two Indians returned to their camp at the mouth of Hardin's creek. Here they sat down beside Allen Crawford, a white settler, and his sons who were camping there on a hunting trip.

This was the peaceful ending of the last Indian alarm in southern Ohio.

Direct descendants of the Nathaniel Pope family today are members of the Fred Pope family who reside on East Walnut street, in Hillsboro.

Now one of the reasons for settlers coming to Highland county was that the Indian situation was not serious. Many of them had suffered harrowing experiences at the hands of hostile Indians in states south and east of the Ohio river.

Probably no more thrilling story can be found than that of the

Jolly family who emigrated from West Virginia to Chillicothe following the massacre of Mrs. Jolly and others of the family by the Indians. Driven away from Chillicothe by the *sickly Scioto*, they came to live near Hillsboro. Two of the Jolly boys, Joseph and William, had been taken captive back in West Virginia.

Joseph, a frail child, was killed because he could not keep up with the Indians on their march. William, robust and fearless, was admired by his captors and adopted by an Indian woman who had lost her own son in battle. He was renamed *Thunder*.

Years later William was found to be alive and living with the Cherokee Indians on the Coosa river in Alabama. His elder brother, David, Jr., went on horseback from Hillsboro to find him and bring him home.

The Indians gave him up reluctantly, and just as reluctantly did William come with his brother to Hillsboro where he struggled to learn the white man's ways. He was finally reconciled to his new life and lived in Hillsboro for two years. Then he went to Wisconsin where he settled and married a girl of his own race. His three brothers, James, John, and David, Jr., were among Highland county's leading citizens. The father, David, Sr., died at Chillicothe.

Another interesting story is that of Thomas Dick, born and educated at Belfast, Antrum county, Ireland. A teacher by profession, he came to this country for better opportunities and became a teacher in western Pennsylvania where he married.

He had just returned from a business trip to Pittsburgh in March, 1791, and was eating dinner with his wife and a neighbor, when his house was suddenly surrounded by Seneca Indians who fired through the open door. The neighbor was killed instantly. Mr. and Mrs. Dick were both taken prisoners and hurried away to the northwest in the direction of the Ohio river.

Mr. Dick was sold to a trader who took him to Detroit where he was purchased by the English commander of the fort and released. Now began the search for his wife.

A trusted Indian was paid to scour the Seneca towns and locate Mrs. Dick. She was found very ill with rheumatism. The Indian secured the help of a negro woman who, although she had been a captive for many years, was allowed the freedom of the camp. The woman carried Mrs. Dick, in the night time, while the Indians were soundly sleeping, to a waiting canoe. After perilous days the Indian arrived safely in Detroit and delivered his charge to her husband.

The Dicks left Pennsylvania and went to Kentucky to live. They did not like it there and emigrated to Ohio, to the Scioto valley, and thence to a short distance east of Marshall. Their son, C. G. Dick, was the first white child born in Marshall township. Mr. Dick, one of the founders of the first Presbyterian church in the county, was also Marshall township's first teacher. He taught, in his own house, during the winter of 1802, *"spelling, reading, and perhaps writing."*

Many other incidents in which famous figures of history were connected, lent color to the early history of our county.

There was Daniel Boone who was said to have been brought through this county as far back as 1778, a prisoner of Indians who stopped to rest and hunt near the Seven Caves. The beech tree he was tied to for safe keeping was identified later by markings and scars.

There was James B. Finley, a traveling Methodist minister and missionary who visited the Indian village of Etnah overlooking the Seven Caves and wrote about it in his journal.

The noted Colonel Logan was believed to have passed through Highland county when, in 1786, he led 700 men from Washington, Kentucky, across the Ohio River at Limestone (Maysville) to the Pickaway towns, to punish Indians for horse stealing.

Simon Kenton, famous Indian scout, is said to have broken up the Indian camp at Etnah when, in 1791, with his band of border soldiers, he pursued some Etnah Indians accused of crossing the Ohio river into Limestone to rob and burn homes and to murder white settlers. The Indians discovered they they were being followed, broke camp and fled, leaving most of their spoils behind them. This incident marked the end of Etnah, for it no longer had become a hiding place.

Once Andrew Ellison, an inhabitant of Massie's Manchester settlement on the Ohio river, was brought along the Seven Caves trail by Indian captors who encamped there and turned Ellison over to the women and children to torture. It was at this time that General Massie, in hot pursuit, missed the trail, but found instead the Paint Creek valley and saw its possibilities. Followed then the opening up of the Paint and Scioto valleys and the founding of Chillicothe.

Another story about Simon Kenton tells how he was stripped and tied by Indians to a wild horse when he was taken captive, and was carried on a wild ride across our county by way of Marshall and Rainsboro.

The tragic Colonel Crawford, who met a horrible death at the hands of Indians during the expedition against the Wyandot towns in 1782, is claimed to have passed through Highland county.

Israel Donalson, a member of the convention that framed Ohio's first constitution, was on a surveying trip with General Massie on Brush creek in the spring of 1791, when he was made prisoner by the Indians and taken north to their camps on the Miami river. Donalson and his captors are believed to have come through New Market on their way and to within three or four miles of Hillsboro. A thrilling escape was made and Donalson reached Fort Washington (Cincinnati), safely.

Cornstalk, *"the greatest chief among the Scioto Shawnees"* is connected by legend with the legendary Indian maid, Etowah, who is supposed to have leaped to her death from a cliff at the Rocky Fork gorge at the Seven Caves, because of her unrequited love for him.

Cornstalk has been called *"war chief in battle and a mediator in time of peace."* With his father, Whitefish, Cornstalk went among the eight or ten Indian villages on the Scioto-Deer-Paint creek plains gathering up captives, stolen horses and Negro slaves in fulfillment of the treaty at Camp Charlotte following the Battle of Point Pleasant.

Legend claims that Greenfield got its name when General Duncan McArthur, exploring his land grant, assisted an Indian woman in carrying a deer she was taking to her camp. Emerging upon the green tract of land, he found at last the right site for a town he contemplated, and the inspiration for its name.

King Solomon, a peaceable Wyandot Indian from Logan county, used to camp on Rocky Fork creek, about four miles east of Hillsboro. With other Indians he hunted in the Brushcreek Sunfish hills and traded bear's meat and venison to settlers for salt.

Two colorful figures remotely connected with our Indian history were, Chief Monocue and Chief Between-the-logs. Both were Wyandots, missionaries, and licensed Methodist preachers. When the First Methodist Episcopal Church was dedicated in Hillsboro, the two chiefs were present.

Monocue was the son of an Indian chief and became a noted missionary and orator among his own people. He is described as *"quick in his motion as thought, and fleet as the roe in the chase."*

Between-the-logs, son of a Seneca father and a Wyandot mother, was born about 1780. He lived with his father until he was nine years old, his parents being separated. When his father died, he went to live with his mother. His sympathies were with the tribes of his own race, and he went to live with Tecumseh's Shawnees to learn what their grievances were against the white people. He did not regard their complaints as justified, and refused to join them in contemplated battle.

When the U. S. Government took the Indians' lands in 1817, Between-the-logs, as chief speaker of the Wyandot nation, headed a delegation of Wyandots to Washington. His pleas were so effective that reservations were enlarged and annuities increased. His influence among his people was great, and he joined with other Wyandot chiefs to aid General Harrison in the Battle of the Thames. Shortly thereafter he embraced the religion of the white man and became a Methodist.

By 1842, all Indian title to Ohio land was acquired by the United States, and the Indians were located on reservations in Kansas and Oklahoma. Some time between 1840 and 1850, surveyors found that a farmer, Philip Roads, living between Rainsboro and New Petersburg, had no deed or title to his farm. The story came to light then that the original owner of the land had sold off parts of his land but had reserved about 60 acres on which Indians lingered, loath to disturb them. Mr. Roads had obtained the land by making a bargain with the Indians, trading them horses and ponies for it. The Indians then left for reservations or for parts unknown.

Mrs. Elizabeth Gossett Cochran, aged 96, a native of this county, says that her grandparents migrated to the county and settled on land near Harwood Chapel, on the North Fork of White Oak creek. She recalls that an Indian used to come and wander about the neighborhood, lingering at the mound known as Fort Salem, calling it Indian Mountain. This had been the home of his people, he said, and he pointed out as proof pictures and signs carved by Indians on beech trees.

What connection we have to Indian history has become so complicated by a misty past that there seems to be no unraveling the mystery of the presence, in the hill section of the county, of a pocket of storybook characters who claim to have descended from the Indians. This pocket is in the Fort Hill area and borders Adams, Pike and Ross counties.

This hill country is unequaled anywhere for the simplicity of its rustic, woodland beauty. Untouched by battles and events that made historic shrines of other parts of Ohio, the region remains primeval in a large sense.

These people claim that they are descendants of the Shawnee Indians who hunted here when all was a wilderness part of the Northwest Territory; Indians who loved these peaceful hills so much that some would not leave them for reservations and remained to intermarry among themselves and with the white and sometimes negro races, composing an isolated world, scarcely touched until late years by outside civilization.

"*When the hunters' moon hung high,*" homesick Indians came back from the reservations to hunt and visit. There was good fishing in the streams and the forests were full of berries, rye, wheat, and other grasses, nuts, fruit trees and healing herbs. This was their home. Their hearts were here.

Later, when emancipated slaves journeyed north, many lingered in the haven offered by the hills. Some remained to marry into the already mixed race of Indian-white.

None today will admit his negro heritage, but all are proud of their Indian blood. Their physical characteristics are coppery skin, black or dark-brown eyes, high cheek bones, and straight black hair. Many have retained Indian superstitions and tales, and odd names, such as Honeygrant and Sugargrant, and possess actual photographs of Indian relatives on reservations. Many can neither read nor write.

They do not have a variety of food. Some eat a kind of shortening bread stirred up and baked in a skillet. This bread is dipped in maple syrup or spread with wild fruit such as sugared persimmon pulp. Wild grapes, apples, all kinds of berries, and nuts are depended upon for sustenance. Some are not averse to pilfering when food supplies are low and will travel miles to *"borrow"* from a white farmer. A number have been arrested and have served terms in the county jail for *"borrowing."*

Some inhabitants make their living by basket weaving. They are quite adept at their art, using strips of white oak. Some work in the timber regions among the *"paper wood"* as they express it, preparing wood that is taken to the paper plant at Chillicothe. Some gather herbs and sell them to the general store keepers who are steady customers. Some manufacture corn whiskey which they peddle to the white man's town, or use it for their own consumption.

Child-like and friendly, they are fond of their pets and when a cabin door is opened, often chickens, dogs, cats, a pig, and *"young uns"* tumble good-naturedly out together, to make room for the caller. Many of the women like their pipes, and almost all of them like to chew tobacco.

Brush and rail fences often form the boundary lines between the properties. Narrow strips of corn patches make little belts along the roads. Nestling in secluded places are the mud-daubed log cabins and shacks, and thin smoke from wood fires curls about the tree tops. From under a cabin or a rickety spring wagon, a gangly coon dog stretches its legs, staggers slowly to its feet and gives a dismal howl.

In an isolated hollow encircled by mounded hills you will come upon a queer cemetery. Graves are high and sprinkled with crushed bits of red, yellow, blue and green glass. Rows of plants have been planted down the length of the center of some of the graves. Identifying head markers are usually of wood or stone and some of them are pathetic as, *"Biddy, ag 2."* People of Indian extraction were buried *"heads west to face the rising sun"* from an old Indian custom.

One grave, legend says, contains the leg of a man. The story goes that when he lay gravely ill of a leg injury many, many years ago, a doctor from Hillsboro was sent for. *"He came all teed up with liquor and chopped off the leg."* When the man regained consciousness and saw that his leg had been taken off his heart was broken. He had a *"piny box"* made for it and it was taken to the cemetery. On fair days as long as he was able the poor old fellow kept vigil beside his leg's grave, never quite forgiving *"that new-fangled doctor from the county seat."*

When spring comes, these winter-bound people will rejoice, for now they will be warm again. They depend on signs and watch eagerly for the peewee rains to come, bringing the chattering peewees back to quickening trees. Then the first crocus will peer up from the grass; and the doctor woman will come out to traipse the hollows, poking about in the dead leaves with her walking stick for a tender herb to cure the *"gatch"* (gas) in her stomach.

Part white, part Indian, she is short and stooped. Her face is lined with a thousand wrinkles and she has crinkly, quizzical, pale-blue eyes. Tobacco juice drools from the corners of her mouth. The greatest honor she has to bestow upon you is to give you a drink of water from a spring that the *"Jedge man from Hillsboro"* (Judge Joseph M. Watts) once drank from and thereupon made it a magical place.

She was once, she will tell you, *"the ornriest, cussedest gun-totin', knife-throwin' woman in Pin Oak holler, 'count of the guv'-ment liquor I got to using."* In a drunken stupor, she lay in a ditch one freezing-cold night in winter, and almost froze to death. If you want proof, ask her and she will take off her high-top shoes and stockings and show you where part of her heel is gone, frostbitten badly that night.

She will tell you how she crawled to her cabin, locked herself in, and rolled and threshed upon her earthen floor until she had cast out the devils in her and had received the *"old time religion."* Her feud with Aunt Tildy over the subject as to which of them had the *"genuwine"* old time religion, was the talk of the hollows. Aunt Tildy used to roll big stones down from her hill-top home against her enemy's hound-dog guarded shack below, at the foot of the hill. They had to *"call the law to the holler to settle the fittin'."*

Sketches of these quaint folk alone would fill this book. If we could fit the pieces together, we could determine these people's connection with the history of Highland county and accord them their rightful place in it. But there are too many missing links. So we accept them as we find them and attempt to preserve what little history we know about them, for they are a part of this county and the county is a part of them.

CHAPTER FOUR

THE WHITE MEN CAME

WHO THEY WERE:

WHEN Robert M. Dittey, one of Highland county's most brilliant attorneys, wrote the introduction to Daniel Scott's History of Highland County, 54 years ago, he pointed out that Highland county settlers were exceptionally intelligent and cultured people and that they possessed advantages far superior to those who settled in many parts of the Northwest Territory.

Be that as it may, we know that they must have possessed indomitable courage to have left their birthplaces to journey into the unknown. Driven by the urge for peace, their journeys were more or less journeys of desperation. Rivers and oceans, forests, mountains, wild animals and hostile Indians did not stop them. A study of their separate journeys is to excite our admiration and give us inspiration.

Why did many of them seek Highland county?

Here was a climate, they had heard, where the sickest person would regain his health. Here was a region where friendly Indians lived. Here the water was good and of medicinal quality. Here there was plenty of game and wild vegetables and fruits were everywhere, just waiting for some one to pick them. Here was a place when you could worship God according to your belief with no fear of molestation. Here was a heavenly place where you would find peace.

Some trekked the long, perilous traces to this county on foot, or horseback, or in covered wagons drawn by horses or oxen, to claim large acreages they had been awarded by the Government for their services during the Revolutionary War. Here they would found towns and establish the homes, churches, and schools they thought were best; here they would push forward the frontier line.

Still others came from distant states because of accounts that had drifted to them by way of letter or word of traveler, of a wondrously healthful land abounding in opportunities for their families, free from the plagues of agues and chills, and dysentery. Tired of battling with flood-ridden lands along the Atlantic coast, tired of participating in terrible Indian uprisings, tired of other restrictions they were experiencing, they came to find peace and safety, and to purchase land.

Some were the strong, far-seeing sons of the cavaliers of Virginia and North and South Carolina who came by way of Limestone (Maysville), Kentucky. Some were liberal minded and refined pioneers of the Chesapeake Bay region who came by way of Fayette county, Pennsylvania.

Some were the gallant border soldiers who came in enactment of duty, or the spirit of adventure. The first traveling ministers who rode circuits through this part of the Ohio wilderness, Presbyterians, Methodists, and Quakers, came, bringing the Protestant religion. They were of the Irish, Scotch, English, and Dutch nationalities.

Came the French who had fled the persecution in France, crossing the ocean in cattle boats or crude sailing vessels, driven westward from the eastern part of this country by unfavorable circumstances; the Quakers, *"the plain people,"* because they wanted to possess freedom of religion; and the Scotch because they did not think the laws of Scotland just.

Doing his bit in opening up Highland county was the traveling shoemaker who came at intervals to *"shoe"* the family; and the hatter, to *"hat"* them.

Some who came were helpless pawns of fate, as the little *"bond"* girls and boys, usually orphans, who had been bound out to settlers for a number of years in payment for their care, protection, and training. Sometimes one of them ran away from an unsatisfactory environment; but more often he or she remained to become a worthy citizen.

Slaves who had been freed by owners who did not believe in enslaving them, came to be near their beloved masters and mistresses. This accounts for many Negroes in the county today bearing the names of well-known Highland county persons.

Luxuries were practically unknown and undesired. Their wants were simple and wholesome, except for a demand in general for a popular brand of whiskey known as the old Monongahela double distilled. There was no demand for coffee and tea, rare articles in those days. There was an abundance of deer, bear, buffalo, turkey, and fish.

Drawn together by common aims and interests, the respect of the community was more to be desired than the acquiring of wealth and property. Should one arise to disturb the peace of the community, he was banished forever. They used each other's given names in salutation.

The men hunted and fished in their spare time and in the evenings the young people often danced the hours away. Women stayed close at home, for this was the custom then. Their duty was to minister to the sick, instruct their children, tend their homes, and make the clothing.

Books and reading matter were scarce, but almost every family possessed a family Bible with carefully kept records and important papers between the pages for safe keeping, and sometimes a copy of *"Pilgrim's Progress."* No pictures hung on the walls except perhaps a picture of *"Daniel in the Lion's Den," "Washington Crossing the Delaware,"* or a marriage certificate, unscrolled, and framed in pine cones.

Social affairs were called *"functions"* or *"infairs."* A gathering of settlers to cut wood for a new cabin was called a *"chopping frolic."* The whole neighborhood was invited to everything that went on and the young folks danced jigs, reels, and square sets to the tune of *"fiddles."* There were wrestling matches, taffy pullings, quilting bees, singing schools, spelling matches, flax breakings, fishing parties, and wool pickings. A few of these, described in Dr. William K. Ruble's incomparable classic of local Americana, *"Stirring Events in Lives of Settlers of White Oak Township,"* are herewith reproduced, as related to him by his grandmother, Millie Kibler Davidson:

BUILDING A CABIN

WHEN men met to raise a building, they would choose two captains, and they would divide the men into two squads. Each captain had two corners of the building to manage and carry up, and of course, each captain tried to get ahead of the other, and such hallooing and laughter as they had until the building was finished. All of the neighbors seemed to wish each other well, and if you had any kind of work which you could not do yourself, they really felt slighted if you did not ask them to help. If your neighbor needed your horse and you were not using it, you loaned it to him. It was borrow and lend, and no one thought anything of it as it was the custom to ask for that of which you were in need.

During the summer time, if one man took a notion to have fresh meat, he invited the neighbors, and they killed and divided it and they fried it down, as the saying is, and they could thus take care of it until it was used. Then some other neighbors would butcher, and so it was, always help and pay back, or borrow and lend. Why, I have loaned my dresses, shoes, moccasins, shawl, hat and hood, many a time, and there was nothing said about such things. Things they did not have, they could borrow and they were welcome.

Corn Huskings

BEN HAULED up some dry hickory logs with the oxen and fired the two heaps which he had made so that the air was warm enough to be fairly comfortable, and he had plenty of wood to renew the fire.

Instead of husking the corn in the field, the men just snapped the ear and husk off of the stalk, and this was piled in a long row to be husked at night. Ben had piled a long row between the two log heaps to be husked that night.

The crowd selected two captains to choose their men and then divided the corn into two piles as equally as possible. Each man would ask a lady to help him, and if there were not enough girls to go around, then the extra men had to work by themselves. Each captain watched and encouraged his crowd, and as they husked the corn, they threw it in piles. When they were all ready, the fun commenced, and how the corn did fly!

Then they danced and ate pop corn which I had popped in my big ovens, and had warmed honey and poured just enough to make it stick so that I could roll it into balls, and I had also made taffy out of tree molasses. Corn huskings were very popular and the young people surely enjoyed them.

Flax Breakings

WHEN the flax was ripe and ready to pull, the young people would make parties and the young men would choose their girl partners to help. They would work together pulling the flax and placing it in bunches.

After the stalks dried and became brittle it was run through hand-made machines called flax breaks, which broke the stalks into short pieces and separated them from the bark or lint. The bark or lint was then scutched or whipped until the rough bark was beaten out of it, then it was placed in the sunshine and rain for a long time to bleach it. Then it was gone over carefully by hand, picking out everything that would interfere with making good thread.

Then we would spin it into thread and you would be surprised how fast a good spinner could make thread. The thread could then be woven into linen cloth, or be used as the chain and filled with yarn made from wool, and that made cloth called linsey-woolsey. The linen cloth was very strong and serviceable, and the linsey-woolsey made warm cloth for dresses, blankets, etc., and the cloth could be colored to suit the owner.

Wool Pickings

WOOL pickings were usually attended by the women and girls of the neighborhood, but quite often the men would come for dinner.

In the spring of the year, after the weather became warm, the men would shear the sheep and take the wool to the creek and wash it, and when it was thoroughly dried, then little bunches of it were taken and carefully separated. All of the curly locks must be picked apart, all burs, Spanish needles, or foreign substances of any kind, be removed. Then it was ready to be made into rolls and the rolls were then spun into yarn.

The rolls were made by using two specially made brushes with wire teeth, called card-brushes. A small bunch of wool was spread out over one brush, then with the other, it was carefully worked into a roll about 10 to 14 inches long.

Finally there was a factory built at Hillsboro. Then all we had to do was to wash and pick the wool, and take it to be carded into rolls, or it could be made into yarn, or we could have it woven into different kinds of cloth for ladies' dresses, men's clothing, woolen blankets, or whatever we wanted, which was a great improvement over the hand-made cloth.

GIGGING FISH

THE YOUNG folks used to gather along White Oak Creek and indulge in their favorite game of gigging. They would make up a party for a certain night. The boys went along the banks and gathered tall, dry horseweeds. Tying them in bundles they scattered them along the banks where they intended to gig, the places usually being at the back waters of a dam.

One boy carried a torch made from the horseweeds. Others waded in the water and searched for fish. They gigged them with gigs, long spear-like sticks with two iron or steel prongs fastened in one end.

When a fish was caught, the boy called to his girl and tossed the fish upon the bank to be strung. The girl, using the stick she carried with her for this purpose, pushed it through the gills of the fish. The boy who caught the most fish had the privilege of kissing the girl who carried them.

COURTING

WHEN your grandpa asked Uncle Lewis Coffman for Sallie, the old man says mighty short like, — "No sir, you can't have my Sallie. It ain't that she is too good for you, 'cause she's not, though there is no better girl in this neck of woods, and you are a mighty fine man, but this thing of all of the Coffmans and Rubles amixin' up just like they can't marry no one else has got to be stopped, and I want you to keep away from my Sallie."

Your Grandpa was an awful nice man, and while he dearly loved Sallie, he never went to see her again, and he wouldn't ever take her home from parties or meetings. We all felt awful bad because we knew that there must be some cause for his quittin' but we could not bear to ask them and they never said a word. Both of them were so nice to me that I used to cry, because I thought that they loved each other and I wanted them to go together, but I never thought of the real cause.

I noticed that your two grandpas went together more than ever, and I was awful glad, because I thought they seemed lonesome, for since your grandpa Davidson had quit goin' with Polly Roberts, neither of them seemed to have a *"regular"* girl, as we called them in those days. Of course your grandpa Davidson would walk home with me from places, but we never called them *"regulars"* unless they sat up with us at night, and I was counted too young for that.

Your Grandpa Davidson carried notes from one to the other but he never told me till just about three weeks before they were married, and of course I never let on to Sallie that I knew a thing. He told me that he was going to help steal Sallie out some night and that they were going to hurry to Squire Pulliam's to be married and they would need witnesses and that he would like to have me go with him and that he would ask my father and mother and he would take good care of me.

To make sure that everything would be all right he came and talked with my parents, telling them the arrangements, and explained about the witnesses, and said that Sallie would rather have me than anyone else in the world and that they were determined to marry, and that there was really no sensible reason why they should not, or he would have nothing to do towards helping.

Because Father and Mother thought so much of John and Sallie, they said they would say nothing about the arrangements, and for him to come when they were ready and that I could go.

Squire Pulliam's cabin was the farthest north of any in the settlement, and he had cleared several acres of land and put a rail fence around his cabin so that the stock could not come close to it, which was considered a great improvement, as many of the settlers had never fenced in their homes, but just fenced in their fields to protect their crops; and there was no cleared land between our home and that of Pulliam's except that which the settlers had cleared and fenced in, as he had done.

There were really no roads except what you might call paths, leading from one neighbor to another and marked by blazing trees along the trail, that is by chopping a patch of bark from the side of trees along the trail so that you could follow from one tree to the other if you became lost in the woods.

The settlers were not far apart, but from our house to the Squire's was about three miles, and from our house to Coffman's was over one mile, and Davidson's lived south of us a little over a mile.

Your Grandpa had told the Squire to be on the lookout for them on Thursday night, and that they would be there sure if Sallie could slip away, and if the Coffmans followed them, that he would begin to hollow for him as soon as they had crossed * Smoky Row Creek and that he must be sure to be ready to marry them quickly.

Pulliam said, "*You raise the yell and I'll be ready,*" and so it was all arranged.

But the next trouble was to get Sallie. Of course we were naturally anxious for them until Thursday night finally came, and to make troubles worse, the rain just poured down and we were afraid that Smoky Row would get so deep that we could not cross, and there was no foot log upon which we could cross.

The Coffman cabin had a hewn slab floor overhead which formed what we called an attic and to get into that place they had to cut a piece out of one of the logs which formed the gable, big enough for one to crawl through, and when they wished to go up into the attic, they placed a ladder against the end of the cabin on the outside and climbed up.

Sallie had told your Grandpa Davidson that her father made her sleep up in the attic and they would take the ladder away every night, for you see that they were afraid she would run away and marry Ruble.

The boys came to our house soon after dark on that Thursday night and waited quite awhile, hoping that the rain would cease, but it just kept on raining and we finally started.

We went on horseback. The boys didn't have saddles in those days, but some of them used woolen blankets, etc., though not often, and others used bear or sheep hides, which they strapped on the horses' backs with raw hide thongs. They call them surcingles now.

Brother Henry had a big black bear skin which he gave to your Grandpa Ruble for a wedding present, and said to him, "*I surely wish you good luck, and I think that brother John and I will go coon hunting tonight, and we'll take our axes and cut through the woods afoot and strike Smoky Row at that steep bank just below Pulliam's ford, and we'll fell one of those tall sugar trees. It will reach across the creek and you can cross on it, if there is too much water at the ford. If you find it to be dangerous to cross, hollow and we will answer, then you ride down the creek and leave your horses at the top of the hill. We will stay right there till you come.*"

We knew that they were not going to hunt coons that rainy night, although a rainy night is a good time to hunt, but I just want to tell you how much interest they took in Sallie's wedding.

Your Grandpa Davidson and I rode Dan. That was the name of the big gray horse. I sat up behind him on a big sheep's hide which had been tanned brown by soaking it in ooze, which had been made by boiling walnut hulls in water.

Your Grandpa Ruble rode a blaze-faced bay horse named Billie and he carried his ax with him, and when we arrived at quite a

---

* *Smoky Row Creek was so named after Smoky Row, a settlement of Irishmen about three miles south of New Market, which got its name from a cherished locality in Ireland.*

distance this side of Coffman's cabin, he chopped down a small sapling, trimmed the limbs off pretty close, then walked and carried it on his shoulder, and we followed, leading Billie.

I was so excited that night, but I knew not to talk above a whisper. The rain was still pouring down but Mother had doubled a linen sheet four double and pinned it over my head and shoulders and also gave me one for Sallie.

When we arrived at the spring branch, which is about 300-400 feet south of the Coffman home, we waited there and let your Grandpa go after her.

My, how I trembled for fear that they would hear him, but your Grandpa whispered to me, "*Don't be afraid, everything will be all right when we get Sallie.*"

Of course she was supposed to be on the lookout for us, and your Grandpa Davidson was to mimic a big owl, which he could do to perfection, and that would let her know that we were near so she could be ready, because she had to wear her everyday clothes.

We could see a light in the cabin but as it was getting late your Grandpa slipped up and placed the sapling against the cabin and Sallie climbed down, and they came hurrying to us.

They must have made a little noise, for we heard old Uncle Lewis making an awful racket trying to get the boys awake and we heard him call, "*Sallie! Sallie!*" Then he jerked the door open and ran around to the end of the cabin and called to her again and of course he received no answer, and he knew that she had escaped.

He was almost sure that she had gone, so he hurried back into the house, and he and the boys were soon ready for a mad pursuit.

They didn't know how Sallie would get to the Squire's but they were almost certain that they would find her there, and they knew that they could make better time through the woods at night on foot than on horses, and with more safety.

We kept mighty still until he was in the house again, then we hurried as fast as possible through the dark woods. The trail was pretty easy to follow from Coffman's to where our uncle Peter Surber now lives, and we could make pretty fair time from there to where Michael Winkle now lives, but from there to the creek we had to go very slow, as it was down hill.

We finally arrived at the ford, and it was so dark there among the big trees that we couldn't very well see, but from the noise, we knew that the water was deep and swift. I can't recollect of any of us having spoken a word since we started as John and Sallie had taken the lead and we followed, keeping mighty close.

While the boys were trying to make out whether it was safe to cross (Mercy, I never will forget how I was scared!) we heard the Coffmans coming just a short distance away, and running like Indians.

Men think quickly at such times and your Grandpa Davidson

said, "*Wait a minute, John. Millie, jump off,*" and I jumped. He plunged his horse into the water and crossed, then shouted back, "*Sallie, get astride the horse, and for God's sake, come on, John.*" Then they plunged in and were safe on the other side, while I was alone on this side, and the Coffmans coming nearer, but your Grandpa said to John and Sallie (he could swear sometimes), "*Go like the devil was after you, and we will soon be there.*"

Now, how do you suppose I felt standing there in the dark and I could hear the Coffmans breathing as they ran?

Just as soon as they started, your Grandpa Davidson hurried the big gray horse back across again and jumped off and threw me upon him astride, then jumped on behind me, and the big horse again plunged into the creek and the water came at least half way up on his sides, and we had to hold our feet up to keep them out of the water, but they couldn't have gotten much wetter anyhow; and just as we got to the other bank the Coffmans arrived at the other side and called to us to stop, but we never answered them.

All at once your Grandpa Davidson began to yell, "*Squire Pulliam, Squire Pulliam,*" at the top of his voice, and then brothers John and Henry also commenced to yell for Pulliam, then crossed the creek on the tree which they had felled and came running toward the cabin. They had heard the Coffmans call to us to stop and thus knew that they were close after us, and while they did not like to mix in their troubles, they were going to see that John and Sallie were treated fairly and anyhow they wanted to see them married.

John and Sallie beat us to the rail fence in front of the Squire's cabin and my brothers arrived about the same time, having cut across the woods from where they crossed the creek. The Coffmans had either swam or waded the creek, I don't know which, and were already shouting, "*Hold on. Hold on 'til we get there.*"

And my brothers and your Grandpa Davidson were calling to Pulliam to hurry up. We could hear him scrambling around in the cabin and talking to himself like he was about half mad, and all at once he jerked the door open and stood in the door in his shirt tail and said, "*Are you John Ruble?*" and John answered Yes.—Then he inquired, "*Are you Sallie Coffman?*" and Sallie replied Yes.

"*Then I pronounce you man and wife, —— —— you.*"

It would sound awful for any one to use such language now days but he seemed greatly excited and perhaps was not fully awake as he hadn't had time to dress, but in later years, he joined church and did considerable preaching.

We turned to go home and there came the Coffmans as mad as bulls, but my brothers stepped in front of our horses and tried to reason with them, for Henry said: "*You fellows know that John Ruble is one of the best fellows in this settlement and that he will* take good care of Sallie and the best thing is to forgive them right now and take them back home with you."

The boys hadn't much to say, but the old man said, "They can just shift for themselves, and I never want them to bother us."

Sallie and John didn't say a word, but I could tell that Sallie was crying and I cried, too, but both men consoled us, and my brothers told us to follow them and they directed us to the tree which they had felled. Then my brother Henry said,

"You boys help the girls to cross on the tree and John and I will take the horses across at the ford, for we won't risk drowning these girls again tonight."

The boys led us and we finally worked through the tree top and then across the trunk to the other bank, then climbed the hill and walked down to the trail to where the boys were waiting with the horses, having forded the creek without accident.

Sallie hated to go home looking as she did in her wet clothes and no others for a change, so brothers and I soon settled it. We told them that they must come with us until some arrangements could be made, and I knew that Mother would arrange about clothes for Sallie, and so they decided to go.

We finally arrived at home and soon had a good fire by which the men could dry their clothes and Mother soon had us girls fitted out in dry clothes and as it was past midnight, we made taffy out of maple molasses and talked and joked and before we realized how time had passed, it was four o'clock and time to get breakfast, and after having eaten, the boys went home.

Your Grandpa told Sallie that he would see her that evening and that he was going to clear off a patch of ground for their cabin that day, and the men would help him to hew the logs and that they would have a home within a very few days.

Now this is what the white men and women were like who succeeded the Indians. These were our ancestors — people like these whose home-spun stories have been left for our enjoyment and appreciation. They knew our county intimately when it was young because they lived so close to it.

We know what they have left without putting it into words. We feel it within us — their courage, their faith, and hope.

And perhaps none are more aware of the richness of our heritage than our own gallant Highland county men and women who donned uniforms and went bravely forth to the vast global battlefields willing to die for her to keep her always HIGHLAND COUNTY.

WHAT THEY DID:

CAPTAIN JAMES TRIMBLE of Woodford county, Kentucky, was one of the first to come to Highland county, where his son, Allen Trimble, was later to become governor of Ohio and the father of the celebrated Mother Thompson of the Woman's Temperance Crusade.

The Trimbles were Virginians, Captain James Trimble emigrating to Kentucky from Augusta county, Virginia, in 1783. When only 18 years old, Governor Dunmore sent James out as a scout, on a military expedition against the Ohio Indian tribes. On this expedition, the youth got as far as the Scioto valley, and then Highland county, where he was impressed by the beauty of the land he had traversed.

Ten years later, Trimble was captured by Indians and was one of several who escaped and fought their way from the Cumberland Gap to Lexington, Ky. He was one of the bravest of the border soldiers in Kentucky.

He did not forget the beauty of the Ohio land he had seen when on the mission for Dunmore, and, after Wayne's victory had restored peace between Indians and whites, he decided to return to Ohio. He explored Highland, Ross, and Scioto counties in 1796, and chose several tracts which he afterwards located and surveyed.

In the meantime, during the winters of 1792 and 1793, Nathaniel Massie, Joseph Williams, and a Mr. Wade were exploring and locating lands in what is now Ross county, and they explored the Paint and Clear creek valleys. Massie, formerly a general in the Revolutionary War, held a land warrant for one of the largest and best portions of Ohio land. He was a noted Ohio surveyor and was the founder of Manchester, on the Ohio River, which was the first settlement in the Virginia Military District, and the fourth settlement in Ohio. In March, 1795, Massie and other surveyors explored the land on Brush creek in Highland county and then the Rocky Fork and Rattlesnake creeks.

Thomas Beals and Nathaniel Pope, Quakers, on their expedition to Ohio about 1795, crossed the northern part of Highland county, where they were to return later and settle permanently.

Then John and Asahel Edgington and one other set out from Manchester in Adams county, on a hunting and canoeing trip to Brush creek, in Highland county. They were known to have made camp at a place between West Union (Adams county) and Fairfax (Highland county).

Simon Kenton, who may deserve the name of Ohio's Daniel Boone, made the first entry of land in Highland county, three miles east of Hillsboro, near Rocky Fork, September 7, 1791. This entry was for 500 acres and was made on four military warrants in the name of Samuel Gibson.

The honor of being the first white settler in Highland county goes to John Wilcoxon in spite of claims made by some that a man named Daniel Hair was first.

The following location of the spot where Hair settled proves the point that he was not first, for this location is definitely in Ross county and was never a part of Highland:

"They reached the banks of the Main Paint, a short distance below the mouth of Rocky Fork. They erected a cabin on a clearing of 60 acres, at the mouth of what is now known as Massie's Spring Branch on the south side of Paint creek about two miles west of where Bainbridge now stands."

John Wilcoxon emigrated from Kentucky in the spring of 1795, searching for a new home in the wilderness where the best hunting grounds lay.

All of his worldly possessions were packed upon the back of his strong horse that was ridden by his wife and child. Wilcoxon, his dog at his heels, went ahead, taking the direction of the renowned Scioto and Main Paint country.

Daniel Scott's description of their journey into the wilderness of Highland county, best describes this event:

"He traversed the hills for several days, camping out at night and frequently remaining four or five days at a place to hunt and rest his wife and horse.

"The weather continued delightful, it being the latter part of April, and nature in the first dawn of vernal beauty presented for several days a peculiar charm to the eyes of the lonely emigrants. The long days of bright, warm sun, succeeding the cold winds and rains of the early part of the month, had already covered the sunny banks and hillsides with early plants and flowers.

"Already the elm, sugartree and buckeye had shown their green leaves, and the early wild grass not only supplied abundant pasture, but covered and adorned the surface. The nights, too, were more charming, if possible, than the days in those graceful woods. The very stillness was sublime, and the mild rays of the moon, penetrating the forest and tracing long lines of light and shade upon the irregular surface, presented a picture that none could fail to enjoy. As an accompaniment, and to enforce the consciousness of utter loneliness, the melancholy and spirit-like song of the whippoorwill arose at intervals, mingled with the distant howl of the wolf, the hoot of the owl, and the scream of the panther.

"But when the early dawn effaced the night scenes and hushed the sounds which had added to their peculiar beauty, the aroused tenants of the tent were more delighted with the music around them. The whole forest appeared alive with birds, and each one resolved to excel all the others in melody and variety of song.

"The few and simple preparations for breakfast were soon over, and Wilcoxon, his wife, child and dog, sat down to their roast of *fresh venison, with appetite, contentment, and surroundings that the palace of no monarch on earth could rival.*

"They did not then fear the Indians, as it was known that they had agreed to go into treaty with Wayne, and therefore hostilities, for the present, were not apprehended.

"But this genial weather and these fascinating scenes and sounds could not always last. Several weeks had now passed in this leisurely half hunting, half emigrating journey, and the cold rains of May commenced. The little party was not entirely prepared for this change, but through a little exertion erected a bark camp under cover of which they were enabled to keep dry.

"The rains continued several days and the time passed gloomily enough. Hunting was disagreeable, and provisions became scarce in the camp. In addition to this, the horse, growing weary of his position in the cold, beating rains, broke his halter and wandered off.

"As soon as the storm abated, Wilcoxon took his rifle and dog and set out in pursuit of the horse. It was difficult to follow the track, owing to the effects of the rain, and, unfortunately, the bell had been stopped with leaves while the horse remained at the camp. He, however, made a thorough search, and after several days found him and returned to camp.

"During this excursion he discovered in a beautiful valley an unusually large and most remarkable spring, which furnished a great abundance of most excellent water.

"Fancying this spring and the country around it, he determined to strike his tent and go to it. He was also induced to make the location permanent by the necessity of having something for bread for his family.

"When he arrived at the spring, which is now known as Sinking Spring, in Highland county, he went to work in earnest to make an improvement and build a house. First he cleared off a small patch of ground and managed to plant some seed corn he had brought with him from Kentucky. Next, he went to work with his axe and cut poles or small logs, such as he, aided by his wife, could manage to get up, and carried and hauled with his horse to the spot near the spring which he had selected for his cabin. In the course of a few days it was so far completed as to serve the purposes of the family for a summer residence.

"The luxury of a bed was attained by gathering up leaves and drying them in the sun, then putting them into a bed-tick, brought with them. For a bedstead, forks were driven into the ground, and sticks laid across, connecting with the walls of the cabin, on which was laid elm bark. On this was placed the tick filled with leaves, which in those days was considered a very comfortable bed.

"Next, Mrs. Wilcoxon busied herself to plant some garden seeds which she had brought with her. This accomplished, and a chimney built something over six feet high, made of poles and mud, with backwalls and jambs of flat rock, and a rough clapboard door for the cabin, domestic comfort seemed to be complete, and the new home by the Big Spring was a joy to the simple, honest hearts of the lonely settlers.

"Time passed on. The small patch of corn and pumpkins grew finely and promised an abundant yield, while in the little garden at the end of the cabin opposite the chimney flourished the gourd and the bean, the lettuce and potato. Around the door clustered the morning-glory, and in a carefully protected nook by the wall grew the pink, violet and other favorite garden flowers, the seeds of which had been carefully brought from Kentucky. These little souvenirs seemed now, to the eyes of Mrs. Wilcoxon, to be more beautiful than they were when she first learned to love them in the garden of her old home, and they recalled to her mind many pleasant scenes of her girlhood days — bringing back and re-endearing to her lonely heart her little circle of distant friends.

"Early one morning in July Wilcoxon started out with his axe on his shoulder and a large wooden pail in his hand, the result of his own skill as a rough cooper, to cut a bee-tree which he had discovered and marked a few days before in his rambles. The tree stood some two miles in a north-easterly direction from the cabin. It was quite large and required considerable time to cut. He had fallen it and gone with the pail to the part occupied by the bees, leaving his axe at the stump.

"The honey appeared in great abundance, and was but little damaged by the falling of the tree. Large sheets of beautiful white comb were taken out until the pail was filled and piled up to the height of itself above the top, and the supply not half exhausted.

"While vexed at the smallness of his vessel, and wishing it three times as large, he concluded to eat as much of the tempting and delicious comb as he could, and accordingly fell to work with hands and mouth.

"He had been thus pleasantly engaged but a short time, with the clear, bright honey running down over his chin and dripping from his hands to the elbows, utterly oblivious to all around him, when three Indians, who had been watching his movements for some time from an adjoining thicket, noiselessly slipped out, and approaching him from behind, seized him by the arms, which they immediately bound, and thus put an end to his luxurious repast. They had been attracted by the sound of his axe, and reached the spot soon after the tree fell.

"After helping themselves to as much of the honey as they wanted, they carried the pail with its contents to their encampment, three or four miles east. They manifested no disposition to hurt Wilcoxon, but took him along as a prisoner.

"When they reached the camp he discovered them to be a war party composed of about twenty Shawnees, who, having refused to go into treaty along with other Northwestern tribes with Wayne, had been on an expedition to the north-eastern part of Kentucky and were returning with some stolen horses and considerable plunder. The three who had so rudely intruded upon him and appropriated the proceeds of his morning's labor were out on a hunt.

"Shortly after their arrival at the camp, the Indians resumed their march, taking their prisoner with them. They took the direction of the Indian towns on the North Fork of Paint, and apprehending no danger from pursuit, they traveled very leisurely, stopping frequently to hunt and amuse themselves.

"On the third day after the capture of Wilcoxon, they struck Main Paint not far from where Bainbridge now stands, and passing down the right bank of the creek to the point where the turnpike now crosses it, encamped for the night. They sent some hunters out in the morning, and after they returned, and had prepared and eaten breakfast, preparations were made for resuming the journey, when, greatly to the surprise of the Indians, who had taken no precautions, believed themselves entirely free from danger, they were suddenly fired upon.

"Not knowing who the assailing party was, nor its strength, the Indians made a precipitate retreat across the creek, leaving everything behind them except their guns. In the midst of the terror and confusion, Wilcoxon managed to escape. The attacking party was under the command of General Massie.

"Wilcoxon arrived sound and well, only minus his axe, pail and honey, at his cabin by the Big Spring, much to his own and his wife's joy.

"He was disturbed no more by the Indians, or indeed by anyone else, for no human being seemed to be aware of the existence of his cabin and corn patch, as none ever visited him.

"In the fall he gathered quite a little pile of excellent corn, and made all necessary preparations for passing the winter, by daubing the cracks of his cabin on the outside and lining the walls on the inside with bear, deer and other skins.

"The long winter passed off pleasantly. He hunted when the weather was suitable, and when it was not, he remained in his cabin dressing skins and, with the aid of his wife, manufacturing them into clothing for himself and family, all of whom were dressed in skins of wild animals. Their bedding for the winter was all of the same material, as was not at all unfrequent with the early settlers. They made hominy of the corn, which, when cooked in bear's grease, is said to be most delicious.

"Early the following spring (1796) a small party of emigrants from Kentucky, going to join the settlers at what is now Chillicothe, accidentally took the route from the river which led them to Wilcoxon's improvement. These were his first visitors, and he entertained them in true pioneer style while they chose to remain.

"He and his wife were so pleased with their society after so long a separation from their fellow men, that they reluctantly consented to abandon their little home in the wilderness and accompany them to Massie's settlement on the Scioto."

And so, the account says, when the autumn came, the Wilcoxons had left for Chillicothe, and their cabin came to be occupied by Timothy Mershon and his family. By this time a sprinkling of settlements made by other Kentuckians and Virginians had begun throughout the county.

Quakers were trickling into the northern part of what is now Highland county, where the soil was fertile and suitable for farming. At Leesburg, a woman preacher, Bathsheba Lupton, rode horseback through the community preaching to and scolding the youths, men, and Indians who spent the Sundays together, playing games in the forest.

Then came the settlement at New Market, Highland county's first town, and the first county seat.

New Market was first thought of and planned by Henry Massie, a younger brother of Nathaniel Massie. Soon after Manchester had been founded, he came from Virginia, to assist his brother in exploring and surveying his grant.

While Nathaniel was busy with the growing settlement at Chillicothe on the Scioto river, Henry located and surveyed the lands on the headwaters of Brush creek and the hill regions southward, in the summer of 1796 and the summer and fall of 1797, because the rich bottom lands of the Scioto and Miami rivers had already been taken.

While on these surveying trips he came upon a wide upland. He entered this land and surveyed it for himself. He chose the land not for its fertility, but for its fine position. Some day, he thought, it would be chosen for the site of an important town, possibly a county seat, and therefore, it would bring him a fortune. Since this land lay in the center of the only towns that had been formed in the Virginia Military District, and another county was certain to be carved out of the country north of Manchester, his belief had foundation.

Henry and his assistants returned to Manchester and that winter Henry visited Nathaniel at Chillicothe. When he saw how Chillicothe and the surrounding territory had grown, he visioned a town similar to it, laid out on the pretty upland that had been his choice. Nathaniel approved of Henry's plan and promised aid in the project.

Then, on April 5, 1798, *"the spring having been very late, Henry set out from Manchester with a small company to lay off the town on the uplands and commence the foundation of a permanent settlement."*

Two days later, in the evening, they arrived at a spring near the tract. The next morning they began building make-shift shelters.

They came well-supplied with meal, bacon, salt, and axes and other tools, brought on their pack horses.

Henry Massie's company was small. It was composed of himself, Oliver Ross and Robert Huston who had come from Ireland a few years previous, another man whose name is not known, and Ross's 15-year-old daughter, Rebecca.

Massie was so positive that his town would be the rival of his brother's Chillicothe on the Scioto that he proceeded to lay out the town in a grand fashion. He gave Rebecca a lot in the town when it was platted as a special honor because he believed her to be the county's first white woman settler.

Universally admired as a plan for new towns, Philadelphia, capital of the United States and also of Pennsylvania at that time, was chosen for the model. The land was divided into regular and compact squares intersected by streets at right angles. All the streets were 66 feet wide except the two main cross streets which were 99 feet. The in-lots each had a frontage of 82½ feet and were 185 feet deep. There were over 400 acres in the entire plat. The public square was the northwest corner at the intersection of the two main cross streets and was designed for the court house. It contained four in-lots. One lot was for a school and an out-lot was donated for a cemetery.

After the town was blazed out in the forest, Massie had a hard time selecting a fitting name for his town. He finally decided in favor of a loved village in his native Virginia, NEW MARKET.

Hand bills were speeded to settlers along the river banks at Manchester, and they carried sensational and wonderful accounts of this model town, New Market, mecca in the Ohio wilderness. So absorbed were these settlers of New Market in the business of rounding out their town that the death of George Washington, under whom many of them had seen service, touched them rather remotely. Many days passed before word reached them of this great man's death and then appropriate services were held for him in the meeting house.

One of the most poignant stories coming to us out of the mist of these first years is the story of the Harris, Berryman, and Vance families who were among the first to come to the young New Market.

There were Jonathan Berryman and his wife and Eli Berryman, who started for Kentucky on October 1, 1798, according to an old county diary, — started from the New Jersey coast, their goal New Market which had been described to them by a traveler. The place exceeded their fondest hopes of a Utopia and they wrote vivid descriptions of their new homes back to their New Jersey relatives.

One of these relatives, a youth named Oliver Harris, was the son of one of two Harris brothers, cobblers by trade, who with their wives and children were among the small band of Baptists in a ship load of Quakers fleeing to America. They were not disloyal to the

Crown, but they had refused to conform to the established Church of England.

In New England, where they landed and settled, they found that they had merely *"jumped out of the frying pan into the fire."* Baptists and Quakers were not welcome there. Their religions were tolerated in New Jersey, however, and there they found a haven.

Oliver's family stopped in the northern part of New Jersey, free people at last. They saw their first Indians, friendly Indians who taught them many things while they lived among them; where to find the best fish and wild game, fruits and berries; Indian remedies for certain illnesses; how to make an Indian dugout that was light and suitable for the tidewater streams that embroidered the sandy soil.

The southern portion of New Jersey, the natives told them, was mostly swamp land, broken only by pine wastes and treacherous thickets. The seacoast was worse, dotted with numerous wild soggy salt marshes, sandy stretches of thickets, and bad harbors.

When the northern part of New Jersey became over-crowded with settlers they were obliged to spread out. Some pressed southward to find themselves blocked on the east by a vast forest. They took the Delaware River Route as far as Salem, some drifting in the meantime over into Pennsylvania as they came, others stopping on the eastern bank of the river in New Jersey, in the Quaker settlements.

To the south, near Bridgetown which resembled a New England village, with its broad streets, quaint homes, and Quaker meeting house, Oliver's family settled. Murmuring past their cottage was a little stream and the soil along it was good for raising oats, rye, and flax. All around were valuable stands of virgin timber and waters yielding fish and oysters. In summer wild geese and wood ducks swarmed over the marshes.

Oliver's family did not find the happiness they sought there. Ill health beset them and it became apparent that the mother must be taken away from the flood-ridden land and the swamps or she would surely die. So Oliver's father had a vendue and sold off the farm. They set out in a covered wagon for Highland county and this marvelous high and dry place called New Market, bringing with them nothing much except the nostalgic memories of fishing and oystering adventures and salt air.

Many of these first settlers are buried in New Market's two cemeteries, the tombstones old and stained by the years. And as you walk among the mounds, scanning the inscriptions, you will find yourself dreaming and wondering when you come upon an inscription such as this:

RACHEL
Wife of William Vance
Died May 1, 1873
Age 90 years, 3 months, 4 days.
The mother of 20 children.

In 1805, when Highland county was organized and Ohio severed its connection with Ross county, New Market was made the county seat of Highland county. Three associate judges, Jonathan Berryman, Richard Evans, and John Davidson were elected by the State legislature to administer justice. The first term of the Highland county court was held in the woods, May 16, 1805.

The judges were seated on a long bench made of a puncheon, with young David Hays, clerk protem, and Dan Evans, the sheriff, on hand to keep order. This it was hard to do, for on the first court day, several fights took place, with one rascal on horseback riding up before the magistrates and flourishing a bottle of Monongahela under their noses and loudly demanding that they take a *"snort"* with him. However, in spite of many interruptions, the dignity of the court was upheld.

George Barrere, a Kentuckian, who came to New Market from Clinton county in 1802, and whose tavern was the most popular for miles around, was chosen Senator; and John Gossett was chosen representative to the State legislature.

In the autumn of 1801, at the close of a cloudy, raw day, an *"athletic young man of medium height,"* dressed in the rough, simple style of the day, arrived at the town by way of the eastern trace from Chillicothe. He wore on his head an 18-gallon copper kettle. Strapped to his back with buffalo tugs, was a large bundle, and he carried a smaller one under his left arm. In his right hand he held a hurl bow.

This was Michael Stroup, who had come to establish a hatter shop. He was a journeyman hatter, but seven years before this when he was only 17 years old, as a soldier under *"Light-Horse Harry Lee,"* he had fought in the Whiskey Rebellion in Western Pennsylvania, against the *"Whiskey Boys."* In the kettle on his head were his hatter's tools and in one of the bundles were a few pounds of wool for hats.

"He was a go-ahead fellow and speedily had his kettle set in a cabin, and soon the sound of his bow was heard preparing the wool for the fulling process. He colored the hats and finished off a few which he sold readily."

When, in 1802, George Parkinson, a hatter from Pennsylvania, arrived, the two hatters built a shop of hued logs and lap-shingles which was the first hued house with a shingled roof in the region. They sent Thomas Kincade, a carpenter, to Lexington, Kentucky, for wool. The hats, when finished, were sold for 18 dollars a dozen.

Logwood was used for the black coloring, at a cost of 25 cents in the block.

One year later, Michael Stroup, the hatter, and Polly Walker were married and their wedding was deemed a most fashionable affair.

"The bride's dress was a very light-figured calico dress which cost one dollar a yard. She wore a nice plain cap on her head, white silk gloves, a plain white collar, and shoes and stockings. The groom was dressed in brown dress coat and pants, white marseilles vest, white socks, and low-quartered shoes, and white kid gloves. The wedding took place at two o'clock in the afternoon. They were married by the Squire. When the wedding banquet was consumed, the guests spent the afternoon in various amusements, shooting at a mark, running foot races, playing hide and seek, and winding up with an all night dance."

Gone now were the leather hunting shirt, breeches, moccasins, and coonskin hats. Home-spun, bark-colored linsey, wool hats, and shoes made of calf-skin, became the style. Ginseng, ashes, salt, and skins used for currency, were now succeeded by real money. More and more settlers drifted in. Besides the log cabin schools, a *"classical school"* had been opened in the Finley cabin on White Oak creek where classes were taught in Latin, Hebrew, and Greek.

As New Market was the county seat, roads naturally trended towards it, or connected with these roads. The roads usually followed old Indian trails or traces, and were just wide enough for a wagon or sled to pass through. Timber rolled to each side formed a fencing or enbankment sometimes as high as five feet. The settlers, absorbed in other pressing matters, had time only to keep the roads barely passable. A traveler along the road was an eagerly-looked for event, and he was usually warmly welcomed.

One of the first roads was that made in 1802, when Michael Stroup, the hatter, William Finley, and George Caley, were employed by Simon Kenton, to continue a wagon road that had been cut from Maysville to New Market, on to Springfield. This was called the Old Mad River road. Following an old trace that had been made by Kenton, the work was accomplished in 18 days. The men had a wagon pulled by a horse and ox. Their wages were one dollar each, a day. Through rain and snow, under terrible conditions and excruciating experiences hardly to be endured, they toiled, and at last returned to New Market, their clothing in shreds and almost starved to death.

All this time, whisperings had gone the rounds that the majority of the inhabitants of the county thought that the county seat ought to be located in a more central spot. John Kerr, who now owned large tracts of land around New Market, and had sold lots with the assurance to purchasers that the local seat of government would remain there, had commanded that the citizens raise money and erect, at their own expense, the necessary public buildings. This accomplished, the matter would be settled.

Kerr and Barrere, leaders in the plans, made arrangements for a barbeque and the first public county July 4th celebration to be held in the town. The whole county was invited with the hope that the people could be persuaded not to remove the county seat from New Market. The streets were thronged, and up and down marched the New Market militia with a fife and drum corps at the head, following an old tattered flag that had once seen service in General Wayne's army.

Stirring orations were made on a rough platform raised for the occasion and appeals made to the people to keep New Market the county seat. It would be nothing short of treason, not to do this. A savory roast ox, pig, and sheep were served, and enthusiasm was rising to a high pitch. Some kegs of whiskey were opened. This was to have been the auspicious moment for obtaining the subscriptions of money for the buildings; but, in consuming the whiskey, the purpose of the day was blissfully forgotten, and thus the cause irrevocably lost.

Hugh Fullerton humorously describes the scene in an article, "Book-Lover Finds Some New Facts of Ohio History," and points out that Billy Hill's land on Clear creek was favored by some as the new county seat. Hill was a popular and well-respected citizen who held militia drills in an impressive manner on the greensward along the creek. Mr. Fullerton says:

"It was decided to lay out a new county town, largely because of Irish Revolutionary soldiers, including Alexander Fullerton. and Clear creek, where Captain Billy Hill of Revolutionary War fame had started a settlement, both wanting the location of the new town. This led to 'the great knocking down,' in which battle in front of Barrere's inn at New Market, more than 100 men were knocked down before the chief battlers were arrested and imprisoned in a well after they had lifted the jail off the foundation and escaped.

"It was decided that the new town should be on the highest land nearest the intersection of the principal survey lines, and that this highest spot was on the ridge between Clear creek and Moberly's branch, in Billy Hill's territory; but it was found that the land two miles south of there was higher, and so the site of Hillsboro, named for Captain Billy Hill was chosen. New Market, after a struggle, surrendered, and has grown smaller and smaller, especially since Dusty Miller moved away to Wilmington and the town mostly set out to corn."

It was in 1807 that the State legislature appointed David Hays, an energetic and capable young man, to select a more appropriate site than New Market. He almost selected Eagle Spring, now owned by James Hogsett, one mile south of Hillsboro on the *"New Market pike,*" but finally decided on the land on which Hillsboro rests as nearest the center of the county.

Hays entered into negotiations with Benjamin Ellicott, who owned the chosen land. For the sum of $200.00 Hays received a deed for 200 acres of land from Phineas Hunt, attorney for Ellicott, September 7, 1807. The new county seat was given the name of Hillsboro.

The sale of the lots took place about the first of October of that year, on what is now East Beech street, east of the Armory location. Mr. Hays was in charge. What is now Hillsboro was then a virgin forest of oak, hickory, walnut, and beech with undergrowths of dogwood, spice, and hazel. Good springs were especially plentiful here and this may account for the sale having been held on this spot.

Constable John Davidson, of New Market, came in to sell off the lots; and near his stand, Christopher Bloom and his wife, also from New Market, had put up a little tent where they sold ginger bread and whiskey to the crowd. Accounts say that many were overcome by the liquor and had to be locked up for the night.

Quakers wearing their broad-brimmed hats moved with dignity among the customers who were an interesting group of English, Scotch, Irish, and Dutch. The price asked for the lots were within everyone's means, ranging from $20.00 to $150.00.

The first lot was bid off to John Campton, a tanner, from New Market. According to a record at the Court House, this was lot number 112 situated on the southeast corner of what is now Beech and East streets. Beside a bubbling spring he put up his shanty and thereupon became Hillsboro's citizen number one. His shanty faced what is now the John Conway residence. For some time no other house was built between Campton's shanty and the present location of the Masonic Temple building, and the ground between was called the *"Commons."*

The southwest corner lot of Main and High streets now occupied by the Columbus and Southern Ohio Electric Co., (formerly owned by Sam Scott and previously known as the Smith corner) was bought by Allen Trimble for $150.00. The Hillsboro Bank and Savings Co., southeast corner of Main and High streets, (the Johnson corner) brought $150.00. The northeast corner of High and Main streets, The Merchants National Bank, (the Fallis corner) was reserved.

Main and High street lots sold for from $40.00 to $75.00. Hays bid off the northwest corner of High and Walnut streets. This corner was known as the Mattill corner and a log tavern,— legend calls it *"The Sign of the Blue Boar,"* was located on it. This building, now clap-boarded, is the oldest business building in Hillsboro and is occupied by the L. E. Griffith Hardware store. For many years it was occupied by the Ballentine Hardware store. The original small-paned windows, characteristic of buildings then, are still in use.

David Reese bought the northwest corner of Beech and High streets where the Gamble property now stands and where once was the residence of Joseph Woodrow. What is now the Standard Oil Service Station, West Main street, (then the Joshua Woodrow corner) was bought by Allen Trimble.

The lots were sold on a 12-months' credit basis. The out-lots sold for from $20.00 to $25.00 and contained from three to five acres. The northwest corner of Court and High streets was sold to Richard Trimble by Allen Trimble, its first owner, for $30.00.

About one month after the sale of the lots in Hillsboro, John Knox put up a log cabin tavern with clapboard roof, on the present site of the Parker Hotel on West Main street. Town meetings were held here, as was the spring term of the Common Pleas court in the spring of 1808.

You could have gotten board there by the week for about $1.25 and you would have had your choice of the season's best offerings, — venison, turkey, bear (bear's feet roasted were considered quite a delicacy), pork, beef, fish, quail, and various other wild game, roasted to a delicious juicy brown for you on a spit over the fire or in the Dutch oven. Ground hominy, corn mush, corn bread, buckwheat cakes, and wild turkey breast were used for bread. Other items on the menu were vegetables, milk, maple syrup, wild honey, berries, corn whiskey, and apple brandy.

You could have sat there with the best of them, listening to the tales of adventurer, or traveler, or to the latest court news; and you could have been the first to have heard, if your ears were sharp, the galloping hoof beats of the approaching pack-horse mailman, and among the first to greet him when he blew his horn loudly outside.

Then if you had returned a few years later on a visit, you would have been amazed at the change of the new county seat. You would have found that the tavern had changed hands and was known as the Eagle Hotel for the refreshing drinking water carried in barrels from Eagle Spring; and you would have been amused, no doubt, at the *"hotel's"* nickname of *"Pigtail Done Tavern,"* so-called because one of the town's dignitaries thought that was what the bell seemed to say when it called him to dine.

Thus was the county seat of Highland county fixed, 139 years ago, and a new era begun.

CHAPTER V.

THE COUNTY GREW

WROTE Martha Hussey, in 1899, at the age of 90 years, of her childhood in Highland county:

"*Father looked around for a place to settle on and soon found one to please him on the head waters of Clear Creek. He bought 300 acres of good land and he and Uncle Alexander went to work, and in a short time had a cabin raised, and in a few weeks we were comfortably installed in it, and on the 18th of November, brother Joshua was born. There was a great deal of beautiful weather that fall and winter and Father and Uncle cleared nine or ten acres of ground and had it ready to plant corn in the spring. Uncle soon found land to suit him and settled in the same neighborhood.*

"*We never suffered for anything to eat as some settlers did, as we raised plenty of corn the next season after we came to do us, and we soon got cattle, hogs, and sheep around us. Father liked to hunt, and he killed a great many turkeys and deer, and he killed one bear. I remember the first summer we lived here Father found a bee tree and brought in buckets of honey comb, full of rich honey. Salt was hard to get when we first came, and they had to go to Chillicothe after it. They would ride horseback and take a sack. Father has paid as much as four dollars for fifty pounds. Five or six years later they went to Manchester on the Ohio River and got it much cheaper.*

"*They were a good deal bothered at first, until they got enclosures for their horses, about having them run away. Sometimes they would find them nearly to the Ohio River trying to get back to where they came from, and Uncle James Underwood had one go away and they never found it.*"

Generally speaking, Highland county awakened slowly to her potentialities as the predominant agricultural county she is today, for the settlers found themselves living in a land of plenty. Manufacturing however began as early as 1799 when Job Wright started manufacturing hair sieves by hand at Greenfield, and manufacturing has continued until today this county is also recognized as an industrial area, with products that are nationally known.

Often several brothers came together to Highland county, bringing their wives and children. They would settle in close proximity, thus forming a rural community where everyone's family name was the same, and the children were all cousins.

The settlers of long ago did their best in tilling the soil. Primitive methods were used, such as hitching a horse to a forked stick by means of bark harness. Then, as now, corn was the main crop, but other phases of farming were innovated by visionary settlers.

There was James Carlisle, son of the abolitionist, Samuel B. Carlisle, who was the first tobacco planter and manufacturer in Highland county. Some of the tobacco was made into twists of two or more pounds for *"eating"* purposes. Some was made into smoking tobacco that became widely known.

There was Jonathan Berryman who brought with him from New Jersey to New Market, choice selections of apple and peach seeds, and who journeyed to Manchester on the Ohio river to obtain cow manure to fertilize the soil, carrying it to New Market in sacks on his back. This, in spite of the fact that a vague legend persists that Johnny Appleseed planted Highland county's first orchard on the site of Etnah Woods, at the Seven Caves.

There was Allen Trimble who recognized the possibilities of sheep raising and began the growing of wool extensively on his farm near Hillsboro. He was one of the first farmers in this state to raise sheep, and to advocate it. His article, *"Fine Wool,"* appeared in a farm journal published in Columbus about a hundred years ago.

Wonderful possibilities for farming lay before the first Highland countians, but tanning, milling, lumbering, distilling, wool-carding, pork and beef packing, were the first industries to which the settlers most diligently applied themselves. Streams were dotted with grist mills and iron forges.

Possibly, since wild growth was so abundant and farm implements were rare, farming could wait while hides were tanned for needed leather, lumber was prepared for the better homes that superseded the log cabins, and iron forges shaped nails and the like that until then, settlers had to journey on pack horses to obtain, as far away as Pittsburgh.

The slaughtering of trees has taken practically all of our virgin timber. Many a bare place exists in the county that was once a fine stand of walnut, or a maple grove where maple sap ran copiously into buckets in the spring.

Lumbering, until about 1900, was a very important industry. There were numerous lumber mills and yards throughout the county. Lumber was kept in yards *"on stick"* until it was seasoned. Oak was, and still is, the standard wood used for building purposes. Poplar, oak, and elm trees once were used in the local manufacture of veneers. Native wood is scarce now, and much that is used is shipped in from the South where it has been steam dried and cut.

A unique contribution to the world today is the result of the establishment of the C. S. Bell Foundry on West Beech street in Hillsboro in 1858, by C. S. Bell from Cumberland, Md. The foundry was moved a few years later to its present quarters on Railroad street.

The main products were plows, cooking stoves, sorghum mills, feed and grinding mills, both power and hand, cane grinding mills, cane and maple syrup evaporators, and a machine called the *"Tortilla,"* used in Mexico for crushing hominy. Later, coffee and rice machines were featured products.

Then Mr. Bell accidentally dropped a piece of metal. Its resonant tone gave him the idea of making bells of iron instead of the more expensive brass or bronze. By 1899, bells for churches, schools, alarms, and farm purposes were being shipped to many parts of the world.

When an emergency order at the beginning of World War II limited the use of bronze and brass to actual combat essentials, Virginia Bell, executive director of the foundry, and granddaughter of the founder, realized that the thousands of United States ships being built would have to have bells. Since Navy bells are bronze, she immediately went to work on the idea of supplying bells for these ships.

She sent her production manager to Washington to solicit a trial order for bells. As a result, since that eventful day, more than 26,000 bells were cast for the Navy, for civilian defense, and for the Maritime Commission; and this included all kinds of fighting ships, cruisers, flat-tops, and landing craft.

The remarkable thing about it all is the fact that these bells are made from a secret formula known only to two persons, Miss Bell, and *"Old Clarence,"* the colored cupola tender who has been in the employ of the foundry for a life time. They guard the secret carefully. Officials of the foundry say the bells are made not from copper, tin, or zinc, but from *"steel alloy."* Before they are shipped, the Reverend Ignatius Lee, a Presbyterian minister, inspects and blesses them.

These are our leading crops: corn; fruit; tobacco; wheat; soy beans; hay; rye; buckwheat; barley; honey; berries. Corn, our largest and most important crop, is grown on the rich, deep bottom lands. The yield has been as high as 124 bushels of corn to an acre on a 10-acre farm, but the average yield is 35 to 40 bushels, with much of it running from 50 to 70 bushels.

The average length of the growing season is approximately 170 days and extends from about April 15, to October 1. Crop seasons are about the same as those of surrounding counties.

The most common and best rotation of crops is the biennial rotation of corn, wheat and clover, which produces three crops in three years. Another, widely used on bottom lands, is that of corn, wheat, sweet clover and timothy. There is still some virgin soil that has never been cleared. More than half of the county or about 60 percent of the land is meadow land.

About 75 percent of the farmers of Highland county own their own farms. About 10 percent employ labor, some hiring by the year and some by the season. *"March is moving time in Highland county,"* is an old but true saying. At this time, often earlier, many farm tenants make changes from one tenant farm to another.

The average size of a Highland county farm is from 100 to 124 acres. There are many smaller farms and a few very large farms from two to three thousand acres. Highly specialized farms as The Highland County Poultry Farm, at Buford, The Sunlight Farm, near Lynchburg, and Mary and John Jones' Turkey Farm, near Samantha, conduct extensive businesses. Many farms specialize in the raising of cattle, hogs, fruit, tobacco, and turkeys.

Chickens are raised on the poultry farms for dual purposes. These are: Plymouth Barred Rock; White Wyandot; Orpington; Rhode Island Red; English White Leghorn. The latter is raised chiefly for eggs. Geese, ducks, and guineas are also raised on some farms.

Cows for dairy farms are for the most part imported from Texas and Colorado and are shipped in as calves weighing from 250 to 300 pounds. Favorite breeds are Hereford and Short Horns, but some Angus, Jersey, and Holstein are also raised. Beef is an important product.

The method of marketing beef in Highland county long ago is in quaint contrast to the methods of marketing today:

"When Jacob Saylor was 19 years old, he lead a steer from Circleville, Ohio, to Boston, Mass. He was employed by a man named Hamlin to lead the guiding steer at the head of a big drove of cattle which was being driven to New York to the market. When they reached New York the market was not satisfactory so they drove the cattle to Boston where they were sold."

Hogs are raised for dual purposes. Breeds usually raised are: Poland China (spotted and big type), Berkshire, Hampshire, and Tamworth. The latter is raised for bacon.

Farm flocks are constantly being improved. Thirty ewes may produce 60 lambs and if one dies, as one farmer quoted. *"It pays its own funeral expenses."* Pure bred sheep are imported from the northern part of the state and the Livestock Company at Hillsboro is a distributing center for the county.

Fruit farms cover from 18 to 20 acres each. Apples are the chief crop. Highland county is in the Roman Beauty belt and this apple is produced abundantly. Other kinds are the Winesap, Jonathan, red-gold Delicious, and Baldwin. Apple trees are planted about 35 feet apart and peach trees such as the Elberta, J. H. Hale, and Champions, are used as fillers.

The production of honey is now a minor enterprise but the scientific raising of bees is slowly developing, marked contrast to the days when honey was obtained by marking a bee tree and, after it was filled with wild, sweet honey by the bees, smoking the bees out and chopping a large hole in the hollow tree to get the coveted luxury.

The planting of berries in gardens is coming in in a big way throughout the county. Raspberries, blackberries, and strawberries are being planted in gardens and are fast becoming a major enterprise. Highland county is just outside the strict Burley tobacco belt and tobacco raised in this county is among the finest raised in the United States.

Pheasant preserves were established in several wooded sections a few years ago. Grouse were released at Fort Hill State Park where, also, young trees were set out in areas where soil erosion had taken serious toll, gullies were filled, and soil dams built. Streams have been restocked with fish and trees have been planted in various spots.

There are many farm agencies in the county which have united to assist the farmer with his problems. These are, namely: Farm Bureau; Production Credit Association; Livestock Improvement Association; Farm Security Administration; Agriculture Adjustment Administration; Dairy Improvement Association; 4-H Clubs; Soil Conservation Service; County High School Vo-Ag Instructors; Grange; Game Conservation; Producers Cooperative Association; Rural Electrification; Federal Land Bank; Farm Credit Administration; Farm Labor Assistant; Farm Forester; War Food Assistant.

One of the first of these to organize was the Farm Bureau Cooperative Association, in 1920, for the purpose of supplying a ready market for county products and farm supplies purchased by Highland countians on a cooperative plan. The association has been defined as *"a cooperative association of farmers endeavoring by organized producer and consumer action through education to achieve economic freedom and social advancement for themselves and all fellow humans; and a spokesman for the farmer in legislative affairs."* It consists of farm bureau offices, warehouse, and petroleum bulk plant. The warehouse provides space for feed, seed, fertilizer, machinery, and other merchandise stocks, and a small storeroom space and a retail store combined on the second floor. Complete automobile fuel and lubrication service are supplied at the front of the building. It is the headquarters also for the Highland County Credit Union, and the Inter-County Rural Electric. It sponsored the Livestock Shipping Association on a cooperative basis.

Until 40 or 50 years ago, Saturday stock sales in Hillsboro were the main events in the lives of this rural county. Farmers brought their horses to town and trotted them up and down the streets to show them off and prove that they were sound and free from the "heaves." Shortly after daylight you saw the traders going up and down the main streets, often one farmer leading several horses. Many horses were imported from Belgium, one trader making special trips abroad to bring back fine Belgian stallions. *"Stock-*

sales Saturday drew a large crowd to Hillsboro," a local paper stated 40 years ago. *"Thirty-two horses and mules were sold to foreign buyers. Prices ruled a shade lower than at last previous sale."*

The crowning event of the year was the county agricultural fair held at the Fair Grounds, in Hillsboro. A news item from a local paper 40 years ago, says of the fair: *"A large crowd attended the celebration of the glorious Fourth in Hillsboro. Harness races at the Fair Grounds were witnessed by at least 5000 people. Rain interfered with the program. Lovely fireworks at night."*

"Dear old days of early morning feeding and milking," said the late George L. Garrett of his boyhood on a farm near Rainsboro about 75 years ago. *"Why, we hardly had any night at our house. My good mother used religiously to begin to call us about three o'clock in the morning, sun-time, and we just had to get up. I think we burned enough coal oil and fuel waiting for daylight to have put us boys through college and to have bought the hired girl a good delaine dress.*

"We shedded our cows at the straw rick and always milked on the south side, because we supposed it to be warmer, although this operation of separating a cow from its lacteal fluid always occurred an hour before sun-up, or an hour after sun-down. In the real cold winter, the milk would gradually freeze on our fingers until they would hardly bend. Then, a little later in the spring, when we began to go barefoot, and when the dew was heavy as rain, and as cold as ice, the cows were turned out to early pasture, and we always had to go to the other side of the pasture field for them.

"We had our farm mostly sowed in dew-berry, or running briars. When we would start for the cows and be on the run, suddenly one of those briars would get between two of our toes, and before we could stop, it would act as a rip saw does when engaged in ripping lumber. I think those briars made all my toes about twice as long as they ought to be. And when we did reach the old cow, to find her peacefully lying down chewing her long green or cud, how pleasant it was to stir her up so one could stand where she had been lying, and warm those briar-torn feet!"

OUR HOMES:

THE log cabins were small, but they were durable, because they were made of fine, local resources of timber. They not only housed the large families of the pioneers in comparative comfort, but there was always room around the huge fireplace for one more weary traveler or guest. They were our first churches, schools, and public buildings.

Then good building stone and clay suitable for bricks were discovered. Skilled masons fashioned houses after their former homes in the East. Wherever you found a good bed of clay, you usually found a kiln with bricks in the process of baking. Brick houses were more fashionable than stone. Many of these homes are in use today and are in excellent condition.

The frame houses that followed closely were adaptations of the Georgian (English). They were built on simple lines, accented by small towers, and bay and dormer windows. Some had deck porches supported by stately columns. Examples of these homes are often found in the most unexpected places as the Norman Overman farm house near New Petersburg, and Governor Allen Trimble's home in Hillsboro.

Greek architecture was revived in the East in 1820 and crept into Highland county about 1830. It was an outgrowth of the Roman Revival for which Thomas Jefferson's initiative was responsible. Doric columns, porches, and doorways modified the popular Colonial style. Another popular style promoted by Thomas Jefferson out of his love for geometry, was the octagon house. Only one such example is in Highland county. This is the old high school building in Sinking Spring, on the village commons, on the main street.

Regardless of the style and the materials of these homes, all were patterned mostly from memory after old southern homes. Highland county has never lost this original charm. It has faithfully retained the flavor of the old South even in modern architecture.

The Greek Revival house can be distinguished easily from the Colonial house because the former tends to imitate the classic Greek temple with low-pitched roof at the entrance supported by large columns that support a dignified portico. The first Colonial house had the effect of being square or blocked and had no columned portico.

Our court house is of old English Colonial design with Roman columns, built by a Virginian. An article in the American Home magazine March, 1938, entitled, *"The American Homes Pilgrimages,"* includes it among the most beautiful homes and public buildings in southern Ohio. It is described thus: *"The Highland county court house at Hillsboro, northeast of Cincinnati, exemplifies a Roman structure."*

Reference to Highland county's court house was made by I. T. Frary, in his *"Early Homes of Ohio,"* published in 1936. Mr. Frary says: *"The early courthouses were inevitably classic in design. As temples of justice there was a natural tendency to revert to the Roman temple forms, even as lawyers who function in them revert to Roman codes. Moreover most of the older courthouses of the state were built when the classics were a veritable obsession in cultured circles, and Thomas Jefferson's classic Revival was at its height. So we find some of the designs reminiscent of Jefferson's flair for things Roman, as for instance the Highland county courthouse at Hillsboro, Ohio, while others reflect the more sturdy structures of the Greeks."*

Churches of modified Gothic (pointed) type are found in the county. St. Mary's Catholic and St. Mary's Episcopal churches at Hillsboro, illustrate this. The Catholic church is of stuccoed brick, surmounted by a gold cross. The Episcopal church is of gray stone covered with clinging ivy, and further enhanced by priceless stained-glass windows. Other examples are the Hillsboro Presbyterian church and the Greenfield Methodist and Presbyterian churches. The red-brick Hillsboro Methodist church is of early Colonial architecture. The flavor of old New England is in the quaint doorway and the stairway on each side leading to the auditorium of the church proper. Its twin was the Presbyterian church known as the Crusade church which preceded the present Presbyterian stone structure.

The taverns of the county were important places. Here many of our first public meetings were held and many housed our first post offices.

"The Traveler's Rest" at Greenfield, was representative of the first class Highland county taverns. Noble Crawford erected it in 1811, and was not only its landlord, but the postmaster. It was the first stone house built in Greenfield. Once a week, when the post boy's horn heralded the arrival of the postman on horseback, in from Chillicothe by way of the old College Township road, villagers hastened to receive their letters and papers and to hear any news of interest from the outside world. This tavern is now a rest home for the aged and its name, carved in the coping over the doorway, has long been covered with mortar.

Most of the school buildings in the county are modern and hold to the Colonial pattern. The McClain High School at Greenfield is of pure classic design and inspiring Georgian beauty and is the costliest and most magnificent edifice in the county. It is rated by critics as one of the most complete and beautiful school plants in the United States. The Hillsboro High School, of red, pressed brick, is modern Colonial. It follows the semi-circle plan of entrance and exit and a giant, century-old maple tree sentinels the entrance to the building.

The Colonial residences are among our most beautiful heritages from the past. Representative examples are the Dr. Roy S. Rogers, Sr., home (Caspar Collins' boyhood home); Forest Lawn (The Colonial Inn), recently razed, built by Governor Allen Trimble and Attorney James Thompson as a wedding gift for the former's only daughter, Eliza Jane, who became Mr. Thompson's bride and the famed *"Mother Thompson";* and the Samuel P. Scott home, now a part of the Hillsboro High School plant. These homes sit well back from the street, with tree-shaded driveways forming graceful entrances and exits. They have the familiar Colonial porches with two sets of columns. On the second floor of the 24-room Colonial Inn, bedrooms were arranged around a sitting room which open on to a balcony. Still another very lovely old home is the Smith residence on East Main street, now in the possession of the Ann Quinn Ottewill heirs.

Many of these old homes have been sold during recent years, and their contents auctioned at public sales. In July, 1944, an immense crowd of 2000 attended the sale of Will Richards' antiques at Forest Lawn, following which Mr. Richards left to make his home in California. Sales were made to residents of Oklahoma, Indiana, Michigan, West Virginia, and Kentucky, in addition to Ohio, and was possibly the finest collection of antiques ever offered by a Highland county family.

The bidding was spirited. The prices many of the pieces brought showed how rare and valuable they were. A top price of $800 was paid for a Governor Winthrop secretary's desk; and a Grandfather Hall clock sold for $525.

Other high prices were: 2 pairs of lace curtains, $64; 1 Roseback rocker, $120; 1 Lyre base night stand, $125; 5-piece tea set, $100; 2 small Staffordshire vases, $86; 2 oval pictures, $68; 1 fireplace set, $151; a pair of scissors, $9.00; 6-piece China tea set, $54; 4 open arm chairs, $230.

This sale, typical of many which have been held in recent years in this county, is best described by the late inimitable Attorney Burch D. Huggins who was present that day, and published in Granville's Barrere's *"Side Slants,"* in the News-Herald, July 20, 1944:

Well, well, the Richards sale, out at what used to be known in former days as "Forest Lawn," has come and gone, and as usual, some things sold high as a cat's back, some less than their real worth. It takes experience, and sales resistance to buy wisely at such auctions. The auctioneers are, or act like they are, in one devil of a hurry, and it was noticed that at times timid or inexperienced bidders were overlooked. On several occasions this unofficial reporter for the News-Herald noticed that higher bids went unseen or were disregarded. We would advise timid bidders to sing out in stentorian tones, to be not afraid, and act like they attended such sales every day and twice on Saturday. What provokes this unofficial News-Herald reporter is the rattle-brained prattle of most auctioneers, making it quite impossible to tell whether the particular sum they keep repeating is the old bid they already have, or the new bid they are trying to get.

Sometimes funny things happen, and often the old saying that "he laughs best who laughs last" is well illustrated. For example the Richards' auctioneer wanted a bid on a miscellaneous and very odd lot of old waiter's coats, and finally asked this unofficial reporter to give him a start at fifty cents, which said reporter, ever the good Samaritan, at once did. Yep — you guessed it — he bought the coats and at once became the butt of many so-called smart jokes, the victim of much good-natured, and supposedly funny, badinage, for paying so much for a "bunch of rags."

Well, the very next day, said unofficial reporter sold those coats for twenty-five cents each, or a total of $3.00, a little matter of 600 percent profit. It should be remembered however that we figure income on investment by the year, which contains 365 days, so the real percent of profit was 365 times 600 percent or a snappy 219,000 percent. Any old fogy can sit around and do no thinking but it takes initiative, and sound judgment and knowledge of values and vision and faith and experience to see a bargain and reap an honest profit. It is this very same self-reliant courage and fortitude and industry that carved America out of the wilderness, yes, that made America great. Selah.

But to return to the sale itself, the crowd of buyers, the curious who came only to see, the crying of prices by the auctioneers, their loud and persuasive urgings for higher bids, the milling through the house and in and out, by scores and scores of people, all these things brought many a pang to all *"old-timers"* one of whom was this said unofficial reporter. Here, in these very rooms he had attended many a dinner, or dance, or other party; here had been one of Hillsboro's most distinguished homes, one of the social centers of the village; here music and laughter and hospitality and generosity and welcome reigned supreme; here the latch string always hung outside; here were Misses Elizabeth and Martha and Sarah and here were Mr. Eddy, and Fred and Will. How many *"old-timers"* remember the reception and dance following the wedding of Miss Elizabeth and Mr. Flint Rockhold? Here was Mr. Joseph Richards, ever the genial host; and here, presiding over all, with a charming grace that was hers alone, was Mrs. Richards, hostess supreme, envoy of friendliness and neighborliness and good-will and charity, gracious in her every thought, kindliness in her every deed.

Yes, the doors of Forest Lawn are no longer open, its latch string pulled in. We old-timers see these old homes where much of the social life of Hillsboro was centered, closed one by one. Other days and other ways crowd upon us. And this unofficial reporter is frank to say he does not like it. Perhaps he may be pardoned for reflecting, in a sense, on the glory that was Greece, and the grandeur that was Rome, yes, on the social life that once was Hillsboro, and is now gone, never to return.

OUR SCHOOLS:

TEACHING began in the homes almost immediately after the first log cabins had been constructed.

Settlers living near the Adams county town of West Union lost no time in sending their sons across the county line for a three-months schooling, until their own log schools could be built. It was not considered necessary for girls to go, for girls in those times took no active part in public affairs.

The first teachers in Highland county were the mothers who would take a little time from their household duties each day to instruct their own and neighbor children. Soon, however, schools were built and teachers employed. Most of these teachers were Revolutionary War soldiers who had seen service among the Indians, and the strict discipline they had known in the Army carried over into the methods they used in the school room. They were boarded around by the school patrons and this was the way they were paid for their services.

Sometimes an educated man taught what was called a *"classical school"* in his cabin. To such a school went those who would learn Latin and Greek.

Pupils in the log cabin schools ranged from kindergarten to young men and women in their early twenties. People in those days were firm believers in the *"rod"* and grown men and women were often whipped for misdemeanors *"until they fairly jumped off the floor."*

The *"scholars"* as they were called in those days, sat on benches of split saplings and their desks were hewn slabs. Pages from copy books, decorated with ink, and greased, were used for the window panes. Ink was manufactured from maple bark. The pupils' only supplies were a Webster's Spelling Book, Pike's Arithmetic, a piece of slate and a goosequill pen. Children hummed their lessons aloud when they studied and thought nothing of it when a bear, passing, poked an inquisitive nose in at the door.

However strict the old-time teacher was, there was no squelching the bubbling spirits of the pioneer children and they often disrupted the school routine. One of the customs was that of pupils barring the teacher out and refusing to let him in except on their own terms. The terms were usually a day's holiday and a treat to apples, cider, and ginger cakes. A relative of a young teacher starting his first term of school at New Market, in 1805, says in his diary: *"Reuben was locked out of the school house this morn and so he quit his school."*

The schools showed rapid progress. A monitorial system originating in England utilized older pupils as monitors and in a degree as assistant teachers. As teachers were scarce, this appealed to intelligent people. The system was called the Lancastrian System and emphasized writing and spelling. Nothing was taught beyond the common branches except bookkeeping. Although both sexes were taught in the same building, they sat on opposite sides.

The first Lancastrian school was opened in Hillsboro in 1818, and existed until 1823. It was opened by John McMullen, a Virginian, in a new log house on Main street.

Often a man and his wife opened a school jointly, the man instructing the boys and the woman, the girls. Or a woman would open a separate school for girls and a man would open one for boys. This ushered in the era of seminaries, institutes, and academies. There were singing and dancing schools on certain nights to which pupils were required to bring their own fuel and light.

The Hillsboro Academy and the Oakland Female Seminary, at Hillsboro, and the Greenfield Seminary at Greenfield were examples of these. The Oakland Female Seminary later became the Highland Institute.

The Hillsboro Academy (Methodist) for young men was founded in 1827 in a *"handsome brick building purchased by its trustees on a beautiful eminence."* It gave particular attention to training young men as teachers but later became co-educational. Rev. Joseph McDowell was the first teacher, but later Prof. Isaac Sams superseded him. The white brick building overlooking the town was situated opposite the present high school building. Its many-paned windows glittered like fire at sunrise and sunset and was a familiar landmark until it was torn down in the summer of 1922 to make room for residences.

The Oakland Female Seminary (Presbyterian) for young ladies, was founded in 1837, in what was until recently the Children's Home, on East Main street. Rev. Matthews was the first teacher. Later, Miss Emily Grand-Girard, a cultured teacher from the French settlement of Mowrystown, became the instructor. Her father is said to have spoken thirteen languages fluently. When the school became co-educational, it was called the Highland Institute. Physiology was the most fashionable subject studied in 1880. After the demise of the school, the building was leased in 1890 for use as a high school and a part of the primary grades. (A three-year high school course had been adopted in 1872, with Prof. Henry S. Doggett as teacher.)

The Greenfield Seminary was founded by J. B. Blair in 1845. Students came from a radius of 50 miles and at times the enrollment was 185. Diplomas were granted to *"meritorious females,"* and the first to receive them were Lavinia Smart and Mary L. Dunlap, in the year 1849. An academic department for the instruction of young men was also established in addition to the seminary. This was noted for its debating societies.

There was a vast difference between the subjects taught boys

and girls in the seminaries and academies. Boys were taught such subjects as reading, arithmetic, bookkeeping, trigonometry, surveying, gauging, geometry, and algebra, and the like, but girls were encouraged to study subjects as, reading, writing, and sewing.

At one time it was considered the thing to do, if finances permitted, to send girls to the School of the Brown County Ursulines. This school, though Catholic, was attended by girls of both Protestant and Catholic faiths, from prominent families in various parts of the United States. Highland county sent its share of pupils to this school.

Not long after this school had been founded, in the summer of 1845, eleven young Ursulines, dressed in black garments and poke bonnets, arrived in Brown county, near the boundary of Highland county, to be its teachers. In *"The Cross in the Wilderness,"* by Sister Monica, the story of these young heroines is related. Never expecting to see their homes and loved ones in France, again, they crossed ocean and wilderness to bring their priceless culture to the new world.

The teaching aim of this school, Sister Monica said, *"was to form young ladies to virtue, ornament their minds with useful information, accustom them to early habits of order and economy, and to teach them how to take their places properly in the family circle and in society likewise."*

Besides the teaching of German, French, Italian, Latin, and Spanish, the girls were taught tapestry, sewing, and waxwork, and Astronomy and the Use of the Globe, Mythology, Biography and the Antiquities, Philosophy and Chemistry, Botany, Geography, and Rhetoric.

Typifying the pioneer teachers of Highland county was Isaac Sams. He was a colorful figure.

He was born in the cathedral city of Bath, England, in 1788, the son of Joseph and Maria Sams. His early childhood was spent in the mountains of Wicklow county, on the coast of Ireland, where his father, a Baptist minister, preached on a circuit. He was sent to one of the finest schools in Dublin.

When Isaac was 10 years old, the household was stricken with scarlet fever. Both parents died. The boy and his sister, Mary, were left without any close living relatives.

Mary was taken to rear by Lord and Lady Carleton, of London, but Isaac was given into the care of a distant cousin who was a woolen goods manufacturer in the little town of Rathdrum, near Dublin. His guardian put him to work at once.

Once he ran away, unable to endure his unhappy existence in an unloving household. He walked the long road toward Dublin and slept in a hollow tree at night. He finally decided to turn back and make the best of his lot, finding solace in church and good books.

The Greenfield School Plant at Greenfield

Hillsboro High School

The Old Church

The Crusaders

Praying before saloon on North High Street, Hillsboro.

The Crusaders

Destroying the whiskey on the public square at Hillsboro.

The Crusaders in front of J. W. Bales Saloon.

"Mother" McDowell, upraised hand. Mr. Bales in doorway Mrs. Stevens, to right of Bales.

When he was 16 years old he asked his master for his indentures and for permission to leave. This was granted. He went to Dublin and worked first in a lumber yard, then in a carpet warehouse. When he was able, he went to London and found Mary. Mary's benefactors obtained a position for him as secretary to Admiral Pickmore, on the Man of War, Caledonia. He spent three exciting years on the Baltic sea. In the meantime, he had mastered the French, Latin, and Greek languages, and their literatures.

It was after England's war was over and he was corresponding clerk in the Treasury Department of Greenwich Hospital in London that Isaac heard Morris Birbeck's vivid description of America. Instantly, he saw his life's work here, and was inspired to come to this country and establish Lancastrian schools. He arrived in Baltimore, Maryland, in June, 1816.

He found several excellent families of means who desired a teacher for their children. Isaac took out papers declaring his intention of becoming an American citizen and then organized his first school near Baltimore. In his diary he wrote: *"I have not yet had to resort to corporal punishment with my children. By my system I keep shame alive and they shed tears when I speak severely."*

His reputation as a teacher spread. Pupils came from far and near. He removed to a more favorable location near a place named Ellicott's Mills, and opened the Rock Hills Academy, a school for boys. Fifty boarding pupils enrolled at the start, many of them former students who had followed him from Baltimore. His school and his reputation as a teacher were phenomenal. When he was persuaded to go to New York City and open a school there, the governor of Maryland wrote him a letter of deep regret.

In New York, Prof. Sams was stricken with ill health. Hearing of the healthful climate and conditions in southern Ohio, he exchanged his property at Ellicott's Mills to the Ellicott brothers, for a tract of land of 1000 acres near Hillsboro, Highland county. He came to Hillsboro in 1835 and occupied himself with some farming until he had regained his health. Then he became the teacher of the Hillsboro Academy for Boys.

His personal appearance was striking. A pupil described him thus: *"He carried himself erect as an Indian and was always active and brisk in his movements. He had something of a military bearing, and always attracted attention wherever he went."*

Another former pupil paid him this tribute long years afterwards: *"The story of his life exemplifies how learning may be attained by perseverance and industry, and how good a use may be made of it when once acquired. His career as a teacher shows what may be accomplished by the true teacher who feels the glorious inspiration of his calling. He believed the work of the teacher* second in importance to none other, and he always acted and taught in accordance with that belief."

Henry S. Doggett, a pupil who later became one of Highland county's leading teachers recalls for us in his book, "*Life and Service of Isaac Sams*," his own first day at school:

"Most of us had seen him as he strode through our street, erect and with an imposing carriage, and it was whispered from one to another that he was an awful savage. As the custom of flogging was still in vogue, we about made up our minds that we would 'catch it,' if we were not uncommonly careful. While exchanging our views on the subject the cry was raised, 'Here he comes,' and looking out of the window we beheld him whom in our lack of veneration we had dared to call 'Old Isaac,' riding up on a small dun horse. He was clad in a long white great coat, buckled around his waist with a surcingle and covered as to his head with a huge fur cap.

"Soon the door opened and Mr. Sams entered, holding in his right hand a short cowhide whip which projected straight before him, and, with a military salute he marched across the room into another apartment where he disposed of his wrappings. Soon returning he held some consultations with a few of the parents who were present and then commenced business.

"'Young gentlemen,' he began.

"We looked around to see whom he was addressing, for we had never been so flattered before, and as we saw none to whom he could be talking but ourselves, we each straightened up about a foot, more or less, and began to think he was a pretty nice old gentlemen after all.

"'All hands attention!' he proceeded. 'Come forward and matriculate.'

"We gazed at each other dumbly. What he wished us to do we could not imagine for 'matriculate' was a word not yet introduced into our vocabulary. However, he called up one of our number, entered his name, and then proceeded to enroll each in his turn, with a turkey-quill pen which he manufactured in our presence by about three clips of an immense pruning knife which he waved in the air like a saber. To me the whole scene was indescribably funny, although my fun was mingled with fear and trembling.

"Soon my turn came. He pulled down his skull-cap with his left hand and raising his turkey-quill in his right, as though to stab me with it, looked at me, as I thought fiercely, and said in an interrogative tone, 'Name?' This I also answered. 'Tell me how many are 16 times 16, quick, quick!' fairly shrieking the last word. I giggled. 'Ah,' said he, 'I see, mercurial, frivolous, but, my dear boy, we will do better by-and-by, we will improve.'"

Prof. Sams was greatly interested in the Common Schools of Ohio, but he considered them weak. He thought that pupils were not thoroughly taught and that Ohio teachers were carelessly and superficially examined. When he was appointed school examiner for Highland county, he adopted a fixed method of strict examination of applicants for certificates which resulted in weeding out the weak.

"His examinations were a terror to inefficient and poorly qualified teachers, but gave true merit and good scholarship the fullest recognition. He insisted on 'personal cleanliness of hands, face and apparel.' Applicants who came with dirty hands were dismissed with a short lecture on the virtue of soap and water."

Other improvements in Ohio schools accredited to Prof. Sams were: a county society of teachers known as the Association of Teachers of Highland County; the first Teachers' Institute; school libraries; the establishment of an educational paper. Recognizing the advantages of graded schools, he urged their adoption, with success, and Highland county had graded schools. Prof. Sams was employed to teach Ancient Languages and Higher Mathematics in the Hillsboro schools at the age of 70, and until his death at the age of 90, he received a few pupils at his home and gave a series of public lectures.

In the country, as in the towns, local resources were utilized in building frame and red brick school houses from whose doors many a future noted person went forth into the world. The names of these school houses are mostly memories for they have been turned into residences. Each was situated in a certain numbered district as, Washburn School, District number nine. Names of others were: Oak Ridge; Point Victory; Pleasant Hill; Dead Fall; Rosebush; Persimmon Ridge; Head's College; Briar Hill. Two alone of these schools, have survived the past and these two are located, one at Danville, and one on the Danville-Buford road.

The late George L. Garrett said, in an address at a school reunion of teachers and pupils at Briar Hill College, in August, 1917:

"It was not only in this old red school house that I taught my first school, but it was here I earned my first dollar and here, therefore, that I laid the foundation for my career.

"How well I remember the hurrying and scurrying to get off to school before the 'first bell would ring.' Then the old dinner basket we took with us filled with home-made bread, biscuits soaked with butter, doughnut, cakes, pies, — and stomach ache. I remember a pie my Mother used to make with a solid crust for a foundation, filled with old-fashioned apple butter, and finished up with a lattice-work top, which I wouldn't trade, if I could sample it today, for the choicest bit of pastry made by Bradley Fletcher's Palm Beach Hotel. And I almost forgot to mention those molasses ginger cakes. My brother Harvey, who now sleeps 'mid the green fields of Virginia, far away, once wrote, in part:

> "I yust to think it was a month,
>   Before bake day would come;
> 'Peared like I wanted cake so bad,
>   I'd nearly die fer some.
> But when the wisht-fer day would come,
>   We'd chase the hens and make
> 'Em lay some eggs fer whitenin'
>   'Fore Mother baked a cake."

"There were the happy recesses and noons, when we didn't have to "stay in", — with all their pleasing games, "Three-cornered cat," "Town ball," "Bull pen," "Fox and Geese," "Hidy-hoop," and then, when the boys and girls played together, such games as "Drop the Handkerchief," "Ring around Rosie," and the "Needle's Eye." I have stood patiently and expectantly a whole recess or noon, in the ring, and never once been "it." If, perchance, some freckled-faced, spindle-legged girl did act the Good Samaritan and dropped the handkerchief behind me, I'd pick it up, and then, in turn, try the same thing on some pretty little girl, she would either refuse to pick it up, or if she did, wouldn't run after me any faster than a lame duck."

Pupils labored over such problems as this: If 2000 honey bees fill a beer quart measure, how many bees are there in a swarm of a conical shape, the base of which is 16 inches in diameter, having the apex 15″ from the center of the base? Answer: 28,620 bees.

A typical lesson in Orthography, as Spelling was called, was:
1. smesis; 2. quassia; 3. monostick; 4. marcidity; 5. liturgy; 6. liquety; 7. incinerate; 8. guerrilla; 9. sluicy; 10. sweat.

The pupil's greatest reward back in the early 1800's for a series of good lessons was to receive a "ticket" which as a rule was treasured all his life, often used for a book mark. The ticket, which was lavishly bordered by drawings of flowers, had penned on it in the teacher's best example of old-fashioned, flourished hand writing, something like this:

TENTH TICKET

This is to certify that Elizabeth Ann Evans of the first class on the evening of the 8th day of August 1828 by good spelling stood at the Honorable Head ——— Timothy Brown

Later, as of 1880, one of the greatest rewards was to see his name in the local newspapers. For example:

"We learn from Miss Rickly, teacher of the Intermediate Department of the Union School (Webster), that Jennie Oreans and Charlie Smith, two of her pupils, have recited 5 lessons daily during the past term, and have not had but two imperfect lessons. Maggie

Paley and Ernest Beeson have recited the same number of lessons and have had but three imperfect lessons. Well done!"

THE EDWARD LEE McCLAIN HIGH SCHOOL
(Greenfield)

No more worthwhile exemplification of the influence of our first teachers can be found anywhere than in the achievement of Edward Lee McClain who gave to Greenfield, his home town, in 1915, the Edward Lee McClain High School, one of the most magnificent school plants in the United States.

He gave the Vocational Building to the town, in 1924, which included the agricultural laboratories, the swimming pool, the cafeteria, and the workshops. He purchased two entire city blocks at the rear of the high school, razed the buildings and made of the site a model playground and athletic field. Modern cottages were erected for the custodians.

The Elementary School which cares for the first six grades and the kindergarten, was erected by the City Board of Education.

The plant has a pupil capacity of 2200. It was designed by William B. Ittner, of St. Louis, architects and engineers. The cost of the three buildings, excepting grounds and equipment, was $950,000. The total cost was $2,000,000.

"A triumph" in Georgian architecture, this group of three buildings, elementary, vocational, and high school, are arranged on an open court and connected by vine-covered pergolas. They occupy one city block in width and two city blocks in length.

The buildings are of matt finish brick which rests on bases of hammer-squared random local stone. Bedford stone dignifies the entrances and marks horizontal divisions. Pictorial panels in Moravian tile mosaic relieve the broad wall surface and four in tints, — two on the front and two on the rear, — are inscribed thus:

Non omnia sed bon et bene (Not everything but things good and well done);

Ars coronat laborem (Art crowns labor);

Litera scripta manet (The written letter remains, i.e., Literature is everlasting);

Scientia regulat domum (Knowledge governs the home).

Words inscribed over the doorways are: Opportunity; Courage; Duty; Purpose; Work; Achievement.

The interior walls are of harmonizing French gray, with three murals by Vesper Lincoln George: The Apotheosis of Youth; The Melting Pot; The Pageant of Prosperity. The Frieze of the Parthenon is on the first floor, and there is statuary on all floors. There are 165 masterpieces in the art gallery.

The floors are of concrete and the finish is quartered oak.

The sills are of glazed brick, and the blackboards are of slate. The stairways and main entrances are finished in marble.

There are three gymnasiums, a community auditorium equipped with pipe organ, stage scenery, radio and motion picture equipment, and two libraries containing 10,000 volumes open to the public. The swimming pool was the largest ever installed in a public school. There are many special rooms.

The school was dedicated by Mr. McClain, September 1, 1915, thus:

"As promising the Most Good to the Greatest Number for the Longest Time

In sacred Memory of Those of my Own People and of Others Whom I Long and Well Knew and Loved Now Passed Away

In Honor, Respect and Esteem for this Community as it Exists Today

With full Confidence in the Generations yet to come

In Behalf of Higher Education, Purer Morals and Broader and Better Citizenship

This Property is Dedicated By the Donor."

— E. L. McClain

THE HILLSBORO HIGH SCHOOL
(Hillsboro)

The Hillsboro High School, erected in 1935, on West Main Street, opposite the site of the old academy building, is a modern and beautiful edifice.

It is of pressed brick and its Colonial architecture is in keeping with the general tone of the town. Nowhere may be found a more ideal setting, or lovelier landscaping, or a more delightful and refreshing view of the surrounding countryside than on this lofty site. Designed by Henry Ervin, local architect, it was W.P.A. project number 2512, and the cost including construction and equipment totaled $200,000.

The school includes a junior high school course and accommodates high school pupils from Hillsboro and neighboring districts. It is equipped with excellent heating and lighting systems, and also has a complete radio, public address, and inter-communicating telephone system.

Three units comprise the building: the central or school room section, the auditorium with seating capacity of 858, and the gymnasium. There is a football field and a baseball diamond in the rear, also horseshoe and volley-ball courts and a parking lot.

The recent purchase of the Samuel P. Scott mansion and

grounds adjoining the high school by the Board of Education will make this one of Ohio's outstanding school plants.

OUR CHURCHES:

Not only were the log cabins the first buildings erected for homes and schools, but they were the first buildings erected for churches. They were set up in the wilderness along with the schools after the homes had been established. Until their construction, preaching was held in the log cabin homes.

To those log cabin homes came the itinerant circuit preacher astride his faithful horse. It did not matter to the settlers whether he were Methodist, Presbyterian, or Quaker, just so he came. When he arrived, he found settlers for miles around crowded together in one cabin on benches or makeshift seats, eager to drink in the words that were to fall from his lips.

The reality of Heaven and Hell were as real to them as Indians and wild animals.

"*It was a religion well suited to his listeners,*" said Robert M. Ditty, in his preface to Scott's History of Highland County, "*strong, vigorous, actual and positive. Creeds there were, and denominations, but the end was sought along the same well-blazed trace. Theories of the creation had not mystified them, scientists had not cast doubt upon the existence of Adam and Eve. Darwin had not announced the doctrine of evolution and aspersed the progenitors of the human race, nor philosophers discovered that Hades did not mean a place of unceasing torment.*"

A young emigrant from the East newly arrived at New Market, looked in awe upon camp meeting scenes in the woods at New Market before he was converted and became one of the founders of the Baptist church. Accustomed to solemn, dignified meetings in the meeting house on the New Jersey coast, he was practically glued to his hiding place behind a tree, by what he saw.

Following a brief but fiery sermon by the circuit rider, one by one members of the huge congregation leaped to his feet to give testimony, until finally, as of one accord, all were on their feet, gathered in a deep circle. Around and around they went in the circle, moaning, singing, jerking, shouting, crying, and praying, until at last they fell prostrate and senseless on the ground. "*It was a fearsome sight,*" the lad recounted in his journal, "*the like of which I had never before seen.*"

Later he helped obtain 300 boards for seats for the camp meeting, and, in his own words:

"*On Saturday we went to camp meeting in the evening. Mr. Robbins preached from Hebrews 1 and 9. After the sermon the people made a ring before the pulpit and got all that wished to be converted into it. Then he told them all to pray. One of the ministers prayed til his breath was spent and had to quit. He told the mourners to pray on until they received the blessing. This was the strangest worship that I ever saw. After that they were singing and shouting and jumping perhaps most of the night. It was clear and windy."*

Religion had sustained the pioneers on their long, perilous journey into the Ohio wilderness and it sustained them afterwards. It was an indefinable something that was a part of them. It was warmth for them when they were cold and food for them when they were desperately hungry and disconsolate.

They relied much on prayer. When one of the bands of French people fleeing the Revolution in France finally reached the haven of Highland county, one of their most treasured possessions was a written record of the prayer said for them by their minister upon their embarkation and preserved between the pages of the huge French Bible they brought with them across the ocean.

Prayer for Travelers for America

Oh, Lord! who are the protector of those who fear you, and trust in your promises, we profoundly humble ourselves before you to beseech your paternal protection for the voyage that our fellow countrymen are going to undertake, and for those who have gone before them; and inasmuch as your angel stands all around those who fear you, and since it protects them, give charge to him that he keep them, in all their families, from all evil encounters, from all misfortunes, from all accidents, and above all, temptations, which could make them fall into sin, that with this in mind they remember that they are ceaselessly before your sight, that you are present in all their plans, and in all their designs, and that it is only among those who love you that there is good success in enterprise.

They are leaving, oh Lord! their homeland, their kin, their friends, and their homes, but they would not leave you, and where would they go, Oh, our Father! far from you, Spirit! and where would they flee from your countenance? Take away, if it pleases you, from their hearts all which could delude them; divert their eyes from all vanity, from all objects of arrogance, from ease and sensuality; that they reflect frequently and religiously on your judgment, on their death and on eternity, and above all keep them from temptations which are particularly attached to their avocations, that they may be like the merchant who searches for good pearls, and who having found a pearl of great price, goes and sells all that he has, and buys it.

That they never make of the goods of the world their all, nor even their principal delight; that they remember to turn away from avarice, which is the root of all evil, and moreover if goods abound, they do not think life valuable for their goods; that their main attention be to make purses which do not wear out, and a treasure in the heavens which never fails, where thieves can not approach, and where moths spoil nothing.

Oh, their good and divine Protector! different perils, and an infinity of dangers and accidents surround them, may surprise them when they are thinking of them least, but if you are with them, they will fear nothing, even if an entire army should encamp against them, because you will send your light and your truth, which will lead them into the dwelling of the Sovereign; it will be their God in whom they entrench themselves.

Yes, Lord! you will deliver them from all evil encounters, and you will come to their aid all the times that they make an humble appeal. You were with Jacob in his travels, you showed your protection in making him see a mystic ladder, which at one end touched heaven, and at the other end earth, by which your holy angels mounted and descended. You gave him bread to eat, and clothes to wear, and you brought him back in peace to the home of his father; by which you convinced him that you were his God, his protector, his counsel, and may it happen to them likewise, Lord, our God!

And as our life is a continuous voyage toward eternity, may they conduct themselves here below; do not permit that charnal covetousness make war on their souls, may they never swerve from justice and moderation, may bad examples never lead them astray, may they make shine before men the light of their good works, may their conduct be that of citizens of heaven; it is there that after all their pilgrimages on this earth, they will praise you, and will bless you for all your kindnesses.

The Presbyterian and Methodist churches were the early predominant churches. Of these two the Methodist church may more rightly be called the church of the pioneer. This was because itineracy, although common to all denominations, was a part of the Methodist church discipline, and most of these traveling preachers were Methodists.

The evangelist on horseback who rode a circuit through the wilderness to minister to the spiritual needs of the settlers was eagerly awaited for days, when families for miles around would gather at a designated settler's log cabin. Improvised seats would be made of boards. Preaching began early in the morning and lasted all day and into the evening, with time out only for meals. This went on for two or three days and then the minister, mounting his horse, took his leave and disappeared on the trail through the forests.

There were many noted traveling ministers. Peter Cartwright and James Quinn were the first regular ones to travel through Highland county, in 1805. The presiding elder was William Burk.

They traveled what was called the Scioto circuit, which included most all of the territory west of the Scioto and east of the Little Miami.

Their main stopping place was the home of a devout Methodist settler, James Fitzpatrick, who had served as a spy in the Revolutionary War. Fitzpatrick, they say, had the finest peach orchard in the county. He cultivated fields of wheat, rye and corn and raised bees for honey. Out of the honey he made a drink popular in the West, called metheglin. He loved people and his home was considered the headquarters of Methodism in those days.

Cartwright is represented as a strong, eccentric character dressed in buckskin, forceful and argumentative, and *"one of the great men of the century."*

Quinn was the opposite, *"handsome, intellectual, and aesthetic."* He preached the first Methodist sermon in the county in 1805, at the residence of Mrs. Jane Trimble about three miles north of Hillsboro.

"Quinn was the first preacher who ever came to our house," said a member of the Fitzpatrick family. *"He came wandering along through the woods from George Richard's, hunting our house, late one afternoon. We had nothing but a little bench for a table, but we got him some supper, the best we had, and he appeared satisfied and quite at home in our rough little cabin. He remained all night, and sat up late talking, and praying with us. The next morning he left, having made an appointment to preach for us in two weeks."*

It is believed that Quinn founded the Auburn Methodist Church near Hillsboro. He purchased a farm between Hillsboro and New Vienna in 1828 and this was his home, *"Rural Cottage"* until he died. He died in 1847, aged 75. His funeral services were held at Auburn Church and he was buried beside his brother, Isaac, in the Auburn churchyard.

It was the circuit riders, camp meetings, revivals, and baptising in creeks that colored the Highland county scene beyond description. Unbelievers and trouble-makers in the congregation would shout, guffaw, and challenge the preacher to such an extent that he often had to descend among them and engage in battle with the offenders. Cartwright and James B. Finley, another evangelist, often were obliged to do this before they could continue with their meetings. However, strange though it may seem, Finley himself when a youth, had been one of the worst offenders at camp meetings and revivals. As a young, drunken ruffian, he has gone down in local history as *"the New Market devil."*

James B. Finley, who came to the Ohio country with his parents when he was fifteen years old, became the guiding light of

Methodism in Highland county. He is regarded by historians as Ohio's greatest circuit rider, Indian missionary, and itinerant evangelist. There is a monument erected to his memory at Eaton, Ohio.

His father, Robert W. Finley, was a Presbyterian minister said to have been the first preacher in New Market and believed to have been the first who preached (1801) within the confines of Highland county. He had been educated at Princeton University. When he came with his family to New Market, he opened what was called a classical school in his cabin on the banks of Whiteoak creek. He educated his son, John, regarded as the most intellectual of all his sons, who became a licensed preacher of the Methodist church and afterwards Professor of Languages in Augusta, Kentucky.

James, assisted by his brother, John, built a cabin near New Market to which he brought his young bride and his sole worldly possessions of gun, dog, and axe. His bride had nothing, for her father, displeased with her choice of a husband, had forbidden her to take her clothes with her.

The resourceful bridegroom set to work to make the cabin as comfortable as possible. He made a bedstead of forks driven into the cabin floor, laid poles across them, and on top of this he laid elm bark and a tick of leaves he had dried in the sun.

He went to New Market, six miles away, and cut and split 100 rails for a bushel of potatoes which he carried home on his back. Once he worked a day for a hen and three chickens which he carried home in his hunting shirt. With his axe he cleared off about an acre and a half of plum bottom, dug holes, and planted corn, and its harvest brought him nearly a hundred bushels.

The Finley boys were bear hunters. One severe winter, when food was scarce, they tracked down and killed eleven bears, the largest one weighing over 400 pounds. James spent one whole winter tracking bears to repay a financial loss he had sustained by going security for a friend at Chillicothe. He killed a number of bears and sold their skins from three to seven dollars each.

After attending a camp meeting at his father's former congregation at Cane Ridge, Kentucky, James was converted to the Methodist religion and felt the call to preach. He left his home and family and started on his mission as a circuit rider, a journey of 470 miles. For 40 years he pursued his calling. He preached to prisoners. He taught the Wyandotte Indians. He finally presided over the eight circuits of the Ohio district and is credited with having *"saved 5000 souls."*

A very human story told about James Finley is the one when, as a young scamp, he came to the cabin of an Irishman named Joseph Eakins, near New Market. The Eakins family had come to the United States in 1801. Wealthy and unprepared for the hardships of wilderness life, they were at a loss to know what to do when the supply of groceries Mr. Eakins had brought from Pittsburgh, and the barrel of flour from Manchester ran out. Mrs. Eakins was in tears.

James Finley, *"rough, ragged, dirty, and a little drunk,"* walked into the cabin and asked what was the matter. He told them to cheer up, he would make them some bread. Washing his hands, he cut a piece of lard from a fresh-killed hog that Mr. Eakins had just bought from Samuel Evans, rendered it, and put it in a dish of meal. He added salt and mixed it all with water. Then he spread the dough on a smooth johnny-cake board and baked it before the fire. The Eakins family thought it delicious, and the entire countryside learned of it. As *"Jim Finleys"*, this bread was New Market's favorite pastry.

Thomas Hall Pearne, one of the later Methodist circuit riders, was, he said, *"rolled by the iron wheel of the itineracy into Hillsboro, Ohio."* He wrote a book entitled, *"Sixty-one Years of Itinerant Christian Life in Church and State,"* published in 1898, after his retirement.

Sometimes he rode a horse, sometimes a mule. He never feared the weather for he was prepared for it. He wore a broad-brimmed hat covered with oiled silk to make it water-proof. A water-proof shawl, slit in the middle to permit the rider's head to go through, completely covered his body and protected him from the elements. The saddle bags containing his Bible and other belongings were hidden from view by the shawl. The saddle was high in front and back, and from the pommel of the saddle in front was a rope about 40 feet long by which the mule or horse could be staked out to graze. Often the animal slept beside him on the ground, under the stars. The rider's feet rested comfortably in large wooden stirrups protected by front covers.

The Presbyterians, most of whom came from Virginia, brought with them when they came, an unbending adherence to their beliefs and their religion. The first Presbyterian churches organized were Rocky Spring, Nazareth, Fall Creek, and New Market.

Rocky Spring church, organized in 1806 on Rattlesnake creek and named by John Wilson for Rocky Spring, Pennsylvania, ministered to all of Greenfield and the Fall Creek settlements. Its first pastor, Nicholas Pittinger, from Pennsylvania, was laid to rest in 1833 in the cemetery beside the church he had helped found.

So strict in its enforcement of the rules of the church, it did not hesitate to discipline and suspend one of its elders, William Wilson, because he tossed a chip to decide which of two men should dine first. It did not tolerate secret societies and frowned upon the Masonic Lodge as *"unlawful and inexpedient."* In 1853 it reiterated that *"this Presbytery would again declare its opinion that Masonry and Odd Fellowship are unchristian and sinful in prin-*

ciple and practice." This mandate was not modified until 1867, but it still advised Presbyterians to have no connection with secret societies.

Any person not conforming to the rules and regulations of the Presbyterian church was expelled from the communion of the church: It was all right to indulge in spiritous liquors, but one must not become intoxicated. Neither must a member of the church join a temperance society. One of the elders of the Nazareth church conducted a distillery on Clear creek and *"bitters was as much of the daily habits of the preachers and the people as was the morning prayer."*

The honor of being the most renowned church in Highland county goes to the Presbyterian church in Hillsboro. From this church which came to be called the Crusade church, a group of valiant townswomen met and ventured forth to break up the saloons which were demoralizing the town and their menfolk. The story of this crusade is told in another section.

Mrs. Louise Dunlap Watts, daughter of a noted pioneer Greenfield doctor, a few years ago when she was 96 years old, said:

"I can still hear the creaking of store signs as they swung in the wind — they were hung on long chains — Robert Kinkead, bandmaster, used to blow a bugle in the evening to call the boys to practice — how the pigs used to squeal when they were caught in Murray's picket fence across the street — everybody had a cow, a barn and a horse — little girls carrying parasols and marching up and down the streets, two by two, after a party — emigrants from the eastern states coming through Greenfield in covered wagons — the long shadows thrown by the lantern's light —

"When I get drowsy sitting here I always recall how that big fly would buzz during services at the old Presbyterian church and how the men would take catnaps during the sermons — country families having picnic dinner on the church lawn on Sunday — they would come to town for the day — old women puffing away on their pipes, fine old women they were — a family coming to church, dressed in deep, black mourning clothes ——"

In Hillsboro, for years, there were only two churches in the town, the Methodist and the Presbyterian, the courthouse bell calling the two congregations to their respective churches.

Dusty Miller, in his *"Uncle Bill,"* the story of the life of William Hampton Miller, of Marshall, tells of the friendly rivalry of the two Methodist and one Presbyterian churches of Marshall. All three churches held revivals every year called *"protracted meetings"* when the youths used to take turns going to the altar *"to get religion"* on successive nights for the sole purpose of prolonging the series of meetings. Revivals often went on in the three churches at the same time. The *"Amen corners,"* sections where old men sat and loudly A-men-ed the minister as he spoke, waxed strong and sonorous. When one church was reported having more joiners than the other such original expressions of Uncle Bill were recalled as "*The Pres-a-terians are beatin' the Mefodists, ain't they?*"

As early as 1813, United Brethren circuit riders held meetings about four miles west of town on the Danville pike. It was not long until a class was organized and a frame building built about 3½ miles west of Hillsboro. Since the United Brethren church was not heard of in Ohio until 1810, this church is not only one of the oldest churches in Highland county, but one of the oldest in the state. Churches in those days were often called "*chapels*" and the brick chapel that superseded the frame building in 1859 was named Ambrose Chapel for Rev. William Ambrose at whose house in nearby New Market about 1818, the church was started. This chapel, opposite a burial grounds, is now a residence.

Almost every denomination of religion is represented in Highland county today, each signifying a certain strength and beauty of purpose and faith that can not be denied.

There are the Baptist churches which sprang from the efforts of Baptist emigrants who flocked to the New Market neighborhood about 1837. A small group of Baptists, differentiating themselves from the "*Hardshell Baptists,*" met at the home of Oliver Harris June 9, 1838, and, under an appletree, organized the Little Rocky Fork Baptist Church, now the New Market Baptist Church. The following persons joined that day: William Vance, Rachel Vance, David McConnaughey, Prudence McConnaughey, Oliver Harris, Mary Harris, James H. Arnott, Comfort Arnott, Andrew McConnaughey, Jacob Johnson, Lydia Vance, Margaret Ross, Samuel S. Harris, and Mary Wheaten.

There is the Church of Christ, more numerous than any other, one person claiming that 50 or 60 years ago, he had counted seven in one deep valley region as he stood atop a high hill.

In the period when Peter Cartwright and James Quinn were traveling through the country spreading the gospel, in 1805, there was born somewhere "*in the wilderness that is now Highland county,*" a baby boy who was to become the pioneer missionary from Clark county 20 years later. This was Isaac Newton Walters, "*one of the most noted evangelists of the early days.*"

Walters is credited with having crossed the Allegheny Mountains five times, riding thousands of miles and preaching at camp meetings, in the homes, churches, barns, and along the trails. He is said to have had more converts than any other minister at this time. He was editor of the Herald of Gospel Liberty, published at New Carlisle in 1843 and was one of the founders of Antioch College.

The Catholic church had its quaint beginning in the John Fallon residence in Hillsboro (The Hill City Hotel). Here long ago, about ten Catholic families gathered for the masses which were said by two French priests, Father Cheynol and Father Gacon from the historic Ursuline Convent in Brown county, until their own church was built in 1849. The Greenfield Catholic Church had a similar beginning.

The Lutheran and Episcopal churches were established about the time of the founding of the Catholic churches. There is a Lutheran church at Dodsonville and an Episcopal church at Hillsboro.

There is the Dunkard Church just south of Sinking Spring where quaint customs such as foot washings are observed during annual revivals. The choicest young beef, wine, and bread are partaken of at the communion service. Members of the church abstain from *"worldly things"* such as picture shows, dancing and card playing. The men wear stiff white collars minus neck ties. The women during the services always wear little white handsome lace caps gathered around the outside. The older women of the church have retained their long hair. It is only the younger ones who have bobbed their hair in modern fashion. Rev. Mr. Cousman and his wife conduct the services taking turn about. One Sunday is known as *"Jacob's Sunday"*. The following Sunday is designated as *"Mary's Sunday."*

There is the most unusual Mormon church known as the Universalist or the Church of the Latter Day Saints, west of Sinking Spring, near Gall Hill. Offspring of the temple the Mormons built in Kirtland, Lake county, in 1833, this church is one of many which were organized against polygamy and estranged from the Brigham Young branch in Salt Lake City.

There are the Quaker churches where men and sometimes women preach the gospel of the Friends. At the edge of Leesburg stands the old abandoned brick meeting house where, until 25 or 30 years ago, Quaker quarterly all-day meetings were county events. People drove from miles to the meetings, hitching their horses and buggies to racks at the hitching posts. The preaching went on all day except at noon when all stopped to dine under the trees and visit and renew old acquaintances. Many noted Quakers are buried in the large cemetery which is a part of the church grounds.

The church, the home, and the school were as one in those days. With so few books available, the Bible was the most widely and thoroughly read book. It was considered practically indispensable. Regular family prayers were said in the homes mornings and evenings. The spirit of religion went with the children into their school rooms. In many an early Highland county school book, inscriptions such as this were written on fly leaves:

>Caroline Copes is my name,
>America is my nation,
>New Market is my dwelling place,
>Christ is my salvation.

OUR ROADS:

THE Indians, as they shuttled back and forth from the Great Lakes to the far South, followed Highland county's first roads, — the animal paths that led them through dense forests to salt licks and springs and along streams where food was abundant. Many of these trails, made by scouting parties, were faintly outlined by pebbles and broken branches and led along the hills so that the red man could command a view of his surroundings, for protection; and connected with main trails. When the first Highland countians arrived they found that a system of transportation had already been mapped out for them.

Since there are no large waterways in the county, roads have been our chief means of transportation. As early as 1803, the county commissioners realized their importance and gave more and more attention to the laying out and opening up of roads that would connect settlements with each other. Prior to this they depended upon several main thoroughfares.

Skirting the southeastern border of our county is a section of the oldest road west of the Alleghenies, the Zane trace, cut in 1796, now known as State Route 41. It comes up from Aberdeen on the Ohio River, northeast through West Union, Peebles, and Locust Grove, and enters the southeastern corner of Highland county where it forms the main street of Sinking Spring. It proceeds almost parallel with the eastern boundary of the county until, shortly after junction with State Route 70, it dips easterly through the northeast corner of Pike county into Ross.

The part of the Zane trace that travels from Sinking Spring in Highland county to Cynthiana in Pike county is laid approximately on the Pickawillany Indian trail, the trail which extended from the confluence of the Scioto and Ohio rivers to the Indian town of Pickawillany, at the mouth of Loramie creek, near Piqua, where it joined other trails. This was a noted stagecoach line and the means by which many Highland county pioneers reached the interior of the county. It is a winding, scenic road.

Another old road was the *"Old College Township Road,"* State Route 28, part of a well-known thoroughfare west from Chillicothe, and extending from Athens to Oxford. It passed through Chillicothe, Greenfield, East Monroe, Leesburg, Snow Hill, and Lebanon.

Immigrants traveling from Wheeling via Zane's trace, bound for the bottom lands of the Miamis, chose this road to reach their destinations. They came on horseback, or journeyed with their families, in wagons. Often they met merchants coming from Cincinnati, traveling likewise, but bound for cities beyond the Alleghenies. This road was laid out in 1799 by General Duncan McArthur, surveyor, and James Manary, William Rodgers, and Joseph Clark, reviewers. It was afterwards established as a state road and improved.

"The Anderson State Road," United States Route 50, is nearly on a straight line from an old Indian ford on Paint creek, to Cincinnati. It originally was a buffalo trail. Surveyed and opened under the superintendence of Colonel Richard C. Anderson, by authority of the State in 1804-5, it passed from Chillicothe to Cincinnati, and intersected Highland county, connecting Zanesville and Cincinnati. This has always been a noted highway from east to west.

"*The Old Mad River Road,*" cut from New Market to Springfield, in 1802, is one of our most interesting roads, and leaves to us an heroic story of adventure.

Stones were needed for a mill that had been constructed by Simon Kenton on Mad River, on the other side of Springfield. Kenton employed Robert Boyce, of New Market, to transport the stones from Maysville. Boyce succeeded in hauling the stones as far as New Market, in his wagon, but from there on he was challenged by an unbroken wilderness. If Springfield was to be reached, a road had to be cut.

Boyce had been authorized by Kenton to employ other workers who were to precede him and make a passable route, and they were to receive their pay when the mill stones were delivered at Springfield. Three men from New Market volunteered their services. They were Michael Stroup, the hatter, William Finley, and George Caley. They were to receive one dollar a day wages.

"They set out about the middle of February, 1802, taking with them two large pones of corn bread and two flitches of bacon. No surveyor had been provided. A day or two after the party started Caley got sick and had to turn back, leaving Stroup and Finley to do all the work, Boyce being fully employed with his wagon and team, which consisted of two horses and one oxen.

"*The party camped out of course every night and were 15 days engaged in cutting the road, most of which time the weather was rough and cold. They had not time to hunt and consequently were obliged to rely upon the pones and flitches for substance . . .*

"*When within twelve miles of Springfield, the party came near freezing to death. They had traveled several hours in the midst of an unusually severe storm of rain and snow, and were wet through and through. Night came on in the midst of a prairie, and soon became so dark that they could not proceed. They took shelter under* the wagon, and attempted to strike fire, but lost their flint and all hopes with it.

"It occurred to Stroup, however, that the mill stone might be sufficiently hard for a substitute. So he went to work as well as the numbness of his hands would permit, and after repeated efforts, finally succeeded in drawing a spark with his knife from one of the stones in the wagon. But before they could manage to gather fuel on the broad and half-iced prairie, the three men had nearly perished. Their clothes were frozen on their bodies long before the fire was sufficient to thaw them.

"During the night one of the horses broke loose and wandered off to escape the rigor of the storm in a distant grove. Boyce started after it, and traveled several hours over the prairie at the imminent risk of freezing. In the morning they discovered that they had stopped the previous night within a mile of a large Indian encampment, to which they immediately went to warm and cook breakfast.

"When the party arrived at the mill, Kenton was not there, and they could get nothing to eat. So they set off in search of him. They found him at his cabin about four miles from the mill, but he had neither money to pay them for their hard services nor provisions to supply their immediate wants. In this state of affairs they started back and got a meal at Springfield on credit of a hospitable log cabin tavern keeper, recently located at that place. From there they hurried back to New Market, where they arrived on the nineteenth day after they set out to cut the road, almost famished, and their clothes literally torn to pieces. . . ."

Roads opened in 1805 were chiefly through New Market and Fairfield townships. The village of New Market being the county seat at this time, all county roads trended in that direction or to connect with roads passing to or through it.

When Hillsboro was founded and made the county seat in 1807, arrangements were made for locating public highways from Hillsboro. Road making was usually done in the spring or early autumn. It was paid for by the State and usually let out on private contract by the State Commissioners of roads for that district.

The mode of travel in those days was by wagon, horse and stage coach. Travel was tediously slow. Often the traveler had to stop and clear the way or pry himself out of mud by means of a fence rail. Over these bumpy roads came the pack-horse mail carrier, the stagecoach driver, the emigrant, and the circuit minister. Their passing along the road were events and settlers hurried from their cabins and work to watch them pass, and to make them welcome should they choose to stop and rest. Wayside taverns did a big business.

Perhaps the *Whiskey Road*, State Route 126, was cut in the most unusual way of any road in Highland county. Leaving United

States Route 62 south of New Market, it runs south through Sugartree Ridge to Winchester and West Union in Adams county.

New Market distilleries did not supply adequately the wants of the settlers of New Market, but at Winchester there was a famous distillery operated by a Dutch settler from Virginia by the name of Hemphill. He manufactured a whiskey claimed to be as good as the favorite Monongahela brand.

A procession of thirty men left George Barrere's tavern at New Market, December 30, 1809, bound for the Winchester distillery. They were led by Barrere, who was Justice of the Peace and also Senator for Highland and Ross counties. He carried a compass and a staff. The rest of the party carried rifles and shot pouches.

A horse at the rear drew a crude vehicle, a sort of sled, made of two whiteoak poles for shafts which were sloped to run and slide on the ground, with inch pins two feet long in the upper side of each pole, three feet from the lower end. Holes were bored in the upper end and tugs were passed through and fastened to the hames on the horse. A barrel of whiskey was supported by two pins on the slide and from the pins hung tin cups and a side of bacon.

Beside the horse, which had a meal bag filled with corn dodgers fastened under its mouth, walked a boy. The entire population of New Market had gathered to witness the departure.

They struck a southeasterly course, set the compass, and refreshed themselves with whiskey from the barrel. Some were overcome by it, fell by the way, and did not get to complete the journey. They camped out the first night, and played and danced and consumed the rest of the whiskey. Obtaining a barrel of the coveted Hemphill whiskey, they retraced their steps, reaching home the next day with the barrel a little more than half full, but they had cut a permanent road.

Miss Minnie Vance says of her girlhood days at Harrisburg, near New Market, a settlement of Harris families, that when she was a girl living there, there was no road from their house into New Market, the trading center of that part of the county. They rode horseback to the store and to church. Now a road runs directly through the settlement and connects with the West Union pike.

Highland county was too far *"inland"* to be directly affected by the construction of the Ohio canal, only that by this means of transportation, many immigrants eventually found their way to this county. Hardly had authorization for railroads been completed than the agitation for their construction began. The press of Hillsboro was the first in Ohio to quote Davy Crockett, who aroused public interest in railroads by recording his experiences. Quotes this Hillsboro paper:

" I *(Davy Crockett) can only judge of the speed of the cars by putting my head out to spit, which I did, and overtook it so quick that it hit me smack in the face."*

Southern Ohio was the first to experiment with railroads. The Little Miami Railroad operated trains as early as 1841 from Cincinnati to Milford, Ohio.

Shortly after this, in March, 1845, a charter was granted to the Belpre and Cincinnati Railroad Company to build a rather undefined road through the Hocking Valley, beginning at some point on the Ohio River, near Harmar and to connect with the Little Miami Railroad in the western part of the State. This road was intended to serve the greater part of Highland county.

In the meantime, Ross county politicians and investors had made heavier subscriptions to the stock issue and so gained control of the movement. Thus they were able to prevail upon the minority to change the name and organize a new company to be known as the Marietta and Cincinnati Railroad Company. This company was organized on August 18, 1847 and all officers were from Ross county. It decided to make Greenfield the one point in Highland county to be touched and run the road through the northern part of the county.

This procedure caused dissatisfaction among the subscribers in Highland county. They withdrew from the company, and, through the aid of their friends, organized a new railroad project, known as the Hillsboro and Cincinnati Railroad Company and to be operated and owned independently. A road was constructed to Loveland where it met with an important road leading to the north and was completed before the Marietta and Cincinnati Railroad. The new Hillsboro and Cincinnati line passed through Blanchester, and, since the Marietta and Cincinnati line was also scheduled to pass through Blanchester, the latter was compelled to make concessions to the new road in order to run over its tracks to Cincinnati, or take over the completed road. This placed the independent investors of Hillsboro at an advantage.

The Marietta and Cincinnati Railroad Company took over the line from Blanchester to Loveland. When the road was reorganized in the late 70's, and taken over by the Baltimore and Ohio Railroad, the line from Blanchester to Hillsboro was included in the deal and made a branch.

In January, 1880, the Columbus and Maysville Railroad Company was organized in Hillsboro, with C. S. Bell as president. When the line was completed it formed a connecting link with the Cincinnati and Eastern Railroad Company that operated between Cincinnati and Portsmouth which had been chartered in 1876. The first train ran over its tracks in November of 1880. So that Highland county would be provided with an outlet to the south and east, it was leased to the main road without rental. When the Norfolk and Western Railroad leased the Cincinnati and Eastern Railroad in the early part of the 20th century, it leased all the subsidiaries at the same time.

In 1853, the Marietta and Cincinnati Railroad projected a road from Hillsboro through Marshall township for the purpose of connecting Hillsboro with the coal fields at Jackson. Many believed that this would open up that part of Ohio lying between Hillsboro and Jackson and that villages along the line would grow into towns and cities.

The road had been cut to just below Marshall when the railroad company sold out to another railroad company. Overnight things came to a standstill. It is claimed by some authorities that one of the leaders absconded with the company's money. At any rate, on the day the railroad sold out, the workmen were told that they were through, that the work was over. The workmen, a gang of Irish laborers, laid down their tools, wheelbarrows, and wagons, the remains of which were found where they had been abandoned up until recent years. Expecting the work to go on for some time, the workmen had spent their money freely as they earned it. Now they were stranded and penniless. Kindly farmers took them into their homes and gave them work to do on their farms until they could save enough money to get away on.

About 1908, tracks were laid from Hillsboro to Norwood for a traction line which ran parallel with what is now United States Route 50. The depot was in a red brick building called the Traction Building, opposite the county jail, on Court street. Tracks ran up West Main street to the public square, turned north on North High street, then left on court street to the depot, and on around the court house to West Main street. The traction line flourished for two or three years, bringing many people along the line for miles into the schools and the shopping district. The advent of the automobile brought about its ultimate decline.

A survey based on observations made during a period of one year on all United States and State routes radiating out of Hillsboro, and made by the State Highway Planning Bureau in 1937, reported that the most traveled road in Highland county is U. S. 50 west of Hillsboro. This route at the time of the survey showed an average of 1070 vehicles a day, 20 percent of which were trucks. The least traveled highway was St. Rt. 138 which carried an average of 333 vehicles a day, 15 percent of which were trucks. U. S. 50 east, was found to carry the highest truck percentage and St. Rt. 73 out of Hillsboro, the lowest. The average daily number of all vehicles traveling over these routes was 5102 and trucks constituted 16.98 percent of this number.

But only 40 years ago, such news items as this appeared in the News-Herald: *"An automobile passed through Russell yesterday to the great surprise of the natives."*

And adorning the county surveyor's office in the court house is an old wooden sign taken from the Barrett's Mill covered bridge:

5 DOLLARS FINE
FOR RIDING OR DRIVING
THROUGH THIS BRIDGE
FASTER THAN A WALK

CHAPTER SIX

Truth-Is-Stranger-Than-Fiction Stories
MOTHER THOMPSON

Allen Trimble left pleasant memories behind him of a life well spent when he died at the age of 87 at his home on Trimble avenue in Hillsboro, in February, 1870; and to carry on the revered tradition of the Trimble name he left to posterity his only daughter, Eliza Jane, known the world over as *"Mother Thompson."*

Born in Augusta county, Virginia, November 24, 1783, of Scotch-Irish parentage, Allen Trimble settled in Hillsboro shortly after the death of his father, Captain James Trimble, in Lexington, Kentucky, in 1804. He was clerk of the court and records of Highland county from 1809 to 1816, but in the War of 1812 he commanded a mounted regiment under General William Henry Harrison. In 1816 he was elected to the Legislature and in 1817, to the State Senate; in 1818 he was elected speaker of the Senate and served until January 7, 1822 when he became Acting Governor. He was elected Governor of Ohio in 1826, and re-elected in 1828. As Governor he extended and improved the common school system, encouraged manufactures and promoted penitentiary reform. He formed the first company to import English cattle, helped extend the Ohio Canal System, and was one of the first of Ohio's farmers to advocate the raising of sheep.

His first wife was Margaret McDowell, whom he married in 1806 in Woodford county, Kentucky. To this union were born two sons, Joseph and Madison. Margaret died a few years after their marriage and in 1811 he was married to Rachel Woodrow. Three children were born to them: Carey A.; William H.; and Eliza Jane, who was destined to become the renowned Mother Thompson of the Woman's Temperance Crusade.

Eliza Jane was married to James Henry Thompson of Harrodsburg, Kentucky, September 21, 1837. Mr. Thompson was a rising young attorney. They had eight children: Allen Trimble; Anna Porter; John Henry; Joseph Trimble; Marie Doiress; Mary McArthur; Henry Burton; and John Burton. Three of these children, Marie, Mary, and Henry, outlived their mother who died in 1905.

Their first home was *"Forest Lawn"* designed and built by the young husband and his father-in-law. Later they went to live with the Trimbles in their southern patterned home on Trimble avenue. This home, now known as *"Mother Thompson's Home,"* was once part of a large estate fronting North High street from Willow to North streets.

In this pretty brick home, Eliza Jane Thompson led the busy, sheltered life of the women of that day. She was gentle and religious, and a devoted wife and mother, inheriting from her father strict integrity and extremely good sense.

For some years there had been spasmodic temperance movements which had had their days and were gone. There had been the Washington Movement in Baltimore in 1840, when a body of reformed drinkers attempted to persuade other men to abstain from liquor. In 1844, the *"Sons of Temperance"* was organized in the eastern states. Members had to sign pledges of abstinence.

In 1873, a lecturer, Dr. Dio Lewis, toured Ohio to lecture on temperance. His lecture, *"Our Girls,"* in Hillsboro, December 22, of that year, was so warmly received that he was persuaded to remain for a second lecture on the following day.

His story of his mother's suffering because of her husband's drinking and of how she waged a campaign, single-handed, against the saloon dealers who sold liquor to him, moved his listeners so deeply that they were inspired to action. They resolved to start a campaign in Hillsboro to stop the supply of liquor at its source. Before returning to their homes that night they organized a *"Woman's Temperance Crusade"* and appointed Eliza Jane Thompson who was not present, to be their leader. Their first meeting was to be the next day.

Mrs. Thompson's fifteen-year-old son, who was at the meeting, hurried home to tell his mother of the happenings and of her having been made the leader of the crusade. Her husband, now a judge and himself addicted to drink, remarked that the whole thing was just *"tom-foolery."*

The next morning Mrs. Thompson's son asked her if she was going to the meeting at the Presbyterian Church. The family left the room so that she might find the answer to the question in her prayers.

A few minutes later her daughter, Mary, knocked at the door and asked permission to enter.

"Look, Mother," she said, *"it must be that you're to go. I opened my Bible to the 146th Psalm! Read it, Mother!"*

And the mother read what was to be known thereafter as the Crusade Psalm:

"Put not your trust in princes, nor in the son of man, in whom there is no help.

Happy is he that hath the God of Jacob for his help, whose hope is in the Lord his God.

The Lord openeth the eyes of the blind; the Lord raiseth them that are bowed down; the Lord loveth the righteous."

So Eliza Jane Thompson went to the meeting.

The pastors present made fervent addresses at the beginning of the meeting which might be likened to sparks setting off a conflagration. Mrs. Thompson, who had selected a seat in the rear of the church was persuaded to move to the front where she was officially elected their leader. When they called upon her to speak she was weak and frightened. Then the men withdrew that the women might be alone to pray for divine guidance in their new undertaking.

They drew up appeals to druggists, saloon keepers and hotel proprietors. Mrs. Sally McDowell, vice president, made the first prayer before the 70 women started out on their mission. This prayer was described years later by Mrs. Thompson thus: *"It seemed as though the angels had brought down coals of fire from off the altar and touched her lips — she who, by her own confession had never before heard her own voice in prayer."*

They prayed together and sang. A strong religious exaltation ran through them like deep currents. When the service ended, they formed a double line and left the church, singing their *"Crusade Hymn"*:

>*"Give to the winds thy fears;*
> *Hope, and be undismayed;*
>*God hears thy sighs and counts thy tears;*
> *God shall lift up thy head.*
>
>*Through waves, and clouds, and storms,*
> *He gently clears thy way;*
>*Wait thou His time; so shall this night*
> *Soon end in joyous day.*
>
>*What though thou rulest not!*
> *Yet heaven, and earth, and hell*
>*Proclaim, God sitteth on the throne,*
> *And ruleth all things well.*
>
>*Far, far above thy thought*
> *His counsel shall appear,*
>*When fully he the work has wrought,*
> *That caused thy needless fear."*

First they went to the drug stores and then to the hotels and saloons, singing and praying, beseeching the dispensers of liquor to stop selling it. At each place they sang hymns and prayed. Informing the dealer of the purpose of their crusade, they announced that they would return on the morrow. Then they proceeded to the next stop. No place was too low for them to enter although *"it was overwhelming to their finer sensibilities and shocking to their modesty,"* one report says.

For hours the battle raged. The women met with strong opposition. There were 13 saloons in Hillsboro and also drug stores and hotel bars where liquor was sold. These were all visited, prayed in, and the proprietors informed of the determinations of the crusaders. Mother Thompson is credited with being the first woman to publicly offer a prayer in a saloon.

One by one the liquor dealers gave in. Some closed their bars and turned to other occupations. Others left town. Two only were extremely obdurate, Robert Ward, a saloon keeper, and Dr. Dunn, a druggist.

Ward, known as the *"Witty Englishman,"* attempted to make the women appear ridiculous. Opening the door with great ceremony, he held it for the women to enter, and then marched smartly to the rear of his bar. Mother Thompson's gentle rebukes and answers to his arguments completely won him over and he, too, finally joined in their prayers.

Dr. Dunn showed more fight. He insisted that he had a right to sell liquor by prescription to anyone he chose, but that he never sold to those whose families requested him not to. However, after several days of persistent prayer meetings and psalm singing, he, too, closed his doors.

When the women erected a canvas and frame tabernacle in front of the Dunn drug store in which they gave exhortations, sang, and prayed, Dr. Dunn brought suit for *"trespassing and obstructing his business,"* and in one of the higher courts he was awarded five dollars damages.

Mother Thompson's husband, Judge Thompson, vividly described the initial descent of the band of 70 crusaders upon the town:

"A band, a cohort, a troupe of 70 women arrayed in sable black moved in a settled line of march through the cold, still streets of Hillsboro. There was no wind. A light flurry of snow descended from the dark December clouds. Throughout the day all places kept for the sale of liquors heard the devout prayers and songs of these gentlewomen.

"At night consultation resumed at the church from whence the "phoenix-like body," springing from the ashes of the funeral pyre of women's immolation, had emerged in the morning. On this Christmas Eve there were reports, prayers, and singing. And as they journeyed homeward, a last quarter moon gave benediction through the white still streets. Since the movement was divinely inspired only a higher power will limit its effects in the nations of the earth."

This wave of reform that started in Hillsboro spread through the world. It has been called, *"The Whirlwind of the Lord."* One month after it had started, 109 saloons in 25 Ohio towns had been closed and 22 drug stores had pledged not to sell liquor.

The Hillsboro Crusade culminated in the organization of the National Woman's Christian Temperance Union of the United States, at Cleveland, Ohio, on November 20, 1874. A white ribbon was adopted as the official badge of the organization and members were called *"white ribboners."* Almost over night, Eliza Jane Thompson and her band of crusaders had become national figures.

Seventy-three years have rolled swiftly by. Still we remember them, proudly, the crusaders of 1873:

1. Mrs. Eliza Jane Thompson....................*President*
2. Mrs. J. J. McDowell........................*Vice President*
3. Mrs. D. K. Fenner..........................*Secretary*
4. Mrs. Samuel Amen
5. Mrs. Thomas Barry
6. Mrs. Julia Bentley
7. Mrs. William M. Barry
8. Mrs. James Bridwell
9. Mrs. Mary Bowers
10. Mrs. J. M. Boyd
11. Mrs. Lizzie Brown
12. Mrs. Bruce
13. Mrs. S. D. Clayton
14. Mrs. F. E. Chaney
15. Mrs. Helen Cooper
16. Mrs. T. S. Cowden
17. Mrs. W. O. Collins
18. Mrs. E. Conrad
19. Mrs. Dr. Calahan
20. Mrs. Sarah Doggett
21. Mrs. Washington Doggett
22. Mrs. James Doggett
23. Mrs. Emily Dill
24. Mrs. Dr. John Ellis
25. Mrs. R. S. Evans
26. Mrs. Fred Ellifritz
27. Mrs. Henry Foraker
28. Mrs. E. L. Ferris
29. Mrs. Frost
30. Mrs. George B. Gardner
31. Mrs. Grand-Girard
32. Mrs. George Glasscock
33. Mrs. William Glenn
34. Mrs. J. E. Gregg
35. Mrs. Anna Hart
36. Mrs. Paul Harsha
37. Mrs. Dr. Enos Holmes
38. Mrs. Anna Hinton
39. Mrs. Sarah Jeans
40. Mrs. John Jolly
41. Mrs. Jonah Langley
42. Mrs. Elizabeth Linn
43. Mrs. M. Matthews
44. Mrs. Dr. Matthews
45. Mrs. Dr. William McSurely
46. Mrs. William Morrow
47. Mrs. McConnaughey
48. Mrs. J. C. Norton
49. Mrs. William Nelson
50. Mrs. J. K. Pickering
51. Mrs. M. Perkins
52. Mrs. George Richards
53. Mrs. J. Rittenhouse
54. Mrs. Josiah Stevenson
55. Mrs. Margaret Stevens
56. Mrs. John A. Smith
57. Mrs. Mary Simson
58. Mrs. J. B. Shinn
59. Mrs. William Scott
60. Mrs. Fielding Shepherd
61. Mrs. Shipp
62. Mrs. E. G. Smith
63. Mrs. Dr. Spees
64. Mrs. Eli Stafford
65. Mrs. Maria Stewart
66. Mrs. Anna Tucker
67. Mrs. Col. William Trimble
68. Mrs. John L. West
69. Mrs. Moses Willett
70. Mrs. Charles Wilson

CASPAR COLLINS

He was young to die, but the fact that he lay down his life for others has given him an honored place in the county's early history.

Once Caspar Collins was a familiar and admired figure about the village, slender, of medium height, and with fashionable crisp sideburns. Son of Catherine Wever and William Oliver Collins, he came from a long line of distinguished soldiers and professional men. He had one sister, Josephine.

William Oliver Collins was an important Hillsboroan. He was born in Somers, Connecticut in 1809, a direct descendant of Edward Collins who had come to Massachusetts from England in 1830. He came to Ohio in 1833 and graduated from the Cincinnati law school in 1835. After being admitted to the bar he moved to Hillsboro where he took a leading part in civic affairs. He was president of the Hillsboro and Cincinnati railroad company; director of the Belpre and Cincinnati railroad; collector of Internal Revenue for the Sixth Congressional District, for three years; trustee of the Hillsboro Academy; and Highland county prosecutor. In 1861 he was elected to the State Senate.

The Collins estate on Collins avenue was one of the loveliest places in Hillsboro. The vineyard extended from the top of the hill, now sectioned off in homes, to the bridge on North High street. The house is a representative southern colonial home. The father in summer drove a span of ponies hitched to a carriage, his two hunting dogs following close behind. In winter, when the snow was on, he drove two spanking horses behind a sleigh, to the merry accompaniment of jingling sleigh bells. He loved young people and he was popular among them, often taking them on drives with him, or permitting them to use his sleigh or carriage while he visited in the stores.

While serving as a member of the State Senate in 1861, William Collins received a commission as Colonel commanding the First Independent Battalion, Ohio Volunteer Cavalry, and the Eleventh Regiment, Ohio Volunteer Cavalry.

This regiment was sent up to Camp Denison in 1862 to be equipped and mounted. It was then ordered to St. Louis, Missouri, to cross the plains and open up communications that had been cut off by the Sioux, Cheyenne and Arapahoe Indians who were terrorizing western plains and mountains. These Indian uprisings had been precipitated by the immigration into Colorado which began in 1858.

The Indians, incited by rebel agents, had sacked the country, destroying mail stations and coaches and cutting off overland communication with the Pacific States and territories.

Caspar Collins' consuming desire was to accompany his father to war. Before enlisting in the service he had made friends with the Sioux, learning the language. He was 17 years old when he went west with his father to fight the Indians.

Some of the most thrilling incidents of Indian warfare took place in this period. Two important battles, Mud Springs and Rush Creek, climaxed the many skirmishes. Men froze to death in the bitter, sub-zero winter.

For more than three years these troops did service in the Central Rocky mountains. Their service was so effective that from the summer of 1862 to February, 1865, communications were never interrupted on any routes for 24 hours in succession.

Caspar Collins was in charge of a scouting expedition made by Company G of the 11th Ohio Volunteer Cavalry, in the spring of 1862. During their journey of 459 miles they were close to Powder River where the Cheyennes and Ogalala Sioux under Old Man Afraid of His Horses were camped. They were attacked by 200 Indians near Deer creek on May 20, and one soldier was killed.

When Captain L. M. Rinehart was killed during a skirmish with the Indians on February 13, 1865, Caspar was placed in charge of the company. He received a lieutenant's commission on May 1, 1865.

Company G was garrisoned at Platte Bridge which controlled one of the most important crossings of the North Platte river, on the Telegraph and Emigrant Overland Route. On July 25, 1865, Sioux, Cheyenne and Arapahoe Indians gathered in the hills north of Platte Bridge but were driven off after a brief skirmish.

The next day a wagon train under Sergeant Custard and a small band of soldiers was on its way to Platte Bridge Fort from Sweetwater Station at Willow Springs.

Across the river from Platte Bridge Fort, 5000 bloodthirsty savages lay in wait to attack the approaching wagon train. When the plight was seen by the soldiers at Platte Bridge, Major Anderson of the Kansas regiment, tactfully refraining from sending his own officers on a suicide mission, sent Lieutenant Collins with a detachment of 25 men to bring in the wagon train. Caspar's father, now Lieutenant-Colonel, was absent from the fort at this time.

The story goes that Caspar gave his cap to James E. Williamson, a private, before he left, stating, *"Jim, I know that I shall never get back alive. Here is my cap that you have admired so much. Keep it to remember me by."*

Caspar and his men were hardly out of sight of the garrison when 3000 Indians were seen swarming out from the brush and hills to attack them.

Caspar ordered a retreat. It was too late. The Indians pressed them so closely that the fighting had to be hand-to-hand. Although Caspar was shot in the hip as they rode down the hill together, he ignored this, according to one of the survivors.

The party had reached the bottom of the hill when Caspar heard the cries of a wounded soldier who had fallen. He turned and rode back to rescue him. As he was lifting him, his horse became unmanageable and dashed headlong among the Indians. That was the last seen of all that was mortal of Caspar Collins.

A searching party found his body on the morning of July 28, about three miles from the scene of the fight, along a creek which now bears his name. The body had been bound in telegraph wire and dragged some distance over the ground. One hand and one foot had been cut off, the heart had been taken out, and the body horribly mutilated.

The body was buried at the fort with military honors, pending cessation of Indian hostilities. It was exhumed on March 19, 1866 and sent to Fort Laramie and interred. When the 11th Ohio Volunteer Cavalry left Fort Laramie for home on June 14, 1866, the remains of Caspar Collins were brought with them to Hillsboro and placed in the family burial lot in Greenwood Cemetery. The following inscription marks his monument: *"Lt. Caspar Wever Collins, Born Hillsboro, Ohio, Sept. 30, 1844. Killed in battle leading a forlorn hope against the Indians at Platte Bridge, July 26, 1865."*

The name of the military post situated at Platte Bridge, between Deer and Rock creeks, was changed from Platte Bridge Fort to Fort Caspar in honor of Lt. Collins *"who lost his life while gallantly attacking a superior force of Indians at that place."* The fort, which was enlarged in 1866 to garrison 500 men, was abandoned in 1867.

Many school children in Highland county have never heard of the name of Caspar Collins, but in Wyoming he is one of the state's great heroes. A town was named for him, also a creek, and the fort, a book was written about his life, and a monument erected to his memory.

The Caspar, Wyoming, Tribune-Herald, in 1934 paid this tribute to Caspar Collins in an anniversary-of-the-massacre edition of the paper:

ANNIVERSARY OF PLATTE BRIDGE MASSACRE NOTED

Caspar Collins Recalls Last Fight of Gallant Army Officer For Whom Caspar Is Named

July 26, 1866, 69 years ago, Lieutenant Caspar Collins lost his life in a gallant but futile attempt to save the lives of others. History records no more sublime act of heroism. When Kansas officers hesitated to lead their men on a hazardous expedition with almost certain death in the offing, Lieutenant Collins, but recently commissioned in an Ohio regiment, bravely volunteered.

From Sweetwater Station Sergeant Custard with 25 soldiers was conveying a small wagon train to the Platte Bridge Fort.

Across the river from the fort 5000 blood-hungry hostile Indians were lying in wait to massacre the fort's garrison, in a vain attempt to eliminate this frontier guard to civilization's progress westward on the famous Oregon trail.

The little group of mounted infantry sallied forth from the fort on that hot July morning with courageous hearts. The old Guinard bridge was crossed at a trot. They cantered bravely up the hill-side to the open country beyond. A few mounted Indians fled before them in apparent fear. It was a ruse to draw the soldiers farther from the fort.

Suddenly from all sides a horde of 3000 fierce Indian warriors converged from adjacent ravines and gullies in an attempt to surround and annihilate the valiant battalion. It was a moment of terror and consternation. The overwhelming odds were such that none expected to emerge alive from the melee. Battling with every ounce of courage and strength the little troop fought its way successfully back toward the fort with the loss of five men.

As they fled precipitately to safety, a wounded soldier, stricken from his horse, called loudly for help. Lieutenant Collins with chivalric fearlessness, turned back to succor him, but was borne down by numbers to meet a hero's death!

With four exceptions Sergeant Custard's force was massacred in the fiendish manner of Indian ferocity.

It was a day of grief and humiliation for the army. However, the army's traditions were bravely upheld by those heroic frontier soldiers who gave their lives for their country and their fellowmen, that the progress of westward civilization be not stayed.

All honor, glory and guerdon remembrance should ever be paid to the gallant men who held back the forces of savagery when the thinly peopled highway of progress was daily threatened. Their lives were a forfeit to the safety of emigrant thousands of men, women and children.

The army was not slow in recognizing Lieutenant Collins' heroism. An honor guard of soldiers accompanied his remains to their last resting place in his Ohio home town. The name, Platte Bridge Fort, was changed to Fort Caspar. When a little town was established at the railroad's end in 1889 no other name would suffice but that of the Platte Bridge hero.

Some day the people of Caspar will awaken to the opportunity to properly observe the origin of the city's name. They will rehabilitate the old fort and its historic environs with proper ceremonies and patriotic remembrance.

Agnes Wright Spring wrote the book on the life of Caspar Collins. The Columbia University Press, New York, in reviewing this book, said: *"Hillsboro, Cincinnati's near neighbor, may well take pride in its youthful hero, Caspar Collins. His brief, but shining story is told by Agnes Wright Spring in, "Caspar Collins—The Life and Exploits of An Indian Fighter of the Sixties." The famous "Jum Bridger" was revealed in the book as having been one of Caspar's associates in his Indian campaigns.*

Probably no one caught the spirit of the story of Caspar Collins more eloquently than W. H. T. Shade who died recently in California. In *"Caspar Collins,"* a poem appearing in his book of poems, *"Buckeyeland and Bohemia,"* Mr. Shade immortalized this Hillsboro youth.

CASPAR COLLINS
by William H. T. Shade

Far out toward the border, where the Platte's dull waters flow,
And o'er the broad, sun-swept savannahs, prairie flowers grow;
And where the winds in wailing sighs still sound his funeral knell,
There is a spot of sacred earth where Caspar Collins fell.

'Twas in the old Eleventh that young Caspar wore his straps,
And in those weary western wilds he dreamed of fame; perhaps
Of coming days of blessed peace, when he might cease to roam,
And meet again the lov'd ones in the old Ohio home.

A braver soldier never lived; no braver fired a shot,
Or better bore the duties hard that fell unto his lot;
No duty was too hard for him when his it was to do —
A more heroic soldier's blood ne'er stain'd its country's blue.

'Twas in July in '65, a scorching summer day,
His scouting party sought the fort. Young Caspar led the way
Along the cheerless prairie trail until his small command
Exhausted reached the grim stockade, then rested on the sand.

The Cheyennes swarmed the prairie then; one grew behind each stone,
And Carnage o'er that region reigned, upon his reeking throne.
The troops were few and sore-besieged, their red foes none too few,
And death seemed grimly grasping for the little band in blue.

A long, slow, white-topped wagon-train was yet upon the plain;
To succor it seem'd but to fall beneath the arrows' rain,
When spake a young lieutenant: *"Colonel, shall those men die,
And we — within their very sight — to save them never try?"*

With blanched face the vet'ran turned. Far o'er the parched plain
All circled round by savages, the teamsters were. *"In vain,"*
The Colonel said, *" 'twould surely be to try to aid them there,
And from my little, weaken'd force no troops have I to spare."*

Mother Thompson

Mother Thompson's Home

Highland County Court House at Hillsboro

Old Octagon School Building
SINKING SPRING, OHIO

Fort Hill near Sinking Spring

Finest example of a stone fortification in Ohio, second only to Fort Ancient in Warren County.

Caspar Collins Birthplace
Collins Avenue, Hillsboro

This beautiful southern-colonial home of Dr. and Mrs. R. S. Rogers, Sr., on Collins avenue, Hillsboro, was the birthplace of Caspar Collins, hero of the Indian wars in the West

"I can not see them perish thus," the young man answered then;
"Give me but twenty volunteers and I will save these men."
His chieftain sadly shook his head, and said, "Take my men? No!
Who goes will ne'er return alive from yon relentless foe."

"Your men are fresh," young Caspar said; "but if they don't, then I
And my poor, tired Eleventh boys to save that train will try."
ATTENTION! MOUNT! — they waited not; the brazen bugle rang;
Upon their tired and goaded steeds the fearless troopers sprang.

The pond'rous gates swung open wide; the brave men passed without
And onward but to death and fame, with many a ringing shout.
Once driven back, again they rode to certain death the way.
A charge more grand was never made than that led forth that day.

No armor'd knight of ancient time did fiercer fighting do
Than that bold boy of Buckeyeland in braidless blouse of blue;
'Twixt sword and shot with savage blood the scorched sands ran red
E'er gallant Caspar Collins 'mid the prairie grass lay dead.

He died on duty's altar as die the true and brave;
His little band ne'er liv'd to greet those whom they fought to save.
The record of a hero's death and charge most nobly grand,
On history's scroll must be inscribed to that immortal band.

Out where the grim Cordilleras raise many a snowy peak,
Once, with a voice all tremulous, an old scout ceased to speak;
And o'er his bronz'd face stole a sigh methinks I yet can see
As he finished. It was all too true, the tale he told to me.

Far out toward the border where the Platte's dull waters flow,
And o'er the prairies' vast expanse do sweet wild flowers grow,
The wandering winds yet weirdly chant a hero's funeral knell,
Above the hallow'd, sacred spot where Casper Collins fell.

JOHN WOOD GOES TO THE GOLD DIGGINGS
The Adventures of a Greenfield Boy

"Gold many hunted, sweat and bled for gold,
Waked all the night and labored all the day.
And what was this allurement, dost thou ask?
A dust dug from the bowels of the earth —
Which, being cast into the fire came out
A shining thing that fools admire and called
A god, and in devout and humble plight,
Before it kneeled the greater to the less;
And on its altar sacrificed ease, peace,
Truth, faith, integrity, good conscience,
Friends, love, charity, benevolence and all
The sweet and tender sympathies of life."

John Wood wrote this at the end of his journal. How was he to know in the beginning, with his high hopes of youth, that the trek to the gold diggings 96 years ago was only a race with death and starvation; and the heaven he had gone to seek was in Greenfield, the pretty Highland county village he had left behind?

Other youths from Highland and Fayette counties were filled with dreams of fame and fortune to be found in California. All were to travel a perilous road over prairies, deserts, and mountains, besieged on all sides by pestilence, Indians, and death. They were to see many of their comrades perish and help bury them along the roadside in shallow, hurriedly dug graves.

John wrote a daily journal of his adventures which fortunately was preserved and a copy loaned the writer by the late Jacob Schmidt, of Greenfield. There were days the boy was so weak from lack of food and water and from illness that he scarcely could set his words down on paper as he had promised faithfully that he would.

Mess Number 1, of William H. Boggs Company, was the outfit that John Wood joined. Other members were James H. Black and Horace and George Sites. Most of this company met in Cincinnati April 3, 1850 where two days were spent in seeing the sights and purchasing necessities for the journey. On April 5 they boarded the steamer, James Millinger, bound for St. Joseph, Missouri, a busy town of 3,000 inhabitants, situated on the banks of the Missouri river.

Thousands of persons had gathered on the wharf at Cincinnati to see the company off. As the boat moved slowly out upon the waters of the beautiful Ohio river, John wondered if he would ever see his home again.

At St. Joseph, the Boggs Company joined a large train consisting of ox teams which were owned principally by J. H. Robinson and A. M. Ogle, of Fayette county, Ohio. Henry Burnett was captain of the entire outfit and Robert Stuart, lieutenant. There were 72 men and 17 teams now in this wagon train.

Each mess had a coffee pot, a frying pan, and a tin plate and a cup for each man. They had a light sheet-iron stove, but this was abandoned afterwards when wood grew scarce.

The boat reached St. Joseph 13 days later. Here they found at least 10,000 immigrants swarming about the town, preparing to start for the diggings. Many were unprepared for the expenses and difficulties that arose, and, homesick, turned homeward. Others lost their money in the gambling houses that sprang up like mushrooms. There was quarreling and discontent.

Young wild steers were bought which had to be broken in before the long trek west could begin. Moving about 40 miles up the river John's mess spent 12 days at a mill. They called their camp, Camp Brown. During the day they hunted and fished and at night they sang and danced about their camp fire. At last the cattle were broken in and they were ready to break camp and begin the great adventure.

Crossing the Nodaway river, they grazed their stock for three days on grass as they journeyed to Hawk's Ferry on the Missouri river. It took three days to cross the river in a hand-rowed boat. A load of cattle was almost lost in the crossing.

The wooded country was left behind them and they were now upon rolling prairies. Far off, in the distance, could be seen the Rocky mountains. Good weather favored them. The friendly Otto tribe of Indians living in this region visited their camp to trade them moccasins.

Now they reached the Nineshaw river, the banks of which had to be dug down before it could be crossed. The roads began to get bad and were strewn with elk horns and a few dead oxen and horses. A drenching rain lashed them. Men waded through sloughs waist deep to capture the panicked horses. Stampeding of cattle was a frequent occurrence and caused great inconvenience during the entire trip.

A corral was made to secure the cattle at night by placing the wagons in a circle and fastening the tongues of each with log chains to the hind wheel of the one in front of it, and leaving a space or gap of about 20 or 30 feet for a driveway. Guards were stationed around other parts. They finally learned to hold the beasts by driving large pickets in the ground and chaining them.

The section of country they were in was inhabited by the Pawnee tribe of Indians, a miserable, predatory tribe which visited the wagon train to beg for food. Now and then they saw an antelope skip across the prairie and heard the howl of wolves.

When just about to start on a 600 mile journey up the Platte river, a messenger appeared, riding post-haste towards them. His company, part of a wagon train from Illinois, had been attacked and surrounded by 200 hostile Indians. Rescuers, hastening to the scene, found that the cowardly savages had fled. The Illinois wagon train joined the Ohio train, for the sake of safety.

When they arrived at Fort Kearney they were joined by another train making a total of 25 or 30 teams.

Then came the plague, — the dreaded cholera. Robert Duncan, a boy from Highland county, came down with it. The doctor, pronouncing him seriously ill, told him that his end was near. Thereupon Robert asked a Mr. Moore to sing a hymn his mother had sung to him before his departure for the west. Too overcome by emotion to sing the hymn, Mr. Moore read the verses to the stricken boy who died a day or two later.

Many were stricken with cholera. Then another plague struck, — diarrhea. John Wood was so sick that he was unable to walk.

David Wright and John Glenn, two stout-hearted lads, died and were laid to rest in graves on the creek banks. Then later on that day Ellis Dixon was stricken with cholera and died.

Living had become a hideous nightmare to all trains traveling west to the gold diggings. Thousands of immigrants were ill. Many trains stopped along the road to tend their sick and dying and bury their dead sewn up in their blankets. Sometimes there was no time for burial and the dead had to be left upon the ground. The water was muddy and unpalatable. When cattle were lost or died, the trains had to lie by for weeks.

At this point John's company almost decided to retrace their steps home. Finally they resolved to continue their journey and struggled on to an elevation 12 miles farther where they encamped. A storm descended furiously upon them that night and inundated the camp. The cattle got away. Exhausted men awoke to find that they had been sleeping in water six inches deep. The cattle were found 15 or 20 miles away.

In the meantime, Robert Stuart, Robert Hendrickson, Franklin Nitterhouse, and Samuel Wilcox came down with the cholera. Hendrickson did not last long and was buried by the roadside.

To add to the difficulties, food had become scarce. There was nothing to eat but crackers, tea, and coffee, with scarcely any water. Had it not been for their religion, they might well have given up the struggle.

They reached the south fork of the Platte river only to be obliged to retrace their steps to the north fork to ford it, crossing paths made by buffalo coming in from the plains for water. They saw a herd of buffalo and wolves scenting the abandoned camps, and again, their cattle stampeded.

A company homeward bound with a wagon load of sick and dying, warned them that there was no grass ahead and that the cholera was worse. John and Dan B. Clark purchased two milch cows from them.

Just before they crossed the difficult north fork of the Platte river, they passed an old Sioux Indian burial ground. A scaffold had been made by planting poles in the ground and fastening poles crosswise. This provided burial places for the dead who were wrapped in skins and laid 10 or 15 feet above the ground, their weapons buried with them. Wolves had disturbed many of the graves.

A stormy night and wolves howling in the wind and rain outside the camp where lay the dead and dying, made the night eerie. The next morning, after burying their dead, the adventurers proceeded on their way on a level road, in sight of Court House Rock, a large isolated bluff of hard sand on an open plain. By the time they reached the river that night to camp, one tenth of John's company and one fifth of all the wagon train were dying with cholera or diarrhea.

Chimney Rock, an isolated sandstone bluff in the shape of a pyramid and fast crumbling in ruins had thousands of names carved upon it. All who were able stopped to carve their names thereon.

The next day two French and Indian trading posts were passed which had been established 16 years previously. An Indian woman had just clubbed a fat dog to death while the men held it. She dragged it to a fire, singed its hair off, cut it in pieces, and put it into the pot for soup. They invited the passing strangers to stop and eat with them.

On the 23rd of April they crossed the Laramie river and made camp in order to graze the cattle and write letters home. The sick were now slowly recovering. John was still so weak that he could scarcely write in his journal.

The Black Hills, just ahead, must be crossed. The road to them was very bad, the river bottoms were narrow and sandy, and there was little grass. However, as they pressed on, they found that there was plenty of wood. Far in the distance they saw the snowy summits of the majestic Rockies. On either side were plains, scattered groves of pine, and antelope and mountain sheep. They came upon a number of precious cooling streams and always made their camp beside one at night.

They did not find the forage for their cattle in the Black Hills that they had hoped to find and they had to be driven off the path for two miles for grass. The country was barren but wild and romantic looking. The cattle's feet were being ruined by the stony road. The two milch cows they had bought some time back, were a boon to the sick, supplying them with rich dishes of soup.

When at long last they had wearily descended the Black Hills and left them behind, they came to Deer creek. They saw hundreds resting their cattle, fishing, and cooking. Some were shoeing their cattle with sole-leather because their hooves were almost worn out with crossing the mountains. A few days later, and they had to stop and re-shoe their cattle's poor tired feet.

Onward they forged, but with heavy hearts. If the Rockies they were seeking should be worse than the Black Hills, they feared they would never reach the land of gold. They came to the Red Buttes and made camp. There was only one route to California and Oregon until the summit of the Rockies was attained. Then the Oregon road branched off to the right.

On July 2 they crossed the north fork of the Platte river for the first and last time. They were now in the sage brush country. The boats they crossed on were made of timber which grew along the river. The ferry was kept by some immigrants who had started early for the gold fields. They charged five dollars for each wagon and one dollar for cattle, and had made a fortune at ferrying. Thousands were assembled here awaiting their turn to cross.

The water in this region was almost all alkali water, fatal to horses. Many animals lay dead along the way, poisoned by the water. The country was destitute of natural resources except wild sage which was excellent for firewood.

By July 5 they reached the cool, clear, and pleasant waters of Sweetwater river, where Independence Rock, a natural curiosity stood at the foot of the Rockies with thousands of names carved on it of people who had been fortunate to have survived thus far. They camped at Devil's Gate where Sweetwater passed through a narrow defile. The Crow Indians stole a team of horses from them in broad daylight two days later and got away with it. They came upon the sad sight of a man burying his wife and three little children who had been unable to survive the hardships. Indians had stolen this man's horses.

Light cases of mountain fever and one more case of cholera broke out. They made a camp in a beautiful valley where 500 head of stock were found suffering from want of food. Many sick and discouraged immigrants were found. Some were dying.

By this time the entire wagon train was all but starving. Their food up until now had been mostly bread, bacon and coffee with sometimes a little flour stirred into the hot grease, which they called gravy. This food was almost gone and there was nothing to cook but willows.

July 11th, the company started climbing the dreaded Rockies. Robinson and Ogle's own teams were by this time so exhausted that it was believed that they would never reach their destination. A strong wind coming from the west blew sand in their eyes and the men had to wear scarves over their eyes. They were compelled to leave a good wagon behind. All began to throw away anything cumbersome as the ascent grew steeper. Extra chains, rings, and kingbolts were dropped, and some left their worn out teams to perish. Sixteen miles farther, at Willow creek, they stopped to camp and bury their dead.

The next day they continued along the backbone of the mountains and encamped at Pacific Springs, the largest known spring in the Rockies. The water was icy cold. David Puckett, who had been ill, was steadily growing worse.

Many were exhausted by the time they reached the road forks on the following day. The road to the right led to Oregon, via Fort Hall. The road to the left led to the Great Salt Lake and the city of Deseret. James Bridewell and John Murray chose the right road because they feared the company would never reach California. Wolves, hares, antelopes, and elk were everywhere and wild sage was luxuriant.

They were 2,000 miles from home by the 15th of July and were starting down the western side of the Rocky Mountains. They were yet 1,000 miles from California and before them stretched mountains yet to be crossed.

Within 10 miles east of Green river, David Puckett succumbed and they buried him on the banks of the Big Sandy. The poor lad had hoped to get enough money for an education.

A ferry kept by the Mormons at Green river was small and had to be worked by hand. The Mormons charged $4.50 per wagon. It took some time to cross and all had to wait their turns. McClean's cattle were getting too fatigued to go much farther. One of the wagons had to be abandoned and the teams doubled.

The dangerous country they were passing through now was infested with alkali water and the Snake Indians. The soil resembled that found at the seashore. They met again their Illinois friends with whom they had parted company some time back, and found that many of them had died.

Thousands of cattle, mules and horses had been lost up to this time from drinking alkali water. Twenty-two miles were covered before a lake of good water was found. They named it Speery's Lake for the man who discovered it.

Finally they came to the Black Fork, crossed it twice, and trekked 25 miles through a picturesque region to a fertile valley watered by seven pretty streams running through it. The fort was called Fort Bridger for an old pioneer who lived there. A number of French and Indians occupied the fort and lived well by trading furs, moccasins, whiskey, milk, and buckskin pantaloons. Milk was sold at 10 cents a pint and whiskey at $2.00 a pint. The Indians possessed hundreds of fine cattle and horses which they loved to ride.

There were to have assembled there the following day, over 100 lodges of Indians to exhibit 500 horses. The horses were a prize they had taken from the Utah tribe with whom they were at war. Much as the travelers would have liked to stay, they felt obliged to refuse the invitation.

The next day was Sunday and July 21st. When the train stopped to rest, John took a book and went off to read and rest. He was awakened by another traveler who warned him to keep to the road because the Indians in that part were hostile. He and his new friend, in taking what they thought was a short cut, were lost and had to walk 15 miles to find the Bear river. Several cattle were lost from drinking alkali water.

After leaving Bear river they went down a narrow valley into Echo Hollow. On the way, Old Drag, a faithful old steer, gave out and had to be left to perish. They passed more abandoned wagons and chains. Crossing jagged mountains, they wound through long groves of cottonwood, pine, and cedar, and were in a region of sublimity. The timber was larger, with pine the dominant tree. It did not seem that the cattle could hold out much longer.

They crossed a cold stream 30 times in the canyon before they descended into the Great Salt Lake Valley. Journeying six miles up this valley they came to Deseret, a town of about 8,000 Mormon inhabitants, near the Jordan river.

The valley contained about 20,000 inhabitants all told, and was almost surrounded by snow-capped mountains. The Utah Indians, a filthy, selfish tribe, dwelled in parts of the valley, mostly along the Jordan river.

The houses of Deseret were generally one story high and were built of sun-dried brick. The streets ran at right angles and were six rods wide. On each side ran a clear stream of water which came down from the mountain slopes in ditches. Deseret was 20 miles from Great Salt Lake and one mile west of the Jordan.

Produce in the city was high. A bushel of flour sold for $25.00. However, the Mormons, who were busy building a commercial house, were kind and accommodating. John took dinner and supper with them. He paid 50 cents for each meal.

They prepared to leave the Mormon city on the 29th. The road of departure was one to the south called the Cut-off or Hasting's route, which intersected another road at the head of the Humbolt or St. Mary's river about 400 miles distant. The company's doctor decided to take the northern route and so departed from them.

It took only two days to reach the Great Salt Lake. Here they saw Mormons making salt. Three buckets full of water made one bucket of salt. Many took baths in the water which was so heavy that no one could possibly sink.

Before they reached the desert they mowed a large pile of grass for each team and piled it in their wagons and filled their kegs with water. There would be no more springs until they got to the other side of the desert. It might be so far across that they would never make it.

The first 14 miles was over a high, rough mountain road so rough they had to hold the wagons up to keep them from upsetting. The land around them appeared to be an extensive plain destitute of even wild sage. The cattle had to subsist on one quart of water a day.

They passed an elderly woman with a coffee pot full of water. She was searching for her husband who had lost a wagon tire and had gone back to recover it.

The next person they met was a Mrs. Hall from Cincinnati. She had lost her husband who had driven his famishing cattle in search of water he had hoped to find nearby. He had failed to return. John's company gave her enough water to last until morning.

When the wagon train reached the bluffs, they gave the last of the hay and water to their cattle. On the way they passed dead and dying stock. Men from the other side of the desert had hauled water out to relieve the immigrants but were selling it for one dollar a gallon and many were unable to buy any. Finally, all the cattle belonging to the company perished except two yokes and everything virtually depended upon them.

Some uncanny sense seemed to tell the cattle that they were nearing water, for within ten miles of it, they began to quicken their walk and tried to break into a run. They started running when within one mile and the men could hardly keep pace with them. At last they were out of the desert.

When the coveted water was reached, men and animals drank their fill and then, utterly exhausted, slept. They had just come 93 long wearisome miles across the desert.

When they awoke the next morning they found themselves near a mountain where there were good springs and grass. Compelled to abandon McClean's last wagon because the team had broken down, they made pack saddles of the wagon and pads out of the wagon covers and stuffed them with dry grass. The provisions were packed on the remaining cattle.

In the meantime other immigrants began to arrive, all famished for water. Some were cursing while others were praying. Mr. Hall was among them and he was preparing to return for his wife.

John and his company rigged out a team, loaded it with water, and went back to succor those stranded on the desert. Alfred Ogle carried water on his back 20 or 30 miles to relieve immigrants' distress. Eight young men from Dayton, Ohio, joined John's mess.

Still another desert loomed upon them. This one, however, was only 37 miles across and somehow, they made it. They dared not stop for many rests for fear their provisions would run out. On a Sunday night they came to Mound Springs where water gushed out of spongy, mound-shaped knobs. The cattle's backs were sore from the pack saddles.

Still they forced themselves onward and as they went, the country grew better. On July 14th, they were in a deep valley of breath-taking beauty. The ground was lush with grass, and the timber was dense. Springs flowing from the mountain collected in the center of the valley in one large stream of water. The immigrants called the region Fountain Valley.

Twenty-five miles farther south and they were in a land inhabited by a blood-thirsty, thievish, sullen tribe of Shoshone Indians, who visited the camp seeking to exchange stolen horses for guns and ammunition.

A sign at a spring warned them that the Indians had stolen all the horses from some immigrants and seven head of cattle. They were a murderous lot, the sign advised them, and they ought to be on their guard.

Unfortunately, the company had given their guns away some time back, for it was thought that all the Indians were harmless. It was also hard to drive a steer and at the same time carry a gun for fear of ruining the steer's back.

When they had crossed the mountains and were traveling 14 miles northward through knee-deep grass in a small valley along Glover Creek, they came upon a dead Indian near the road. He had evidently been shot by an immigrant. In one hand he clutched a whip and in the other an arrow and it looked as though he had been shot off his horse.

Word got to them that day that five immigrants who had insisted on taking the short cut through the mountains, the cut off, with their pack horses, had been cruelly murdered. Later these five were found and buried. Another sign posted near by stated that six Indians had been shot recently in the vicinity.

That night the wagon train was awakened by the guards and warned of the approach of several Indians. The Indians proved to be none other than white men from Robinson and Ogle's company, A. J. Jeffries and a Mr. Hedrick. They had been separated from their company on the cut off. Believing, as Wood's company had, that the road continued down Fountain Valley below the cut off and then turned and crossed the mountain on the other side, they had concluded to cut across and meet their comrades at noon that day, or night. Deciding that they had made a mistake, they had turned back to meet their teams, after hungering and thirsting all day.

The next day, as they were completing a 30-mile journey up Grover creek through thick clusters of willows, they heard desperate yelling. Arming themselves with guns they borrowed from immigrants who had just come up, they rushed in the direction of the noise. It was almost dark when they came upon an Indian camp. They learned that Captain Robinson and his men had stumbled upon the Indian camp and a battle had followed. The Indians had in their possession a number of horses they had stolen from white travelers.

On the 28th of August they reached the south fork of St. Mary's and the Humbolt rivers. They followed the Humbolt river all day, crossing it 12 times. Descending a sharp canyon, they proceeded cautiously 20 miles. Hunger pains were so acute they were obliged to kill one of the steers for food. They could hear the barking of dogs belonging to Indians but they were not molested.

They covered 15 miles the next day, crossing the river 25 times. When they reached the Fort Hall road they found that they had missed it by at least 150 miles when they had taken the cut off, or Hasting's route. They saw evidences of Indian depredations throughout this region. That night they reached the fork of the Humbolt river.

When they came upon an immigrant hauling bran and shorts to feed his horse, they coaxed him to sell some to them. John bought 12 pounds of rye which were ground in a coffee mill. The bran cost them 20 cents a pound and the rye, 25 cents. They made batter out of the bran and shorts and made it into cakes.

The terrifying word reached them the cholera was raging in their wake. They hastened on over dusty, hilly roads, frequently stopping to clean out their shoes. Their toenails were worn off by the sharp stones. That night they dined on dark cakes, willows, and beef roasted on coals.

The next day some of the men went about the other wagon trains trying to buy some flour and bacon. They met with no success.

There were now 24 men traveling in John Wood's company. Their names were: Mess 1. Henry Burnett, John N. Robinson, James and Morris Rowe; Mess 2. Robert Stuart, John Wood, Thomas R. Grub, George and Horace Sites; Mess 3. David Loofborrow, Isaac Smith, Archibald McGahen, James Williams, Thomas Compton, Harris and Jackson Bryant; Mess 4. Moses Stout, George Decker, David Taylor, William Smith, Michael Turner. Mess 4 was from Dayton, Ohio.

Now the last of the bran and most of the rye and beef were gone. Things were looking bad for them again. They passed several dead horses and cattle which had been shot with poisoned arrows by the Indians; and the graves of two immigrants who had been killed by Indians. When they heard that the Indians were preparing an attack to avenge the death of other Indians, an attempt was made to get off the little traveled road they were on, cross the river, and gain another road four miles away. When they stopped to rest they saw an Indian on a pony in the high grass and gave the alarm.

John and Morris were driving two lame steers at the head of the train. They attempted to reach the ones in front who were rushing to reach the road and crying for the rest to come on.

Several more Indians on horseback appeared who were, apparently, spies. Then, a half mile away, to the left, they saw about 40 Indians on horseback and 100 on foot hurrying towards the immigrants. They were singing a war song. Others were putting out their camp fires. One of the men was dispatched to warn immigrants ahead who were not aware of the impending danger.

On pushed the savages, armed with guns. As they flanked the wagon train, they fired upon John and Morris who were about 500 yards behind the others. The entire wagon train halted and prepared to fight. The youths managed to reach their company which quickly formed into a line. They had in all only two guns but every tent pole and cane available were shouldered. They stood pat, shouting defiance at the Indians.

The savages made a rush at them as though to take them by storm, then wheeled and retreated to their camp where they raised a reinforcement and again rushed them. The immigrants stood their ground fearlessly and the Indians hesitated, as though suddenly struck with fear.

Then to their aid came the immigrants who had been warned by the messenger.

Night was descending. John's company made a break for the road. Indians followed, watching for an opportunity to steal the cattle. One steer stuck in the mud and was left to its fate. At last they reached the welcome fire of a large wagon train which pitied them but would share nothing with them but some tea.

When morning came a force of 35 men was rallied to return to retaliate against the Indians. A four-hour battle ensued and 15 Indians were killed. By this time their food supply was all but gone. They were obliged to eat the last of their beef which was full of maggots but tasted fine because they were so hungry. That evening John purchased 25 pounds of beef and several pounds of beans from another wagon train they met. Assembled at the camp that night were about 400 wagons. Many women and children were in the assemblage.

John tried his best to buy flour and bacon for his company. Hundreds were living on half rations and had had no bread for weeks. Those who had provisions would not part with any of them. There was nothing left in John's company but some coffee. That evening they succeeded in buying 35 pounds of beef and they had a feast of coffee and beef. They came upon a young man who had quarreled with his father and was returning home. He had been subsisting on frogs and wild roseberries, a coarse substitute for bread.

The cattle by this time were quite lean and their feet and backs were sore. They were traveling through bottom land infested with hostile Indians. Wearily they pressed ahead through desolate country over sand, rough roads. The heat was unbearable, there having been no rain for weeks.

Valuable property was seen everywhere on the plains where it had been left to rot. Many were begging pitifully for bread. At least half of the immigrants were starving. Many were glad to die. John's company came upon a large patch of roseberries, feasted on them, and thus were able to get on 20 miles farther.

They wondered how they had managed to escape the cholera raging behind them not many miles back. By this time the water supply had given out and the cattle had grown so weak that they fairly staggered along.

John borrowed a horse from a passing immigrant and paid him for its loan that he might go in search of water. Five miles distant he found blessed water and this was all they had to subsist upon. Other immigrants still would not share what food they had claiming that they were starving themselves.

At last they came upon a 45-mile stretch of desert, a sheer

waste of burning sand. It would be madness to turn back, knowing what they had left behind them, so they forced themselves ever on.

They had not gone far when they came upon a party of hungry men skinning an old ox that had been left to die. They took what they wanted for themselves and gave the remainder to John's company. The beef, which had been blown by the flies, was bad, and it was practically impossible to eat it. Later they found a lame steer, killed it, and obtained a supply of meat. The cattle had only willows to eat. They had to stop every few minutes to clean out their dust-filled shoes. They met some immigrants who had killed a few old cows from which they got 40 pounds of meat.

When they reached the edge of what was known as the Humbolt sink, where they encamped, they were told that the Californians had a large trading post beyond the next desert and that anything could be purchased there. This would have been great news had they had among them the necessary money.

It was now the first of September. They were moving slowly down the sink where the river ended and began to widen into a lake.

The travelers found an old sheet-iron stove and cooked about 30 pounds of beef in it. This they sacked for food supply for the journey across another desert. They saw hundreds of immigrants preparing to cross.

There was a man from Missouri who had a large wagon train loaded with hams and fruits which he sold at 65 cents a pound. With what money they had left they spent two thirds of it for a ham and three pounds of fruit. This was almost devoured the first meal. Casks were filled with water and all that was not absolutely essential was thrown away. There were now only four steers left in John's company. The last of the fruit and beef was eaten that night.

The road they were on was lined with wagons, dead and dying horses, mules and cattle. A steer gave out, then two others. Still another fell. John remained with the last steer to fall and tried to urge it on. Every time he succeeded in getting it up it would drop again. He purchased a gallon and a half of water and both man and beast slacked their thirst.

Sighting some men sitting around a wagon eating boiled oats, John asked for a share of it and gave them money with which to buy water in exchange. He was forced to leave his steer when at last it lay down and refused to budge again.

John reeled deliriously on, trying to overtake his mess ahead, but now he was ill. Sometimes he imagined he was back in his native Greenfield. Again he imagined that he had reached California and was reveling in gold. It was ten o'clock that night when he arrived at the tents of his comrades who were asleep with their steers tied fast to them. They were in a country of thieves.

On the 4th of September they were on the banks of Salmon Trout or Carson river where there were a number of trading posts. All kinds of provisions were sold. Flour sold for one dollar a pound, liquor for 50 cents a dram, and molasses for $4.00 a gallon. Roguery of all kinds went on about them by men who had nothing to do but steal horses, cattle and mules. These men were from the gold mines and had come to the trading posts for this sole purpose.

John's mess had no money now. They killed a steer, sold part of it for 20 cents a pound, and bought flour. The one steer they had left they sold for $22.50 and divided the money among them. The situation was grave and the company disbanded, deciding that it was every man for himself. The day was spent in resting, butchering the beef, and selling it. Hundreds of travelers arrived every hour bringing fearful tidings of cholera, starvation and death.

Three hundred miles still lay between them and the gold mines. They were thousands of miles from home. They must travel faster than ever or know more suffering and want.

A gigantic barrier of mountains challenged them, mountains 16,000 feet high. John Wood, carrying his blankets on his back, forged onward. He was joined by Robert Stuart and Thomas Grubb from Washington C. H., Ohio, and they were welcome company on this last lap of the trek. Each man had some flour, pork, coffee, and molasses, also a plate, cup, and frying pan. Others decided to join in small bands in like manner. Some stayed behind to come on with their remaining cattle.

As they were about to start, several men from Robinson and Ogle's company were met returning from the mountains. They told a heart breaking tale of privation and suffering and of having had to desert their exhausted cattle.

John and his comrades bade them farewell and struck out along the Salmon Trout river. This journey was a nostalgic reminder to John of his boyhood days along Paint creek in Highland county. They dined fairly well during the day on pork, beef, molasses, pancakes, and coffee.

They walked 35 miles, passing a trading post, and then a man digging the grave of his wife who had just died. The man told them they need not fear the Piute Indians in this region for they were friendly.

The next day, after walking 28 miles, they arrived at a Dutchman's trading post. The skin had been rubbed off their feet by their shoes. Here they purchased flour from the eccentric fellow and journeyed on through Carson's valley, a lovely grassy region where countless horses, cattle and mules were grazing. Many immigrants were observed begging their way from place to place.

Good fortune was with them when, enroute to the next trading post they encountered a man named McClelan who offered the boys jobs of driving loose stock over the mountains, on horseback. John and Robert accepted the offer. Each was furnished with a good horse and his board, and started off across the plains to round up the cattle.

Riding was a relief from the tedious walking, but they wondered if their horses could scale the craggy walls of the mountains. Two days of riding and they reached Devil's Ladder, an almost perpendicular hill. Immigrants were clambering laboriously up it and teamsters could be heard whooping and swearing for miles.

Up and up they rode, reaching Red Lake, a beautiful scenic spot dotted with pointed pines 300 feet high and tall regal spruces.

Every two or three miles they passed a trading post where it looked like practically everything any one would want was offered for sale. An Indian was seen perched on a crag with his bow and arrow in his hand, watching the movements of immigrants on the road below him, and looking like a picture in a book.

And at length they passed through what had seemed an endless grove of lofty timber to the peak of the mountain and were ready to descend.

Down they came, passing Tragical or Leak Springs on the way and traversing Onion Valley dotted with several trading posts. They took their cattle to pasture over a sloping road which wound through pine and fir trees. They passed hundreds of immigrants with their blankets on their backs, traveling for dear life. The thought of gold drove each one desperately on and on.

Captain Robinson and his party came up to and passed John and Robert, who stopped at Pleasant Valley to buy hay for 20 cents a pound and barley for 25 cents. The grass had already been eaten off by the hungry cattle of others.

They were only 12 miles from Ringgold, the first gold mining town, on the morning of the 16th. Pulling up stakes for the last time they hurried on and reached the town by one o'clock.

The streets were thronged with traders. Men were everywhere, frantically digging. The miners were called to their meals at the six hotels and boarding houses by bells. Board for one week was $16.00 and the cost of a single meal was one dollar. Gold must have been plentiful for all seemed able to afford these prices.

John Wood, 3000 miles from Greenfield and loved ones, was weak and utterly exhausted. However, he forced himself out to where miners were at work to learn from them the processes of mining. He found men working as though their lives depended upon it, their faces drawn with worry and discouragement.

He saw two brothers, newly arrived, quarreling and separating and was to learn later that this was the usual occurrence. He saw two little girls carrying dirt in a bucket to their father who was rocking out gold. Their mother and brother, they said, had died on the plains and they had helped their father drive the ox teams hither.

So at last John Wood reached his journey's end along with approximately 80,000 other immigrants crossing the plains and mountains that spring and summer. At least 3000 wagons and $3,000,000 worth of property had been abandoned along the way. Every few yards of the long, long trek was marked with the grave of one who had perished.

Did John Wood return to Greenfield a wealthy man? He did not say, and no one seems to know.

Who was John Wood? Who were his parents? Records fail to reveal this. We might call him the indomitable spirit of Highland county pioneers.

He said, at the conclusion of his poignant little journal: *"The fate of more than half no one knows nor ever can. What a blessing to the world, if mankind only knew their wants, and seek for contentment in honest and moderate gain, for true and lasting happiness can come from no other source."*

HILLSBORO'S MYSTERY CHILD

For more than 80 years, the heart of a Hillsboro woman cried out for the answer to this question, *"Who am I?"* She died January 21, 1942 at the home of her daughter, Mrs. L. C. Vance on West South Street, with the mystery still unsolved.

Mrs. Sarah Dorney Stroup never knew her true identity but until the day of her death, at the age of 89, she sought to pierce the curtain of mystery that veiled her abandonment as a child 87 years ago in the railroad depot in Hillsboro.

Even in her waning years, she still hoped that some miracle would reveal who her parents were and how she came to be deserted by a woman believed to have been her nurse.

She spent many years in a diligent search for some clue to her identity. A noted professor took an interest in her case and spent much time and money in an effort to locate her parents, but today the mystery is as deep as ever.

Mrs. Stroup knew that she was brought across the ocean from England by a woman named Ellen Dorney, who represented herself as Sarah's mother but who was undoubtedly her nurse. Ellen was a tall, dark complexioned woman with a fiery temper and she often beat the two-year-old child.

Ellen brought with her also another child, a little boy who greatly resembled her and who, she claimed, was her son.

She had come to America following her husband's death to visit her sisters, Mary and Margaret. It was learned that a brother-in-law, William Park Dorney, had sent her money for the ocean voyage.

When Mrs. Dorney reached Hillsboro, where Margaret lived, she learned that Margaret had become a widow and taken her three children and joined Mary in Indiana. Whereupon she returned to the depot to take a train to Mary's home.

At the depot little Sarah balked and cried out that she did not want to go with her. The woman, according to the conductor, a Mr. Clark, turned and shouted angrily:

"*Whoever wants this child can have her! I don't want to be bothered any more.*"

Pushing the child from her, the woman boarded the train with her son and vanished from the little girl's life.

The tiny stranger, blue-eyed, sandy-haired, delicately-featured, and dressed in expensive, hand-tailored clothes, quite different from the cheap clothes worn by Ellen and her son, soon became the attraction and the darling of interested townspeople.

Four prominent women of St. Mary's Episcopal Church came forward to champion her, Mrs. William Scott, Mrs. John A. Smith, "*Mother Thompson,*" and a Mrs. Skanks, the minister's wife. They paid a motherly widow, a Mrs. Harper, to care for little Sarah, as she came to be called, and kept her in lovely clothes they made for her.

When she was seven years old she was bound out as was the custom to do with poor children in those days. Sarah was taken to the home of General Charles Sheif and his mother to work for her board.

But Sarah missed kind Mrs. Harper and cried for her, so she was taken back to her where she worked out part time for her keep. Mrs. Harper took her with her when she went to live in Indianapolis and here Sarah worked in a boarding house to help out.

She recalled as though it were yesterday when she saw Abraham Lincoln's body lying in state at the state house in Indianapolis. Two years later they came to Cincinnati. Here Mrs. Harper was killed by a train.

Sent back to Hillsboro, Sarah, then 10 years old, went to work at the James Stroup farm, west of Dodsonville. Here she grew to young womanhood and married her employer's son, John W. Stroup, a widower, who lived at his parental home with his child, Eldora.

Sarah's husband took her to his farm near Danville where they lived for what, she said, were 37 of the happiest years of her life. Then she came to Hillsboro.

"*But all through the years,*" Mrs. Stroup said, "*I longed to know my own parents. I went to Indiana and found Ellen Dorney's sisters, Mary and Margaret, but they refused to tell me anything except that Ellen had remarried and moved to some place in Missouri. Then I lost all trace of them."*

Professor Isaac Sams, who had come from Bath, England and settled in Hillsboro, tried to locate Sarah's folks for her at his own expense, but failed. He was sure, she recalled, that she had an English father and a Scotch-Irish mother and that she was descended from nobility.

In those days when a girl stood in line for an inheritance, she often was done away with to make way for an over-ambitious male relative in the family. Sarah's scheming relative, Prof. Sams thought, had had Ellen Dorney bring the child to America and purposely lose her when the chance presented itself.

Mrs. Stroup had but two relics of her childhood, a child's cup of the finest china she brought with her across the sea, and a picture taken of her in her new dress when she was five years old, by Hillsboro's first photographer.

She was proud that she had shaken hands with nine governors and four presidents and that, as oldest woman bearing the name of Stroup at the annual Stroup family reunion at Dodsonville, she was presented with a chair she always prized highly. Never having attended school since the age of nine, Mrs. Stroup practically educated herself.

When she died she left behind her only one known living descendant, her daughter Hariett, (Mrs. Lewis C. Vance) with whom she made her home. Her husband died in 1906; her step-daughter, Eldora Stroup Jonte, died 10 years ago; and the boy she took to rear when he was deserted at the age of 17 months, Charles Mooney Stroup, she lost trace of during the First World War and has never been found.

"As long as I live," Mrs. Stroup often said, *"I shall never stop wanting to know who I really am."*

HIGHLAND COUNTY'S FRENCH SETTLEMENT:

Frederick Druhot
   n'en en France
Dans lac, M: D.
   Audincourt, Fr.
mort le 27 Avril
   1841 paria chutte
d'mm apbre qui
   brullait dans
soutrone age'
   de 51 ans.

Ici repose
   Susanne
Epouse de
   Frederic Druhot
Ne'e en France
   Jan. 1790
Mort le
   14 Mai 1870
age'e de 80 ans.

Quaint inscriptions on thin gray stones, stooped with age, mutely relate the story of the romance of the French lad, Frederick, and the French maid, Susanne, who have been sleeping these many years now in the little French cemetery at the edge of Mowrystown in Highland county.

We wonder: Did the maid and lad come over the stormy sea in a cattle boat, as did many of their kinsman; did they know each other before they came, or did they meet in the log cabin school house when she was a shy school miss and he an ambitious backwoods youth?

Frederick died when he was only 51, but Susanne lingered on and reached the venerable age of 80 years.

There are many inscriptions similar to these on the markers that head the mounds in the French cemetery. The words and constructions, all in old French, are confused; there are improvised words that do not quite make sense; and there is an evident attempt at rhyming. But somehow they piece together into the real and thrilling story of a band of brave emigrants who fled from France in 1800 to make their homes in this country.

During the time of the French Revolution, tumbrels filled with victims rumbled heavily through the streets to the guillotine. The king's soldiers and the people were engaged in a violent conflict. It was a time of rebellion and bloodshed. Mobs ruled and no one was safe, neither king nor subject.

Many sought refuge in caves and lived like hunted animals. For the slightest offense, perhaps for only the humming of a song, or perhaps for no reason at all, innocent persons were dragged before a court to face a trial that was only a travesty of justice, and were condemned to death by beheading.

Some dreamed of escaping to America, where surely was to be found peace at last and freedom from persecution. Here in this glorious young republic they would establish homes and realize security for their children and their children's children. Here they would begin a new France that should be like the old, and yet not too much like it.

Banding together, a courageous number managed to escape. They crossed a tempestuous ocean, making on the average only about 20 miles a day. Often their frail wooden crafts were driven back over the long miles they had just covered and they were obliged to retrace the way. It took several months to make the trip. At last they arrived in Buffalo, New York. Here, and at various other places, they purchased land, for most of them were people of means.

Where one French family went the other finally followed, and, eventually, those who had penetrated the wilderness and settled in Ohio, in the vicinity of Mowrystown, were joined by the rest.

It is said that Capt. Andrew Badgley made the first settlement here soon after 1800. The town, however, was not platted until May 29, 1829, by Samuel Bell. It was named in honor of

George Mowery, whose son, John, and grandson, Abe, played leading parts in the early history of the settlement.

About 1811, a Methodist church was organized about one-fourth mile below the site of the town and was called Sloan's church because it had been constructed by a Mr. Sloan. About 1812, George Barngrover built a grist mill on the creek, several distilleries sprang up, and John Smith opened the first store. The store has vanished but Mowrystown's first cabin, which stood beside it, has been moved across the street and is now being used for a garage. Mr. Smith kept a large barrel of whiskey in the store. To it was attached a tin cup and any customer making a purchase was entitled to partake freely of it.

Joseph Bell was the first postmaster and James B. Finley was the first teacher.

The late John Fenwick, who in 1938 was the oldest living descendant of these French pioneers, related his family history which is representative of all the other family histories of Mowrystown.

Thomas Fenwick, his grandfather, was a Scotchman, who held several land grants in Maryland and Delaware. He came to Buffalo in company with the French Huguenots, having married a French girl. It took them three months to cross the ocean. While living in Buffalo, John's father, William Russell Fenwick, was born.

In 1816 the Fenwicks moved to the state of Delaware. Hearing of the wonders of this part of the country, Thomas decided to bring his family here. With his wife and three sons he reached Fall creek, near Hillsboro. Here he stayed for a short time, then went to Ripley, Ohio, and from there to the state of Illinois. There the Indians were troublesome and fevers and ague were prevalent. One of the children died. The family went to live on Fifth street in Cincinnati but soon afterwards sought their French kin located about three miles west of Mowrystown.

The journeying from place to place after leaving Buffalo had been done entirely on foot, except for the mother who rode upon pack horse. In her arms she carried her sixteen months old baby. Clinging to her waist was her next youngest, aged 18 months, who sat on the saddle behind her.

One of these two little boys was William Russell, the father of John Fenwick.

When a young widower, William fell in love with a pretty brown-eyed maiden named Catherine Cornetet.

Catherine's parents had died when she was only a child. She had been taken into the home of a cultured family named Grand-Girard which was to figure prominently later in the educational and cultural life of Hillsboro. These people reared Catherine into lovely young womanhood.

When Catherine was 15 years old, the Grand-Girards moved

to Hillsboro and Catherine went to live with the Johnson family at Taylorsville, a nearby hamlet.

While attending services in the Presbyterian log church in Mowrystown one Sunday, William Fenwick, from his seat on the men's side at the left, observed the sweet, intent features of the young miss beneath her sober, scoop-shaped bonnet. Catherine was sitting demurely among her elders on the right side reserved for women and girls, dressed in her best home-spun dress which was long and black and reached to the tips of her sturdy brogans. Although conversation was not permitted in the church and full attention must be paid the earnest French minister who conducted the services in the French language, there could be no restriction on the surreptitious exchange of glances.

Services had just begun. Out of their small, mottled black and green hymnals, "*Chants Evangeliques*," they were singing their usual favorite first song, Chantique 23.

The romance that began that day, culminated a few months later when Catherine and William were married in the little French church. She was 16 and he was about 30.

In the spring of 1832 a new wave of emigration took place.

France had not recovered from what has been called the most startling event in European history, the French Revolution, until the Revolutions of 1830 and 1848 flamed.

Napoleon had been banished to the island of St. Helena. There he died May 5, 1821, thus ending the hopes of numbers in France who were anxious that he escape and return to France.

Louis XVIII, now an old man and unequal to the problems confronting him, came to the throne. He was immediately prevailed upon to restrict the liberty of the people. His death occurred September 6, 1824 and the government fell to his brother, the Count d'Artis, who took the title of Charles X.

Charles X created new peers in order to strengthen the influence of the crown. He was hostile to the press and the popular party.

The chamber of deputies was dissolved. The ministers, whose powers had been weakened, resigned, and persons of more liberal politics were appointed. Prime minister Jules de Polignac was placed at the head of the cabinet. This was unfortunate. The name of Polignac was hateful to the French people because of the influence this family was supposed to have exerted over Marie Antoinette.

The discontent of the oppressed people grew until at last mobs surged in the streets. By July 28 of that year, (1829), they were rioting and the soldiers of the king were vainly trying to check them. The king fled to Rambouillet and there, on August 2nd, he abdicated in favor of his grandson, the Duke of Bordeaux. This act was ignored and a mob of thousands prepared to march to

Rambouillet. The king escaped to England and afterwards died, in 1836, in Austria.

Fleeing this scene in 1834 were French protestants who emigrated to America and to Mowrystown for the purpose of religious freedom. Some came through spirit of adventure. The ague raging at Cincinnati drove some hither who might have settled in that city permanently.

The story of the Euverard family is typical of the stories of families who came in this last migration.

A Bible printed in 1772, in French, and in the care of Mrs. John Tolle, of Hillsboro, bears witness to the tale of the flight from the Revolution by a family that settled in Mowrystown after a perilous ocean trip. Descendants of this family still live in and around Mowrystown.

"This Bible," said Mrs. Tolle, "*was sent to my daughter, Lillian, by her great uncle, Frederick, of Sequim, Washington.*

"*Our Uncle Fred's mother, Katherine, was the youngest of 11 children when she came to this country. She was only four years old and soon forgot her old home and the voyage. Her family brought this Bible with them when they fled from France in 1832. Valuable papers and bank notes were concealed between the pages.*"

The Bible, a large, leather-backed book covered with heavy, unbleached linen, is 16½ inches long, 10 inches wide, and 4 inches thick. It was printed in 1772 by J. F. Ostervald, 'Pafteur de l'Eglife de Neuchatel', and is entitled, 'La Sante Bible.'

The comforting prayer that was said for the French immigrants and the translation recorded in the section on OUR CHURCHES, is preserved in it, written in the old time French on paper that is yellow and brittle with age. Pierre Euverard's passport, issued by Le Secretaire general at Dix, France, is also kept in the Bible.

Tired of revolution and strife, two cousins, Pierre and George Euverard of Etobon, France, decided to seek the haven others of their countrymen had found about 30 years before in the village of Mowrystown. An ocean and a wilderness lay between them and their hearts desire.

Pierre, a forest guard, his wife, son and daughter and George, a stone mason, and his wife and 11 children traveled by wagon from the little town of Etobon and then to Le Havre where they took passage on a vessel sailing to America. A revolution was raging in Paris and a revolutionist stole the gun George had bought to bring with him to the new world.

There are many families scattered throughout the United States who trace their ancestry to the two cousins, Pierre and George. George's great grandson, W. H. Euverard, of Greensburg, Indiana, in his history of the Euverards, says,

"*Sometime in June, 1832, the two Euverard families took ship* at Havre. Some say the time required for the voyage was 38 days, others say 60, and some even more. On the way they encountered a calm and had to wait for several days until the wind rose and started on their way again. I remember my grandfather telling of the storm at sea and how waves rolled mountain high.

"On reaching New York the Euverards went up the Hudson river as far as Albany, then up the Mohawk river, and again northword to near the Canadian line where they bought some land and built a house. Their house was made of logs and the roof of split clapboards through which the snow sifted in winter. Everyone went to work, the girls for the sum of 50 cents a week.

"A part of the families came by way of Portsmouth to Cincinnati in 1836, in a horse-drawn canal boat and settled on Broadway. An epidemic of malaria fever drove them, six months later, to Mowrystown, where they spent the winter in a log house near Dr. Funk's store.

"The following spring they bought some land near Stringtown (Maple Grove) now owned by Lloyd Euverard and some of the land adjoining, afterwards known to us as Uncle Fred's house.

"They had cleared off the land they had purchased, which abounded with wild turkeys, hogs and other game. They raised hogs, fattening them on acorns and beechnuts. When they had butchered them they were hauled to Cincinnati and sold for 1½ cents a pound.

"On Sundays they went in farm wagons to the French Presbyterian church at Mowrystown for services which were conducted by the noted French minister, the Rev. Grand-Girard."

Before the persecution, Pierre and George lived in the province of Languedoc in southern France. Sometime during the period of tumult they left that part of the country and settled in the Haute Saone.

The Euverards were a band of craftsmen and were skilled stone masons in France. George was called *"The Mason"* when he lived there. Each succeeding generation of Euverards has had its stone mason.

The late Frederick Euverard of Sequim, Washington, was the grandson of Pierre, the forest guard, and he formerly lived in Highland county. He was present in the church at Mowrystown when the Rev. Grand-Girard preached his farewell sermon.

"Stones in the jail at Hillsboro were set some time after the Civil War by my uncle, Peter Euverard, eldest son of George, who, like his father, became a stone mason," Mr. Euverard recalled.

By 1870, the population of Mowrystown had reached 414 and included a few thrifty German, Scotch Irish, and Swiss families. A United Brethren church was organized, a steam mill erected, and the first tavern opened its doors.

It was along the rambling, placid waters of White Oak creek

that curves its graceful way about Mowrystown like a great, protecting arm and turns reluctantly towards the Ohio river, that legend has it that scraps of the dress worn by little Lydia Osborne were found clinging to the bushes. The child had wandered from her home in Williamsburg and was lost in the wilderness. The roused countryside searched in vain for her for days. Although traces of her were found in a number of places, she was never found and her fate is unknown.

Bear was plentiful along the creek and nothing was more fun for the young French girls and boys than a bear, opossum, or raccoon roast. The boys piled dry hickory wood into a huge pile and set fire to it. When it was in coals, they turned the meat on long sticks over it until it was roasted. Potatoes and corn pones were roasted in the ashes. Tea was made out of sassafras and served with the repast.

There were log raisings, flax breakings, and wool pickings. Young men chose girl partners and were separated into groups. Each group tried to outdo the other. Fun went hand in hand with work.

Horse racing was a gala occasion. The community was noted for its fine horses and here in the village would assemble almost any day the young bloods with their prancing steeds. The racing took place on the main street of the town and everyone turned out for the event.

The houses in the Mowrystown of today are more or less modern but the names of the people have remained much the same. There are names such as Jodry; Tissot; Euverard; Druhot; Rosselot; Marconette; Beucler; Peugot; Mignery; Cornetet; Sauner; Ruble; Grandjohn; Brognard; Pettithory; Winkle; Willett; Fenwick; Fender; Parrott; Pulliam; Moler.

If you were to visit in many of these homes, you might be shown many interesting relics: an old, thumbed hymnal; a garment; a flax hackle; a corn blade; a picture; a dish; Indian relics turned up by plows; a piece of jewelry. Should you happen to find the right home, you might have the privilege and honor of having sung for you in a sweet, trembling old voice, a hymn or two in French.

You would wonder when you see a tear lurking in the singer's eyes if she is thinking of her ancestors sleeping in the quiet French cemetery. There, thick browning grasses sway in the autumn breeze, birds linger in the bright-leaved poplars overhead, and lengthening shadows spread a coverlet as the sun goes down.

When winter comes, snow lies softly and white upon this secluded spot. But the French maids and the French lads will dream on through the countless winters, the steadfast heritage of their faith and courage secure in the hands of those who have come after them.

THE GIST SETTLEMENT:

REMOVED from a state road, in a secluded part of Penn township in Highland county, is a little world all of its own.

The little scattering of houses begins just before you reach a bend in the winding road on which you see a peaceful, shady cemetery, the Cartheginia Baptist frame church, and an abandoned frame school building. Soon a road strikes off for itself to the right and if you should care to follow it, you will come upon the very heart of this strange world and see aged, odd houses that breathe of days long gone. The oldest log cabin to be found in the county and perhaps in the state sits sturdily in a pretty spot as if defying time and the hand of man to demolish it.

Such a friendly, courteous folk they are, that they belie a name found to designate the place on an old atlas of the county, Darktown.

In the church at Wormington in Gloucester county, England (if it, or its replica be still standing), is a blue stone against the north wall within the chancel of the church simply inscribed with the name and age of one Samuel Gist. Below stone steps there is a vault containing a marble coffin which had for years awaited him in a deal case in his stables in Gower street. There one would stand before all that remains of Samuel Gist, mortally.

The world in which he was living almost 200 years ago has probably forgotten him but he is alive in the hearts of the inhabitants of the Gist Settlement today.

Scanning the 28-page will he made June 22, 1808, about seven years before his death, we learn the character of this fine Englishman rather intimately.

He must have been a colorful figure in his day, somewhat contradictory, but well-meaning and lovable. To begin with, he was really fabulously wealthy. He had two married daughters, Mary and Elizabeth. He also was fond of his 268 slaves living on his extensive estates in Virginia and the Dismal Swamp. Horses were a particular hobby and he is credited with bringing the first race horses to America, to his Virginia estates. He was honest, generous, virtue-loving, stern, religiously inclined, home-loving.

He kept changing his mind about some details of his will and added four codicils, the last one, March 4, 1811. Between 1811 and 1815 he died.

In his strange will he decreed that within one year from his death his slaves on his estates in America should be emancipated if the law of Virginia so permitted; that his American estates be sold and the proceeds be held in trust for these slaves and for their heirs forever, by appointed trustees.

Land was to be selected for them by the trustees, homes and

schools built. This land must never be sold but must be handed down from one generation to the other.

"*I specially request trustees and their descendants to attend to the comfort and happiness of my slaves and their offspring,*" wrote Samuel Gist.

Thus it came about that these Negroes, who at that time were located in Hanover county, Virginia, just north of Richmond, were emancipated by the assembly of Virginia. Traditional lore says that about 230 Gist Negroes were located in Erie county, near Sandusky, by Virginia or Ohio trustees. They were dissatisfied because of the climate, the malaria, and the mosquitoes and they walked their homesick ways back to "*Ole Virginny.*" Here they remained for 12 years when they were relocated in Brown, Adams, and Highland counties.

The location in Highland county was near Dunkard and Quaker families and these people accorded the emancipated slaves good treatment, although there was some opposition from other neighbors. Among the names chosen by them were the names of Smith, Rollins, and Turner. None retained the name of their benefactor, Gist.

Joshua Woodrow, Hillsboro, Levi (?) Warner, Chillicothe, and Amos Lewis, New Vienna, were the trustees appointed for the Negroes. The last named was the first Quaker child born west of the Alleghenies.

So many litigations arose over mixed-up land titles that finally the trustees in recent years presented a petition to the state to have the care of the Negroes turned over to the common pleas court. The court now settles their land problems.

Among the common pleas court records is a big book on the top shelf of the back room dating back to 1831 in which was kept court proceedings of appointment of trustees, funds, expenditures, and reports to the court. In the recorder's office is a deed dated 1831, from John Cave to the trustees. In the surveyor's office is a plat by Burnett, 1870, showing the division of land so that it was placed on the tax duplicate; also a plat by Duckwall, a resurvey, 1895.

Most of the original cabins with their stick and mud chimneys, puncheon floors, and latch strings, have been superseded by frame structures, but one cabin believed to be the oldest standing log cabin in Highland county, dating from 1803, has withstood time. It stands on an old French farm now owned by Evert Ross, whose family has owned it for at least 137 years.

The children attend school in the neighboring village of New Vienna but they still like to romp in their deserted school yard. There are no stores and the trading is done in the county seat of Hillsboro, or in New Vienna. They are curiously friendly to the visitor. It is a carefree, easy-going community of only 8 or 9 families, a haven from storms of life a kind man feared they could not combat; but prior to World War II, the population was about 70.

Mr. Gist's will, a copy of which is in the court house, reads like fiction.

He tells of three instances in which he has had business dealings involving money, with John Hiscox, John Wilkinson and John Tabb, respectively. He was granted judgment against them, but just in case he might have been in the wrong and these men may have been cheated in some way, he left a large legacy to each man.

To the Wormington school master he left an annuity of 20 pounds and the residue and remainder of balance of dividends of 1000 pounds of three per cent consolidated bank annuities for purchasing school supplies and clothing for the poor and needy children.

His two sons-in-law received 10,000 pounds of three per cent consolidated bank annuities and out of the dividends, interest and annual proceeds they were instructed to maintain and support six poor men, six poor women, and six poor girls. Six poor boys were to be clothed, educated and apprenticed in Elizabeth's college or hospital. Every year on St. Thomas day five pounds each were to be given to the poor men and women; and 10 pounds to each of the poor boys. Should there be any surplus, other poor boys were to be cared for.

Large sums were left to Mary and Elizabeth. On Elizabeth's marriage to Wilbur Fowke she received a settlement of 12,000 pounds with four per cent annuities which brought her in, annually, 480 pounds in interest and annuities. Should Mary not comply with the requests made of her, she was to be cut off with one (1) shilling. Otherwise, in addition to her legacy of 2000 pounds, she was to receive her father's pictures, books, four silver-covered dishes, silver gilt cup, four pillar candlesticks, silver snuffers and pan, plate, and bed furniture. He had at first bequeathed the furniture to a relative, but at the last decided in favor of Mary, since she *"fancied"* it.

His two sons-in-law, Wilbur Fowke and Martin Pearkes, fared handsomely. A Thomas Darracott, of Virginia, was left his gold watch chain and seals. Each servant received a legacy in accordance with time of service. Thomas Bland, his coachman, received his carriage, horses and harness.

In his last codicil he changed his mind concerning a bequest to John Sellick, to whom he had left 100 pounds per annum. Unless John abandons his idle life and follows a respectable calling, says the will, his legacy is to be reduced to a mere 50 pounds.

Each niece and nephew received 100 pounds, and sometimes more, when a favorite. So did his employees and apprentices. The following received a like bequest: Bristol Infirmary; Christ Hospital, in London; City of London Lying-in Hospital; Welch charity in Gray's Inn Lane; Hospital for the Blind; Vaccine Institution.

On and on read the bequests with full instructions as to how his last wishes were to be carried out. He seemed to feel a divine responsibility for those he was leaving behind. If one could read between the lines the reason for each legacy, out of it might evolve a thrilling story.

Fate seems to be as contradictory as we would believe Samuel Gist's life was, for here in Highland county Samuel Gist lives in the hearts of his black brothers, while in his marble sepulchre across the sea in his native England, he sleeps the years away.

BEFRIENDED DESPERADO:

HE WASN'T a desperado, they say, not really. In spite of the infamous reputation he bore, worthy citizens maintain that he was not as history has painted him.

His name was Robert McKimie.

When the world scorned him, friends who were prominent and well-respected, rallied to his aid. Some of them stealthily carried food to him where he lay hidden in the den at the Seven Caves, to be known thereafter as McKimie Cave.

An intimate friend of his said that after he had served time in the Ohio State Penitentiary at Columbus for robbery, he went to Texas where he changed his name, became a Sunday school superintendent, and finally became governor of a state.

Picture a lad wandering gypsy-like over the hills of Highland county whenever he could escape from school, a handsome, fun-loving brown-eyed chap who was the soul of kindness. In the pretty village of Rainsboro where he was born he was popular with young and old.

Because he loved his home and because he feared the vindictiveness of the harsh laws of the west where he was believed guilty and where he knew he would receive no mercy, they say he pleaded guilty to the robbery charges brought against him in the Highland county courts. His uncanny evasion of the law throughout his life was said to have been because of a protective net thrown about him by loyal friends who believed always in his innocence.

The story of Robert McKimie, as accurate as it is possible to obtain it, makes a thrilling tale of desperate deeds.

As the story goes, at 14 years of age, McKimie went to Columbus and enlisted in the army. He was not heard of for two years. Then his aunt, who had reared him, received a letter containing a draft for $50. He had left the army, he said, and had entered the cattle business in Kansas. Some day, he promised her, he would return with his fortune made.

On a bright day in September, 1877, he returned as he had prophesied, a home town boy who had made good. He had become a man of means and influence.

To the amazement of everyone he married sweet, attractive Clara Ferguson who had been orphaned by the death of her parents and lived with relatives in Rainsboro. Folks liked McKimie, but, knowing his restless disposition, they doubted that he would settle down as a good husband and citizen. But he purchased property in Rainsboro, entered the drygoods business and, to all appearances, turned out to be an ideal citizen. But he didn't live happily ever afterwards.

It seems that McKimie had not quit the army; he had deserted it; he had not gone to Kansas and made a fortune in the cattle business, but had joined a notorious gang of murderers and robbers who haunted the stage coach road in Utah.

Joel Collins, leader of a band of Union Pacific train robbers, received the blame for training young McKimie for his life of crime. His pupil became the most daring of the lot, and the gang called him *"Little Reddy from Texas."*

McKimie's first crime was said to have been the stealing of a horse and the killing of a man in Utah. For this murder he was sentenced to 15 years in the Utah penitentiary. After serving a year he escaped, killing his guard by striking him on the head with a bar of iron.

The Cheyenne and Black Hills stage robbery in February, 1877, was the next deed attributed to him.

The ensuing crime set the whole country aflame. Young Johnny Slaughter, popular stage coach driver and the sole support of his widowed mother, was killed by the robber gang. In March, 1877, McKimie and his gang attacked the stage coach and ordered Johnny to halt. Before he could rein in his horses his heart was filled with buckshot. McKimie claimed later that the fatal gun had gone off accidentally.

After this murder, the desperadoes fled to the crossing at Cheyenne river. Here was a wilderness through which immigrant trains and stage coaches had to pass going to and from the mining regions. Three coaches were attacked and robbed and $14,000 was stolen, of which $11,000 was in gold dust and $4000 was in greenbacks.

There was a *"moll"* in the gang, a woman whom they nicknamed *"The Kid."* Extremely fond of McKimie, she overheard a plot to kill him and a man named Webster and make off with the loot. She promptly informed McKimie and the two turned the tables on the plotters. Securing most of the greenbacks and $8000 of the gold dust, they escaped.

McKimie always claimed that he buried $6500 of the money, but where he would not reveal. He and *"The Kid"* caught a train and went to St. Louis. There he claimed he gave his companion $1000 and went on alone to Texas. From Texas he journeyed to Philadelphia where he had the gold dust coined and sold most of it. Then he returned to Highland county and to Rainsboro, to all appearances a successful young man.

Instead of this being the end of his escapades, he was only getting away to a good start. The story of his riches excited comment and a neighbor wrote to a friend at Ogallala, Neb., of McKimie's sudden success. A great train robbery had just occurred at Big Springs, and the Ogallala friend, M. F. Leach, believing that McKimie might have had something to do with it, notified Seth Bullock, chief of detectives. Accompanied by Deputy U. S. Marshal Lyle, Bullock went to Rainsboro and placed McKimie under arrest. That was on January 15, 1878.

McKimie's case was probably the most conflicting one ever to come up in the Highland county courts. He had many friends as well as enemies. Clara, his wife, believed steadfastly in his innocence. She was permitted to remain in his cell with him.

One day while he was in court, his cell was searched. Behind a sink was discovered a handkerchief containing cartridges for a pistol. Soon after this telegrams arrived, purportedly from Bullock who had gone to Columbus to see the governor about signing requisition papers. They ordered that McKimie be released. The officers, however, dissatisfied as to their authenticity, held their prisoner and learned later they had been forged.

Later, McKimie made a spectacular escape during the absence of Sheriff Newell, who was out of town, and Clara, who was with the jailer's family.

When the sheriff's father and a colored porter went to McKimie's cell to replenish the coal box, McKimie sprang at them with a revolver. The weapon had been smuggled in and kept for him by another prisoner.

Shouting for them to clear the way, he fired, the shots missing. Rushing about the unfamiliar quarters of the jail, he finally found the front door, dashed through, crossed the street and disappeared down an alley.

Mr. Newell fired at McKimie and part of the shot went into his right arm causing the loss of his third finger. The tail of his coat was torn off and spots of blood and his riddled cigaret case gave evidence that he had been hit. But he escaped.

Emerging from the alley, McKimie came to a tanyard. Here he turned east, crossed High street and, following the Rocky Fork creek, arrived at the Belfast pike. He crossed the pike, circled to the town, reached the Chillicothe pike, and turned east again. By 1 o'clock he had reached the Point, in the vicinity of the Seven

Caves, where he found a deserted house and hid until the next day. Then he went to the home of a man named Walter Ogle where he was among friends.

Ogle notified John Gossett, H. O. Cleggett and Frank Messmer, who concealed McKimie in a straw stack. Cleggett hid McKimie in the hayloft of a barn and took him quilts, despite his wife's entreaties to have nothing to do with the desperado.

McKimie stayed in the barn by day. Two nights were spent with Messmer. From there he went to a man named Grandstaff, who agreed to keep him until he could obtain money to get away. He remained with Grandstaff for eight or 10 days.

Cleggett went to Bainbridge and bought a bottle of dye and McKimie's hair was dyed black. With Cleggett and another man named Pepple, they went to Ferguson's at Rainsboro. They claimed that on their way there they met a searching party composed of Bullock, Newell, Lyle, and another officer in a spring wagon, whom they passed undetected.

In the meantime, rewards were being offered for his capture. A famous detective, John T. Norris, of Springfield, was called into the case.

Leaving Ferguson's, McKimie and Messmer went to Cleggett's house, the officers close on their trail. McKimie was hidden in a closet. While the upstairs was being searched, the two men slipped out the back door and hid in a culvert, eluding the pursuers.

Things were getting pretty hot and McKimie hastened his plans for departure. He and Messmer stayed at the home of a man named Perry Rockhold, who cut off some of his wiskers to make McKimie a moustache.

Wearing a pair of brown overalls and the false moustache, he departed from Rockhold's house the next day, riding his host's horse, Snort, as far as Ferneau's mill. Crossing the creek, he turned Snort loose and went on foot to Bourneville to the David Moore farm, where he spent the night. The next day he arrived at Chillicothe and Jim Ferguson's saloon, to find that the officers had preceded him. He peered at them through an auger hole bored through a wooden partition that separated the stock room from the bar in the saloon.

Ferguson would neither harbor him nor give him up and McKimie was obliged to leave Chillicothe. He took the night train east, bound for Charleston, West Virginia, and two weeks later was joined by his wife in Richmond, Virginia. They remained here for some time and then went to Raleigh, North Carolina, for a month, and then to Savannah, Georgia. Becoming uneasy for his safety, his wife persuaded him to go farther away and they went to Nassau on the Bermuda Islands. But here they ran out of money. His $6000 had been spent.

Because McKimie could not pay their board he was arrested

and thrown into prison for debt. He served 41 days and was released. The American consul arranged for him to work his way to New York on a ship.

Leaving his wife at Nassau, McKimie went to New York and on to Ohio to obtain money from his lawyers, Sloane and Hough. He stayed with his friends, Cleggett and Grandstaff. Failing to obtain the money and becoming desperate, he and Messmer robbed an 80-year-old man named Roads of his savings. To Messmer he allotted $10 and to himself $80 with which he returned to Nassau for Clara.

While on his way to Ohio on this first trip, McKimie met New York Charlie. Their paths crossed again at Parkersburg, West Virginia, where McKimie was residing at that time. Wayward Charlie had come from a fine family in Cincinnati. He had, however, served time in a Pennsylvania prison, and had escaped.

Their acquaintance saw the birth of a plot to rob two banks in Bainbridge, Ross county, simultaneously. It seems that McKimie and Cleggett had planned the deed previously, but it was not until some time later that it was to be attempted. At Grandstaff's Cleggett and Messmer joined them.

Suspense and fear had begun to grip the residents of three neighboring counties; no one could be sure at whose house the robbers would strike next.

Redkey's store at Rainsboro was looted by McKimie and Charlie. After they failed to crack the safe in Hulitt's store, the following Sunday they attempted to rob Hillinger's store at Bainbridge for revolvers, and at this village they broke into Pepple's store and secured clothing which they hid in a barn.

At this point a local man named Johnny Jones seems to have become involved with the gang. Their next robbery was perpetrated at the Eubanks' home where lived two aged women. The gang imprisoned them, and scorched their bared feet, thus compelling them to give up their money. Of the money stolen, Messmer got $60 and Jones $200. McKimie took the balance, some jewelry and three sets of spoons. He later presented Mrs. Grandstaff with one set of the spoons.

Leaving the Eubanks' home the desperadoes started for Cynthiana where they intended to rob the Dan Bryant home. Because of sickness within and too many people about, they abandoned this scheme and returned to Grandstaff's.

Now thoroughly aroused, citizens recalled John T. Norris, the famous Springfield detective, into the case. Six days later he arrived and things began to warm up for the robber gang. Cleggett warned Messmer that detectives were on their trail. Messmer, hurrying back to Sprinkle's saloon at Bainbridge, dropped the remainder of his share of the spoils, $45, wrapped in a piece of paper, over the fence among the weeds.

Robert (Bob) McKimie
Highland county's Jesse James.

Beaver Brothers Mill, three miles north of Rainsboro, has been a mill site since 1808 and in continuous operation for 129 years. Two other equally interesting old mills are McCoppin's Mill and Barrett's Mill.

One mile northeast of Rainsboro is the birthplace of Governor Joseph Benson Foraker.

Frankie, a Carmel Indian Woman

The mother of this woman was a full-blooded Cherokee Indian. The father was Cherokee, but had a white (Irish) grandfather. Both were children of Highland county Indians who were removed to the Indian reservations in Oklahoma. When Frankie and her Indian husband were married they came back to Highland county, making the trip in a covered wagon drawn by oxen. Frankie and her parents are buried in the cemetery at Carmel and their descendants are scattered throughout the hill section.

In the meantime Johnny Jones had been locked in the Highland county jail at Hillsboro for some misdemeanor and was absent from the rendezvous at Grandstaff's between McKimie, Charlie, Grandstaff, Messmer, and Cleggett for the purpose of plotting the robbery of the two Bainbridge banks.

Charlie and Messmer surveyed the situation in the unsuspecting town, returning to report to McKimie at Grandstaff's. The plot, as planned, was certainly a most daring scheme.

McKimie and Charlie intended to ride into Bainbridge on horseback and tie their horses in front of the Rockhold, Cook & Co.'s bank in the west part of town. Messmer and Grandstaff also were to ride into town and tie their horses in front of the saloon in the eastern part, near the Spargur, Hulitt & Co.'s bank.

The first moves were to be made by McKimie and Charlie. Going casually into Rockhold's bank, Charlie was to present a draft and while the clerk was cashing it, McKimie was to draw his two revolvers and seize all the money in sight, including that in the open vault. They were to dash out, leap upon their horses, the hitch straps having been partly cut through to facilitate their escape, and flee westward.

While the excited citizens would be gathering at Rockhold's bank, Messmer and Grandstaff were to rush into the Spargur bank, rob it, and escape to the eastward before the crowd in the western part of town returned from their pursuit of McKimie and Charlie.

Had Charlie remained to help carry out the plans the robberies probably would have been successful. But at this time he and McKimie had a disagreement. Charlie doubted that there would be enough money in it and he doubted also that Messmer and Grandstaff would have the nerve to go through with their parts. Moreover, he wanted to be the *"big shot"* of the gang and run things his own way. It ended with Charlie going home and McKimie taking him to Greenfield where he got a train.

McKimie's next move was to head for New York, from where he intended to sail for his wife, to bring her to his uncle's home at Proctor, Virginia. As the draft he offered as payment for his passage was not bankable and it would be 10 days before the steamer sailed, McKimie came back to Ohio, trailed unknowingly by Norris, this time to Waverly, in Pike county, and then to the Grandstaff cabin, near Rainsboro, in Highland county.

Norris knew that McKimie was suspected of hiding in this neighborhood where the robberies had been committed, and that he held frequent conversations with Jones, who always had plenty of money on his person. He questioned Messmer as to where he had been on the night of the Eubanks' robbery; Messmer stated that he was at Cleggett's. Norris knew that Messmer had spent that night with Grandstaff.

Messmer also had made the mistake of having some one change money for him, as, he said, if he himself had it changed, he might be connected with the robbery.

Thereupon, Norris arrested Messmer and charged him with the crime. John, Messmer's brother, was next arrested.

Discovering that a sister of the two robbery victims, the Eubanks sisters, had reared Mrs. Grandstaff, Norris hastened to the Grandstaff residence. Grandstaff and Cleggett were subpenaed as witnesses.

From Grandstaff Norris could get no satisfaction, so after placing him in jail he went to interview Mrs. Grandstaff. She finally revealed the truth concerning the robbery, and turned over the spoons which McKimie had given her and which she had hidden under a stump back of the house. When Grandstaff learned that his wife had told all he confessed and offered to tell the whereabouts of McKimie.

Meanwhile, Mrs. Cleggett had noticed smoke curling out of the chimney of the Grandstaff home. Knowing that Grandstaff was on trial at Waverly and suspecting that McKimie had been hiding at this house, she notified authorities. It was not long before a crowd of about 150 men had surrounded the place.

The story of McKimie's capture was described to me in 1937, by the late George L. Garrett, who was an eye witness to the event:

"It was the most momentous and exciting event in the history of Rainsboro and vicinity, — my former home and my birthplace.

On the day the capture was made near the cabin where he had concealed himself, word was received in our home near Rainsboro that Bob McKimie was surrounded by a body of men near the McMullen farm situated on what was known as *"Anderson State Road,"* and at a point not far from Deer Park, a mile from the Point. We had eaten our Thanksgiving dinner when the word reached us, and my brother Harvey and myself both got astride my father's old pacing horse and started for the scene of action. Just as we reached the cross streets of Rainsboro, on the corner of which McKimie had formerly kept store, and in which he had been previously arrested by Seth Bullock, we met a posse of citizens with Bob as its prisoner. It was a typical mob of about 150 citizens, usually of the law-abiding class, who were armed with every conceivable kind of weapon. Heading the procession was the prisoner, fastened and roped to the horse he was riding, the rope being wound round and round his body, confining his hands and arms, and running under the horse, and tying each leg, so that he was almost as much of a curiosity as an Egyptian mummy. At each side was a man hold of the bridle, leading the horse, each armed with a gun, while behind him on the horse sat another man, holding fast to the prisoner to see that he did not escape.

When first discovered he was concealed in the cabin and one Clay Roads, a young man, went close to the cabin, and with a gun fired blindly through the window, hitting McKimie with shot, in the cheek. It was said that Roads immediately after the shot made a *"bee-line"* from the cabin, and it was told that he was found later in a hollow log, and some one made a picture showing his feet visible, while another frightened citizen was trying to get inside the log and begging Clay to give him room. Upon the arrival of a good many citizens at the cabin, a call was made for McKimie to come outside, but he did not appear, and finally an old bachelor named Isaac Jones and known familiarly as *"Betsy"* Jones, volunteered to go inside and see if McKimie were really in there. He entered alone and found a man bewhiskered and looking like anyone but Bob. Jones talked to him a few minutes and then told him to pull off those false whiskers and go out and surrender. He said, "I know you, Bob." McKimie then removed the whiskers and drew two revolvers, one in each hand, and with Jones, started to leave the cabin, but he commanded him to stay with him and not leave his side. Finally, he came out with both revolvers drawn and compelled Jones to stand right by him to shield him from shots from the citizens.

He was immediately surrounded by from 100 to 150 men, but they did not shoot for fear of killing Jones. McKimie kept the crowd at bay for an hour or so, gradually working his way toward a piece of timber where he hoped to make a dash for liberty. Finally some one took a shot at him and hit him in the face, right at the lower part of the jaw bone, making a bad-looking wound. Another shot was fired which struck him in the region of the heart, but the bullet was deflected by a rib. Seeing that the game was up, he offered to surrender and to turn over his weapons to Jones, provided they would cease firing at him. As he turned them over he said to Jones, *"I give you one of these, as you are the only one who had the nerve to enter the cabin."* He was then bound as described, and a curious looking mob composed of the best citizens of that community, started for Rainsboro. As my brother and I met them, Bob said to us, *"Hello, boys, ain't this a d—— pretty mob?"*

We followed the mob to an old tavern and Dr. McBride and my father probed and dressed the wounds. They found the shot near the heart had followed the ribs and come out near the back bone, or was lodged there. The shot in the jaw had, likewise, followed the bone, and come out near the lower part of the jaw. The shot from Clay Roads had swollen his face until his eye was about shut, and this, with the wound in his jaw, made him a gruesome sight. With his swollen and blood-stained face and neck, and his bodily wounds, his western sobriquet, *"Little Reddy,"* was most fitting.

As the doctors were probing and dressing his wounds, McKimie held up one scarred hand and said, "*There's Uncle Sammy Newell's mark which he left, when he shot at me as I went through the jail yard gate on Main Street when I broke jail.*" This belied the hinted story that his escape was winked at by the officers; and some even went so far as to say that the sheriff, W. C. Newell, had gone from town on the night of the escape, that it might be made. The fact was, the escape was made possible by the kindness of heart of old Uncle Sammy Newell, the jailer, and through his unsuspecting nature he having opened Bob's cell to furnish coal at Bob's request, and being unaware that some friend of McKimie had slipped a revolver into McKimie's cell, which he fired as he made his break from jail. It looked as though he never tried to shoot the jailer, but was firing only to terrorize him.

During the months between his escape and re-capture, he certainly had the Rainsboro neighborhood terrorized. Young boys were almost afraid to venture out after night-fall and no one knew when additional robbery would be attempted. Uncle Phil Roads, a well-to-do citizen, a bachelor, and quite miserly, was one of the victims. He generally kept money in his home, and also kept a live guinea or two in his room for "*arousement*" purposes. On that night the guineas gave the alarm and awakened Barbara Mosier, a niece living in another part of the house, who by the way was grandmother of Hon. Harold Mosier, former lieutenant governor, now a congressman at large from Ohio. She escaped and ran for assistance through the woods. It was said she was clothed only in a chemise.

Going back to the night of the day when McKimie was captured, after the wounds were dressed, Sheriff Newell was placed in charge of the prisoner, who, with a posse of four men deputed by him, started to Hillsboro in an open spring wagon, and just at the upper edge of our farm, and in a small tract of woodland now owned by Mrs. Edith Brown, a gate stood open and a rope was suspended from the limb of a tree, and the sheriff was commanded to drive into the woodland, it being the evident intention of those who made the sinister arrangements to make summary disposal of their fear and anger, and thus prevent any subsequent escape. Sheriff Newell, however, was determined to deliver his prisoner at the jail, and drawing a revolver, threatened to shoot anyone who interfered with his purpose, and he whipped his horses and proceeded without further molestation. One of the posse who was helping guard the prisoner, jumped from the wagon at the time of the demand to deliver McKimie to the persons for hanging, and ran through the woods and made a straight shoot for his home.

At the time of the robberies, the McMullen family lived near the scene of the capture, and John McMullen, formerly postmaster, remembered much that happened. N. P. Clyburn, now an attorney at Washington C. H., also resided near the Point and he, with his cousins, the John Roads boys, saw the crowd gathered about the cabin. John Roads, father of Conard Roads, and John Hulitt, later a resident of Hillsboro, were among those who aided in the capture.

Seth Bullock, who made the first arrest of McKimie, afterward became a warm personal friend of Theodore Roosevelt while the latter was in the West, and after Roosevelt became president he appointed Bullock as an officer in charge of Yellowstone Park, and Bullock visited the President in Washington. While on that visit, R. T. Hough who, as a partner of Ulric Sloane, was one of the attorneys of McKimie, and who, at the time of the visit of Bullock in Washington, was there as a Federal official, met and renewed his acquaintance with Bullock, and they recounted the exciting days of which I am telling you. Just why no further effort was made to extradite McKimie after his term of imprisonment was ended, and to have him returned to answer to the charge of having murdered Johnny Slaughter, was never explained, so far as I know.

I am telling you this as one of the few survivors of those exciting days, and as one, who perhaps, attended one term of school as a beginner while McKimie was a school boy at Rainsboro, and as one who, after his return to Rainsboro from the West, with apparent hard-earned wealth, (for that day), sat in his store room of nights and heard him tell how he mined for gold and thus earned, or acquired the gold-dust which the story he told, was the basis of his modest fortune. And also, as one, who personally saw at least, a part of that Thanksgiving day's events which, if put into a scenario for a modern motion picture, and with a faithful showing of the motley crowd which recaptured him on that day, would make a picture as exciting and as interesting as any present Wild West film, or as colorful as a screen portrayal of the day "*When Knighthood was in Flower.*"

McKimie, again behind the bars of the Highland county jail, showed great fear that he would be taken back to the Black Hills. Because of this he pleaded guilty to the indictment against him in Highland, Ross and Pike counties.

Then again he made an attempt to escape. Authorities discovered in his cell an old knife, a spool of thread, and an old-fashioned musket ball with a pin driven in it to which a thread could be attached. This was to be slipped through a window to a friend who could attach a needed article to it for McKimie. His cot had been broken up. In the corner four bat-like clubs, one for each of the four prisoners in the cell. Severing the irons that held them and armed with a club, each prisoner was to make a dash for liberty.

Subsequently, McKimie and Jones tore away the box of the sink, partly forced a sheet of boiler iron from the pit underneath the cell, and were able to draw out some of the two-inch spikes. Officials found that a wholesale escape of all the prisoners on the first floor had been contemplated. They had just commenced to tear away the foundation wall at the northeast corner of the jail when caught.

Soon afterwards McKimie was brought to trial. He pleaded guilty and was sentenced. New York Charlie had been trailed to Athens and captured by Norris.

Folks in Rainsboro used to like to tell of McKimie's prowess as a marksman. Riding a horse at full speed, he could make a circle of bullet holes in a fence as he went galloping past, they said. One woman told of a relative who visited McKimie while he was in the penitentiary in Columbus and carried nails concealed in her psyche, or hair-do as we would call it, to try to help him escape.

Thus concludes the fantastic tale.

Many folks say that McKimie was just a simple country lad who really went west to seek his fortune but got into bad company; that he was their *"goat"*, never their leader; that one of the men who tried so hard to help him escape his captors was his own father (McKimie's mother was unmarried when he was born); they say that escapes were made easy for him by sympathizing citizens and that officers didn't really try to capture him until John T. Norris came along.

Three Hillsboro Boys Go West

Long ago, in the early 1870's, three Hillsboro youths were fired with the spirit of adventure and went west in search of gold and silver. They were John and James Bullard and John Swisshelm, the latter the father of Charles Swisshelm and Mrs. Cora Priest. Another Ohioan, John Sherwood, *"joined up"* with them.

The men became heroes around Tucson, Arizona and Silver City, New Mexico. They are regarded romantic figures in the local history of that part of the west. Many places have been named in their honor.

The town of Silver City in New Mexico was founded by them and they discovered the silver mines for which the town was named. For many years Silver City was *"wide open,"* and was the home of such characters as Billy the Kid and Deadbeat Johnson, judge; and the Red Onion and Blue Goose saloons.

Silver City was made the county seat of Grant county. Streets and buildings were named for the popular young pioneers, — Bullard street, the Bullard Hotel, and Swisshelm Mountain range. The range was named for John Swisshelm. The youth named Hillsboro, New Mexico for their home town, Hillsboro, Ohio.

Another young fellow named Yankee hunted and prospected with them. Yankee street was named for him.

John Sherwood, it was claimed, had the reputation of locating more good mining ground in Bisbee than any other man. He mined with John Swisshelm in the Swisshelm mountains when it was nameless and sold the Great American mine in that district before Bisbee achieved fame.

"When my father and the Bullards first went west," said Charles Swisshelm when he was interviewed for a local newspaper, "they lived by hunting deer, bear and turkey and other animals and trading with the Indians. After hunting and trading for three years they began prospecting and apparently were very successful.

"My father told me that the reason he escaped being killed by the Indians was that he and the Bullards never followed a pack trail. It was the habit of the Apaches to ambush white men and women along the trails. They would lie in wait along the trails for hours, camouflaged with grass on their heads, and then leap out and kill whoever came along, usually shooting them in the back.

"My father also told me that an Indian was an awful poor shot with a gun but an excellent shot with bow and arrow. They never learned to shoot guns right, and it was practically an accident if they hit anyone with a bullet unless they were right on top of the victim.

"He talked to the Indians frequently and they often told him that they had seen him in the woods. "Why didn't you kill me?" my father would ask. "You hunter. Don't follow trails," they would tell him.

"The Apaches were "snake-like fighters and would lie in wait but would not stand up and fight in the open. Neither would they kill a man if they knew he had friends nearby who might come to his aid and kill them."

John Bullard was to lose his life in an adventure with the Indians. Leading a company of men which included his comrades, John, a Confederate officer, pursued a band of Apache Indians who had stolen horses in Silver City while the men were away hunting.

After chasing the Indians for several hours they finally caught up with them on a mesa some miles away.

John divided his company into two divisions. They closed in on the Indians, cross firing on them, and John carelessly paused to reload his gun after having shot an Indian and felling him.

The Indian pulled himself up and aimed a revolver he had taken from a white man at John. As John's gun was unloaded, he yelled at the man next him to shoot quickly. The Indian and John's companion shot simultaneously. Both were killed.

The party of white men continued their pursuit until all the Indians had been run down. They then returned and got the body of John they had been obliged to leave lying on the mesa.

Western newspapers described the pioneers as a bunch of young, sturdy, ambitious chaps from southern Ohio — Hillsboro, in

Highland county . . . repeating history . . . trail blazers for the succeeding generations of modern prospectors . . . seeking *"horn silver"* and *"coarse gold"* with rifles in their hands and six-shooters in their belts. They were heroic men, the papers declared, and did heroic deeds that live, and they built foundations upon which we of today rest and thrive. They gave names that will live generations after they themselves have been forgotten.

One account of their adventures reads thus:

"But that mountain range was not the only place in the southwest that got its name from these Ohioans. They first discovered the now famous placer gold ground in New Mexico, which they named Hillsboro, after their own home town in Ohio, and they also discovered and gave the name of one of their party to the now well known mining camp of Bullard's Peak in the same state.

"Later prospecting opened up the section around Silver City, which they likewise christened. Not satisfied with opening up two great mining districts they migrated into what is now Cochise county, and they soon fastened their "eagle eyes" on the Bisbee and Swisshelm districts — giving their own name to one and selling their holdings there at such big figures as to enable them all to retire; all but John Sherwood, who concluded to live and die in Arizona.

"When this prosperous "partnership" split up the great American claims had been sold for $100,000 and the Swisshelm claims practically adjoining had been sold around the same figure. This was "going some" when there wasn't a railroad within 50 miles and no mining in the district and no "hole" deeper than 50 feet. But they had a "good eye" and all mining ground picked by them has withstood the test of time, and grows better with work and depth."

Perhaps some day, some one will piece together the absorbing details of this adventure story so that it will not be lost to posterity.

AMELIA'S GRANDFATHER GOES TO AFRICA

CAPTAIN JAMES BOYD HERRON of Hillsboro could not have chosen a more thrilling setting for adventure than his voyage in 1836 to Africa, the *"Dark Continent,"* second largest land mass in the world.

At the close of Europe's wars about 1770, an awakening of interest in Africa brought about a period of explorations. Four years before David Livingston began his missionary journeys, Captain Herron set sail on the LUNA, a two-masted, square-rigged vessel commonly called a brig. A man of culture and deep religious convictions, his mission was to see about and report upon the colonization of the Negro in Monrovia, in Liberia, on the west coast.

Captain Herron kept a journal of his experiences. His granddaughter, Amelia Newby DeVault, former Hillsboro girl, now a resident of Elizabethtown, Tennessee, loaned the journal from which the story of his voyage was gleaned.

He gave Jim Priest, his colored body servant, his freedom and took him to Liberia with him. Jim was to remain in Africa where he became vice president of Liberia and his son, James Herron Priest, became Speaker of the House.

On Tuesday, July 5th, 1836, the Luna left Staten Island and sailed *"handsomely down the bay."* Most of the passengers were sea sick soon after the start, but all gathered daily on deck for morning prayer and a morning sermon. These services were also held each evening.

Each entry in the journal concluded with the latitude, the longitude, the distance sailed that day, the kind of weather, and the temperature. From 50 to 150 miles were covered daily. The entire crossing consumed 45 days.

From the inland country of Highland county, Captain Herron was to see unusual sights which, together with the infrequent passing of other vessels and a supply of good books he read, broke the monotony of the trip. He was to see his first porpoise harpooned, drawn in, and the blubber cut off to make oil, eating porpoise liver for dinner at evening.

Storms and beating rains beset the Luna. Many times they feared the brig would never make it. *"Mother Carey's chickens,"* he said, *"followed us for miles and it grew dark and the clouds were low."*

Sailors firmly believed that when the small oceanic birds they called *"Mother Carey's chickens"* appeared, this was a sure sign of approaching storm.

Captain Herron wrote:

"The transparency of the water when taken in a bucket is remarkable. I have noticed the phosphorescent appearance of the water drawn after night similar to the sparks emitted when a cat's back is rubbed. It reminded me of the phosphorescent appearance of the western country after a long rain when the whole road seemed strewn with sparks . . ."

He continued on Monday, July 18th:

"I took a seat on the stern and looked out towards the west and mused on home. It had an effect on me almost as powerful as the playing the Ranz des vaches is said to have on Swiss soldiers about sundown. In the evening it was announced that Edith Fisher's grandmother had departed. She was brought on deck when a few words were addressed to the company by W. Anderson. She was placed on a plank sewed up in some cotton cloth, a stone put to the feet, one end of the plank put on the rail, the other elevated. Some splash. She was in her watery grave . . . In less than an hour the voice of mirth was heard on deck."

On Thursday, July 21st, he wrote:

"Wind light . . . three humpbacked whales tumbled past, spouting or blowing when they rose out of the water. We saw a flying fish . . . its motion in flight is like a young robin. Sometimes they light on the deck and are kept as bait for Dolphin . . . The sailors are busy mending sails . . . they scarcely ever have any spare time . . . at the wheel or at the needle even on the Sabbath . . . One of the sailors is sick with the sore throat. They evince great affection for each other. There is no murmur heard that their time at the wheel is doubled in consequence of the man being sick. Of all hard lives I have seen a sailor's is the hardest, much worse as it respects labor than the slaves in Virginia . . . They are spoken to in the rough tones of the common, called such names as Sam, Jack, or Jim, and are scarcely known by the officers."

Sickness dogged them all the way across, with bleeding a common method used to cure. The drinking water was kept usable by the mate fixing up a drip through which water percolated in sufficient quantity for the use of all, losing its unpleasant taste and becoming cooler through this method. To detect the course of the winds a dog vane was made of cork and feathers.

On Friday, August 12th, they glimpsed the Cape Verde Islands and other vessels and saw the island of Bravo *"like a cloud low down on the horizon."* That night in thankfulness for their safe voyage, they held meeting *"after the old Methodist style, and it was affecting to hear the blacks pray for the white people."*

Beaten back by a squall, the Luna weathered through to port at Monrovia on Friday, August 19th.

Native Kroomen rowed out and pulled alongside the Luna. They were marked from the tip of the nose to the roots of the hair with some marks darker than the skin on their arms, interspersed with stripes and angular figures. All were naked save for a covering around their waists. It was the custom to meet incoming vessels in the hopes of obtaining rum.

The picture in Monrovia was depressing. The white inhabitants complained of the scarcity of provisions and the resident missionaries gave a discouraging account of the colony. Another colony they told about had contained 1200 but was reduced to only 850 and 100 of these were orphans.

Methodist, Baptist and Presbyterian churches had been established. Pastors received no salary but depended for their slender support on a school. A Miss Caroline Clark conducted a school in the Methodist church. She had 31 pupils and received 250 dollars a year from the Methodist Society. One very young pupil had learned to read the new Testament intelligently.

The Kroomen lived in small huts made of bamboo roofed with large leaves which turned the rain and they did all the drudgery along the coast line. Most of them wore gregories on their arms or around their ankles. Gregories were charms made of roots, beads, or leopard teeth and were supposed to prevent sickness and protect them. The head Krooman, called Jumbo by the white visitors, wore a conical-shaped object larger than a hen's egg, put into a kind of cotton and suspended from his neck.

At the entrance of one village two forked sticks with one laid across the top had a large stone suspended from the center of the top piece. This gregorie was to ward off all evil.

There was a long house where the destitute were kept. Captain Herron when he visited it, found eight inmates in a wretched condition from horrible sores. They begged him to take them away with him. Sores were common ailments. The slightest scratch if neglected became an ulcer. The destitute of the colony each received from the government house one gallon of rice a week and this was their only sustenance.

The cemeteries were odd. On almost every grave was a bottomless wash bowl turned down. Two sticks about ten feet long were placed in this. On the top nearly a dozen pieces of white cotton from one to two inches wide and a yard long floated in the air. Sometimes a rice tray was broken and laid on top of the grave.

The flowers of Africa were described as gorgeous and rich, filling the air with perfume. There were rice fields, lime, lemon and plum trees, some corn, potatoes, banana and plantain trees, cassava, cocoa, and a kind of fruit like the prickly pear, agreeable in taste. Much of the soil was rich and fertile. Goats, sheep and fowl comprised the meat supply.

Only the more fortunate people had the best of these foods. Flour, meat and meal were not found on the tables of the average Krooman. Flour cost $12.50 a barrel, meal, $8.00.

Often a slave ship anchored in the bay and an officer would come to the village to buy provisions. One such ship was returning from a trip to dispose of 180 slaves, bound to the leeward for another cargo of human beings. One English merchant traded an elephant's tooth weighing three pounds for four handkerchiefs and about one pound of tobacco.

On his journeys through Liberia, Captain Herron visited several slave marts, and picked up the following bits of Kroo vocabulary:

bogara	(a hat)
boa	(a pig)
bukka	(a goat)
wora	(pantaloons)
bree	(bullock)
toungh	(canoe)
woodey	(beau)
fallga	(knife)
cantdah	(book)

nuunbukh (river)
shootah (bottle)
darrice (cloth)

One day he visited the beautiful village of Senoa where banana palms were abundant. At the Palover House he saw His Majesty, King George, of England, *"a sober old man."*

Captain Herron traded the top of his umbrella to a pretty native girl for her brass ring.

An attempt was made to stop the trafficking in slaves and volunteers were called to go to Kroo towns and assert the right of the colonel over the land to require the natives to come under Colonial government and to renounce the slave trade or to leave the place. Volunteers paraded the streets training for war or made ready their guns.

Oblivious to this excitement, 20 canoes drifted, fishing, and there were four sails in the harbor, one a Spanish slaver with Portugese colors.

In the midst of all this, it had become time for the Luna to start her homeward voyage. On the 26th of September, *"with a fair wind, we left the cape, bound for home. Dr. Skinner and his daughter and a Captain Homer have been added to our list of passengers, in addition to monkeys, sheep, gnats, pigs, alligators, a guana, a pair of pigeons, and a parrot."*

Landing on the eastern coast of the United States, Captain Herron went to Jackson, Mississippi, thence to Philadelphia, Easton, Harrisburg, and Wheeling, arriving in Hillsboro Monday, November 29th.

His mission finished he turned to teaching school. His journal dwindled and soon came to an end. The most interesting entry was the one on January 25th when *"the Aurora Borealis appeared tonight in the north. The reflection can be seen over the houses. In the morning there was a white frost."*

He spoke of calling frequently upon a Miss Andros and of her entertaining him by playing the piano. However, she was not to be the lady of his choice for he was married later to Elizabeth Wilson, a Virginian. He, too, was originally from Virginia.

His closing entry was, simply:

"Wednesday, May 31: School closed this day."

List of books read by Captain Herron on his 48-day voyage across the ocean:

The Bible
Combs Physiology
Reynolds Tour
J. Alleine

Life of Harlan Page of N. Y.
Life of Bacon
Life of Boone by Flint
Life of Gardner
Christian Pilgrims
Life of S. Foote
Life of Sir Isaac Newton
Life of Z. Collins
Life of Milton
Dick's Improvement of Society
Power of God by Chalmers
Life of Dr. Johnson
Life of Henry Martin
Life of Kirk Whitt
Life of Butterworth
Life of Washington by Paulding
No Fiction by Dr. Reed
Martha by Dr. Reed
2nd volume Landen Travels in Africa
Pilgrims Progress
Life of Wright, Methodist Missionary
Life of Zerah Colburn, Arithmetician
Willard's Journal and Letters
Life of Howard

UNDERGROUND RAILROAD STATIONS

1. The home of Colonel Thomas Rogers, abolitionist, 3½ miles southeast of Greenfield on the Greenfield-New Petersburg road. Colonel Rogers, who was colonel of the militia of Highland county, sheltered runaway slaves and drilled young recruits of Greenfield for service in the Civil War. The house burned.

Col. Rogers' father, William, had come from Loudon county, Virginia, with his father, Hamilton Rogers, about 1700. William Rogers was an abolitionist and because Virginia tolerated slavery, moved to Brownsville, Pennsylvania, about 1783 or 1784. The next spring he moved his family to Lexington, Kentucky where he engaged in the pursuit of Indian marauders. When Kentucky was made a slave state, he decided to come to the Northwest Territory. In 1799, with his sons, John and Thomas, he set out for the Scioto country and arrived at the north fork of Paint creek where he built the only cabin between that place and Chillicothe except for General McArthur's.

2. The home of John B. Black, 2½ miles east of Hillsboro (2 miles east on US 50 and ½ mile right on mud road). This house stood farther back from the road when runaway slaves stopped

here on their way north from Marshall. It had two outer rooms on the second floor at the back entered by an outside stairway.

Fearful that Morgan's raid would be directed this way, Mr. Black, with his daughter as witness, buried the family silver and valuable papers in the back yard. He was the grandfather of Mrs. Helen Rogers Noftsger, Dr. Roy Steele Rogers, and Stanley Rogers, all of Hillsboro.

3. The Jonathan Van Pelt farm, about 8 miles southeast of Hillsboro (about 3 miles east on US 50, turn left and go on the New Petersburg road to farm now known as Valley View Farm, owned by Byron Clark).

Mr. Van Pelt gave protection to many slaves fleeing north via Marshall, hiding them in his fields and hay mows. Once children almost gave some slaves away when they prodded in the hay with pitch forks.

One slave liked the place so much that he stayed on with the Van Pelts. He had given his family up as lost and was trying to resign himself to it. While working in the fields one day he saw an old, dilapidated carriage pulled by a timid horse, coming up the road. In the carriage were a Negro woman and her children, his own family. There was a joyful reunion. Each had thought they would never meet again.

4. The Samuel Ridings home, about 12½ miles southwest of Hillsboro (near Hollowtown).

Mr. Ridings kept a coffin, wagon and blacksmith shop, and at night hid slaves in his house who were brought to and from his house concealed under hay in wagons.

5. The Chapman home, about 7 miles east of Hillsboro on US 50, below Boston, now the Guy Sams residence.

6. The Samuel B. Carlisle home which stood about 3½ miles southeast of Hillsboro, on the Pigeon Roost road, in the center of what is now a field.

Mr. Carlisle was the fourth son of James Carlisle, a Virginian, and was born in Ross county in 1804. He came with his parents to Highland county in 1806.

Although he and his wife (Lucretia Lucas) were the parents of 12 children, 8 daughters and 4 sons, and had a 400-acre farm to care for, they gave shelter to fleeing north-bound slaves. Mr. Carlisle died in 1890 and his wife died in 1893.

7. The Wheaten home (still standing) about 13¾ miles northeast of Hillsboro and about one mile from New Petersburg.

8. The Daniel Lewis home about 10 miles northwest of Hillsboro, on the Donaldson farm, house no longer standing; on the left side of the county-township road which turns into the Gist Settlement.

Mr. Lewis taught school in the Gist Settlement in exchange, it is believed, for the privilege of a home. Slaves, coming this way from Brown county, stopped at the Lewis cabin, sure of protection by the schoolmaster.

9. The Marshall Nelson farm, about 4 miles northeast of Hillsboro on St. Rt. 128, now known as the Nelson stock farm.

George Harris, one of the characters for *"Uncle Tom's Cabin"*, hid in a corn shock for two nights to escape his pursuers, at this farm.

This farm was one of the principal stations.

10. The David Zink home, 6 miles southwest of Hillsboro on St. Rt. 62, on the northwest corner of the crossroads at New Market.

The house had behind it an old, shed-like building with a large fireplace. When anyone noticing smoke coming from the chimney remarked, *"David is smoking a slave,"* this meant that a slave had found refuge.

11. The Pennington farmhouse, a white brick house on a hill to the right of US 50, about 3½ miles east of Hillsboro. (Second house after crossing the Clear creek bridge).

12. The Dick home, still standing, and occupied by Dick descendants, about 8¼ miles southeast of Hillsboro, ¼ mile from Marshall on the Marshall-Carmel road.

Slaves arriving in Sinking Spring were directed to this home. They were hid in secret closets in the walls upstairs, and when the route was clear, guided to the next station by Mr. Dick on horseback.

13. The Moses Tumbleson farm, near the Dick home.

14. The Richard Lucas farm, now the Boyd farm, on Churn creek, near the Tumbleson farm.

Highland County's Ghost Towns

The geography and history of Highland county have somehow gotten mixed up with ghosts, for dotting the county are a number of ghost towns which, if they had survived their founders' dreams, would have changed the whole pattern of the county.

You will find 10 of these ghost towns on old records at the court house. These records represent some person's dream lost in the mist of long years ago. The names of the towns are unusual and interesting but the records accompanying them are so meager that they leave us little but conjecture and mystery.

Here is a brief outline of the 10 towns. You may have driven or walked over one of these town sites dozens of times and never dreamed that you were walking over a ghost.

CARLISLE: Founded October 27, 1818 by Benjamin Gilbreath, somewhere on the east branch of a creek. It had a public square, commons and streets.

FALLSVILLE: Founded April 20, 1848 by John Timberlake and named for the falls. Township road to the falls was formerly the main street of the town. More history and geography are known about this town than any other. (See story following)

GEORGETOWN: Founded March 24, 1817 by John Davidson, somewhere in Whiteoak township near Buford on White Oak creek. John Florence was the proprietor and John Davidson was the Justice of the Peace. It had 81 in-lots and three streets.

MOUNT ERIE: Founded March 11, 1818 by Joseph Spargur, the proprietor, somewhere in Paint township on Rocky Fork creek. It contained 15 acres and 9 poles and had four streets.

NEW EDENBOROUGH: Founded December 27, 1817 by Edmund Wade, and recorded by George Shinn, Justice of the Peace, somewhere in Jackson township. It had 48 in-lots and five streets.

PALMYRA: Founded March 5, 1818 by Michael Sinks and Thomas S. Foot, somewhere on Whiteoak creek, in Whiteoak township, on the survey of James Tutt. It contained 10 streets.

ROCKINGHAM: Founded August 26, 1818, somewhere on Rocky Fork in Paint township.

SALSBURY: Platted and recorded May 12, 1818.

SICILY: Founded June, 1848, by John Newton Huggins and named for its proximity to Sardinia in Brown county.

STRASBURG: Settled about 1849 by John Marconet and named for Strasbourg, a city in northeast France.

In addition to the ghost towns there were several settlements, crossroads, and post offices that might have developed into towns. These were, namely: Gist Settlement; Hansboro Settlement; Lincolnville; Millertown; Shackleton; Sringtown; Bennet's Crossing; Hoagland's Crossing; Morrow's Crossing; Paint Post Office; Frogtown; Turkey; Sharpsville; Sassafras Corner; Nace's Corner; Smoky Corner; Bell Hollow; Pin Oak Hollow; Jack Hollow; etc.

FALLSVILLE: Population, one family; location, about 6 miles north of Hillsboro, 1½ miles on State Route 73 to fork, take Careytown road branching to right, proceed 4 miles to second township road to the left and go on this road about ½ mile to the *"Fallsville Falls"*, and the town site of the ghost town of Fallsville.

The land hereabouts was part of a grant belonging to John Bayhan, a lieutenant in the Revolutionary War. It had passed into the hands of Captain James Trimble, then to his son, William Trimble, who empowered his son, Allen, in 1808, to sell the land. Allen sold 206 acres in 1825 to Simon Clouser who, with his two daughters, Susanna and Charlotte, occupied the gray stone house which had been erected near the waterfall about 1812 by John Timberlake.

Water falling over a triple-shelved limestone incline 35 to 40 feet, was the spot Simon Clouser chose to erect a grist mill. The mill, consisting of two stores and a wooden overshot mill, stood below the falls. To this mill came many of the first settlers to have their corn and wheat ground into meal and flour. A bridge spanned the falls and the road leading from it through the town was named Main street.

The history of Fallsville is obscure. It was not officially platted and recorded as a town until April 2, 1848. When first settled it had three streets, Main street, Mill street, and Cross street, dotted with 6 or 8 houses. Most of the settlers came from North Carolina. James Underwood, Moses Smith, John Holmes, Isaac Woodmansie and the Carey and Brown families, were among the first to settle.

Preaching was held in the homes until the organization of the Auburn Methodist church in 1830. The Clouser family is buried in the cemetery adjoining the church.

It was in this community two years after the platting of the the town, 1850, that the Highland County Literary Society was formed, a society to which the young men of the community belonged. They gave debates, orations, and speeches, and was the most prominent organization for miles around until the founding of the Quaker Society. Oratory was emphasized. The paper Charles Edwards wrote on *"Fallsville, as it will be 50 years hence,"* has been lost to posterity, but he prophesied that Fallsville would become the leading town of Highland county, with limestone quarrying and milling, the main industries. Shakespeare, Byron, and Bancroft's History, were among the favorite books studied.

Several colored people lived in the neighborhood and one of them, Andrew Payton, who bought several lots at the close of the Civil War and lived there until his death in 1893, was Fallsville's last resident. Another colored man was *"Whitewash Johnson,"* who received his nickname doing whitewash jobs for the neighborhood.

Some of the residents of Fallsville believed in witchcraft and it was a custom to sprinkle salt in the footsteps of a stranger to dispel any evil that he might have brought into the village with him.

Legend has it that vain search was made by experts hired by the villagers for gold and treasures believed to have been buried by Indians enroute from the Great Lakes region to the South. On every Christmas Eve, the legend goes, an Indian chief in full regalia would knock on the Clouser's front door and by signs try to tell the aged women where the treasure was hidden. A John Roads from Hillsboro was hired to come and try to interpret the signs. As the eccentric Clouser sisters grew older, it was believed that they, too, buried valuables. Legal documents they had drawn up for them are said to have been sealed with drops of their blood.

Soon after the official platting of the town in 1848, Fallsville began to decline. No railroad came up the valley as they had hoped, and the mills dwindled as other parts of the county became more thickly settled. People moved away. Only the stanch gray stone house of the Clousers remained, the immense mill wheel lay rotting on the site of the grist mill beside a section of stone wall, part of a burr lay at the foot of the pretty falls, and wheat fields took up the village site. For years bits of broken dishes were plowed up in the spring.

Zimri Carey described this ghost town in a poem he wrote many long years ago.

FALLSVILLE

Near where Clear creek's waters calmly flow
A small village stood some years ago;
On a sloping hill-side near the flood
Is where once the pleasant village stood.
On the grassy bank at the foot of the hill
In days gone by stood an old grist mill;
Where neighbors brought grists of corn and wheat
To be ground into meal and flour to eat.
The old mill rose from the bank and stone wall
A few feet below a beautiful fall.
Water power and a great wooden wheel
Propelled the machinery which ground the meal.
In days gone by when the sun was low
To the old grist mill I used to go
With a great sack of corn, or with one of wheat,
To be ground into something good to eat.
Sometimes I would go in early morn
With a great sack full of golden corn.
Sometimes after a rain the waters would pour
Over the precipice with a mighty roar.
Sometimes great clouds of mist would arise
And almost obscure the sun in the skies.
There were stables and houses large and small
In this little village near by the fall.
On many a bright and beautiful day
Little children would run and romp and play.
Those people are now all dead and gone,
Who once lived in the stone house on the lawn,
Those people had ideas all their own,
Which were not to the world generally known.
They believed that witches were round about
And hired a Blackman to frighten them out.
They employed city men to search for gold,
On the old hillside beneath the mould.

But their searching and digging were in vain,
As nothing was accomplished for all their pain,
One son, 'tis said, became a millionaire,
And dealt in gold and diamonds rich and rare.
This son who was both wise and witty
Dwelt for a time in New York City.
'Twas there he acquired both wealth and fame
But I do not choose to make known his name.

CHAPTER SEVEN

TOWNSHIPS — THEIR TOWNS, VILLAGES and HAMLETS

1. BRUSHCREEK:
   Carmel
   Elmville
   Sinking Spring
2. CLAY:
   Buford
   Hollowtown
   Strasburg
   Sicily
3. CONCORD:
   Fairfax
   Sugartree Ridge
4. DODSON:
   Allensburg
   Dodsonville
   Lynchburg
   Webertown
5. FAIRFIELD:
   Bridges
   Centerfield
   East Monroe
   Highland
   Highland Station
   Leesburg
6. HAMER
   Danville
   East Danville
7. JACKSON:
   Belfast
   North Union
8. LIBERTY:
   Hillsboro
   Hoagland
9. MADISON
   Greenfield
10. MARSHALL:
    Harriett
    Marshall
11. NEW MARKET:
    New Market
    Shackleton
12. PAINT:
    Boston
    New Petersburg
    Rainsboro
13. PENN:
    Careytown
    Samantha
14. SALEM:
    Pricetown
    Pulse
15. UNION:
    Fairview
    Russell
    Sharpsville
    Willettsville
16. WASHINGTON:
    Berrysville
    Folsom
    Prospect
17. WHITE OAK:
    Mowrystown
    Taylorsville

BRUSHCREEK TOWNSHIP

CARMEL
ELMVILLE
SINKING SPRING

CARMEL: Population, about 25-30; Altitude, 964 feet above sea level; Location, 12 miles southeast of Hillsboro, on crossroads, surrounded by hills, in Brushcreek township. Can be reached by going to Marshall and turning south at bend; or going east on U. S. Route 50 and turning on to State Route 70 at stone house. Unincorporated.

Carmel was never platted nor intended for a town. It received its name from a log church named Mount Carmel about one mile away on the Marshall-Carmel road. A new Mount Carmel church was built in 1865 in the southern part of what is known today as Carmel, and the older church was called Old Log Carmel. When it was learned that another place in Ohio was named Mount Carmel, the word Mount was dropped. The name originated from the Biblical Carmel, a town in the mountainous part of Palestine.

A post office, now in a tumble-down state and abandoned, was established here about 1876 and T. M. Watts was the first postmaster.

In the hills southwest of Carmel live the descendants of Indians, one of the most interesting groups of people in the county. One winding road weaving its hilly way southward off the main highway from Carmel, passes through a cluster of houses known as Millertown, past one section of Fort Hill, and connecting with State Route 41. Millertown originated from the settling of Miller families beween 1840 and 1860 and named for them.

Carmel has a two-room elementary graded school. High school pupils go to school at Sinking Spring. The one church is known now as the Methodist Church. Residents receive their mail at Ove McCoppin's store at the crossroads, or by rural mail delivery.

ELMVILLE: Population, about 8-10; Altitude, 778 feet above sea level; Location, 16 miles southeast of Hillsboro, near the border line of Highland and Adams counties, in Brushcreek township. Reached by taking State Route 124 through Marshall to Harriet, then turning right on the Sinking Spring road on in to Elmville. Unincorporated.

Elmville was never platted nor intended for a town. A post office was established here, date unknown, with James McIntyre as postmaster and owner of a blacksmith shop managed by a Mr. Jarvis. The place was called Elmville for the stand of beautiful large elm trees on the site.

It is situated in a farming community. Children attend school at Sinking Spring. There is one store, a Christian Union church, and a few houses. Residents are served by rural mail delivery.

SINKING SPRING: Population, about 223; Altitude, 956 feet above sea level; Location, 17 miles southeast of Hillsboro, on the historic Zane trace now designated as State Route 41, in a scenic valley among the highest hills of the county, in Brushcreek township. Incorporated.

Although Highland county's first settler, John Wilcoxon, a Kentuckian, in 1796 built a log cabin beside the spring for which the village later came to be named, Sinking Spring was not platted for a town until November 27, 1815, by Jacob Hiestand, owner of the land. Mr. Hiestand gave it the name of Middletown. This was because of Sinking Spring's location on the Zane trace, halfway between Maysville and Chillicothe.

When a post office was established about 1819, it was discovered that another town in Ohio previously had been named Middletown, so the name was changed to Sinking Spring for the spring beside which John Wilcoxon had settled 25 years before. The spring, which sometimes disappeared, flowed from an underground stream at the foot of a hill in the southern part of the village. Two limestone funnel-shaped depressions above the stream clearly disclosed other underground streams, now no longer visible, because the streams changed their courses. The spring is deep and full of clear, refreshing water.

The platting of the town brought a flow of immigration from Pennsylvania, Virginia, and Kentucky. Many settlers were Revolutionary War soldiers and their families, and they gave an aristocratic, southern air to the town.

Mr. Hiestand hoped that the village would become a county seat. He was so confident of this that he donated a square in the center of the town for a court house. On the spot on which the dreamed of court house was to have been, the first log cabin school was built about 1820. The first teachers were Jesse Dewey and John Wickerham.

About 1851, when the township was divided into school districts, a new school was decided upon. It was erected near the site of the log cabin school, in the southwest corner of the square, and in octagon shape. One German farmer refused to pay the tax levied upon the district for it, claiming that it was ugly and that it did not look like a school house but more like a smoke house.

The octagon building was abandoned as a school in 1844 because of its size and because the law required that school houses must be owned by the district. It stood on public ground. This same year a two-story brick was built on the east side of Main street, but, since it was not centrally situated, it was sold to Isaac East for a residence. Then a two-room frame building was built on Grand street and two teachers were employed, a man and a woman. The man received $40 or $50 a month and the woman between $30 and $35.

During the Civil War the octagon building was headquarters for the home guards and guns were hung on wooden pegs on the walls. It was used in later years for council, court, and other civic meetings, and for high school classes.

Sinking Spring now has a modern school plant on the site of the frame school building, accommodating grade and high school pupils.

By 1880, the population had reached about 197. Sinking Spring had two grist mills, two shoe repair shops, one tannery, two portable steam saw mills, two blacksmith shops, one wagon shop, one wool carding mill, two harness shops, one wheelwright, a chair manufacturing and cabinet shop, several stores, a post office, one Methodist and one Presbyterian church, with outlying Lutheran, Dunkard, and Universalist churches.

Close to Sinking Spring, opposite a roadside park, on State Route 41, once stood a large, rambling yellow-frame hotel with log, columned porches, on a 1,500-acre tract of woodland. From the hillsides flowed many springs of iron, sulphur, and clear water. The place was known as Butler Sulphur Springs, and until it burned 20 years or so ago, was a popular place for vacationists.

In the hospitable log cabin home which first stood on this site, Leonard Butler, (great grandfather of Maude Butler Matthews and Bess Butler) was said to have entertained Johnny Appleseed. It is claimed that George Washington once surveyed through this part of Ohio. Many legends have been handed down, and none more interesting than that of the stage coach driver who was murdered at Station Hill, around the bend from Butler Springs, where drivers changed horses. Robbers lay in wait for the man when he stopped to rest and change his tired horses. To this day, when the nights are dark and stormy, he is supposed to come galloping down the road in search of the men who murdered him, and you had better take to your home and stay indoors, or else you might be mistaken for one of the guilty.

Many story-book regions such as Coon's Crossing, Bell Hollow, Pin Oak Hollow, Potato Knob, Pine Top, Pancake Hollow, Smoky Corner, Beech Flats, Marble Furnace, Pisgah, Shoemaker Hollow, Big Harkleshin, Little Harkleshin, Nace's Corner, Martin Hollow, and Jack Hollow are in the vicinity of Sinking Spring, although some are not in Highland county.

Bell Hollow, striking off from State Route 41 south of Carmel makes a winding, semi-circle to meet State Route 41 again at the edge of Sinking Spring. Bells on the cattle of the pioneers who turned them loose here to graze suggested the name of the hollow. The tinkling bells on the necks of the scattered, roving cattle made pretty music to the lonely ears of the settlers.

Nancy Jane Washburn Gall, who was born February 14, 1847,

near the present entrance to Fort Hill, close to Sinking Spring, and except for 3 years following her marriage to John N. Gall, when she lived in North Union, in Jackson township, lived her entire life in and near Sinking Spring. She died several years ago at the home of her daughter, Mrs. Tom McClure, at Sinking Spring.

Her great grandfather, James Washburn, migrated from Virginia to the land here which he possessed and he gave the plot for the pioneer school known as Washburn School, district number nine. Nancy Jane later taught in this school. This land is now owned by Henry Countryman, but on it is the Washburn family burial ground where the pioneer Washburns were buried. Washburn Hill, nearby, one of the highest hills in the state, towers to an elevation of 1,334 feet. It was named for the Washburns.

"When Grandfather Washburn came here this was a wild country infested by animals. Grandmother Washburn used to tell me about how the wolves used to surround the cabin at night. How terror-stricken they were for fear the animals would get in at the blanket which served as a door!"

Her father, Thomas Washburn, owned a grist mill and saw mill near Sinking Spring, called the Washburn Mill. It later was known as Reed's Mill. He then bought a farm near Fort Hill where his daughter Nancy Jane was born, and near where she was later to teach.

"I shall never forget them," she reflected tenderly, with the mist of tears in her grave hazel eyes, "my girls and boys. A large class of young men attended to prepare for teaching. Among those who became successful teachers were: Anthony Setty, who went away to fight in the Civil War and returned to become an influential farmer in Adams county; Isaac Wesley Jarnagin who died near Hillsboro; P. P. Stultz, who went to the Civil War and latter settled in Indiana where he died; Joe Washburn who died near Barrett's Mill in Highland county; and his crippled brother, Sanford, who spent his last days in Bainbridge, Ohio.

"My husband taught at the Washburn school after our marriage and he was as proud of his pupils as I was of mine. One of his most promising was the late Oliver Newton Sams, of Hillsboro, the best mathematician in school. My husband watched "his boy" become a lawyer, president of a bank, and director of the Federal Reserve Bank of Cleveland; and after my husband's death I had the privilege of watching Oliver forge on to greater honors. Another prized pupil was Mrs. Olive Watts, of Hillsboro, wife of the late Judge Joseph Watts. She was considered the best reader in the school and community. I can remember as though it were yesterday that whenever she gave her reading, "My Mother's Bible," the audience, young and old, broke down and wept. Then there was Mrs. Flo Parshall, now of California, who was a writer of splendid essays; Joe Eubanks, a teacher, now of Barberton; Dan T. Hiser and *the late Marion Hiser, of Greenfield, and the late Ferris Cummings, of Pisgah, all who showed promise and fulfilled my husband's expectations."*

Nancy Jane's son-in-law, T. H. McClure, started his business career in Sinking Spring by hauling kegs of water in his wagon to the cemetery at the top of a high hill overlooking Sinking Spring. For each keg he was paid two cents by a woman who used the water regularly to water the numerous flowers she kept growing on her family burial plot.

Perhaps no more charming spot near Sinking Spring may be found than the Mechlin estate, south of Fort Hill. When Ohio purchased this estate in 1938, it obtained for posterity, important earthworks, circle, mounds, and burials of the moundbuilders and the ideal entrance to Fort Hill state park.

The homestead sits on a spacious lawn against a background of majestic, wooded hills. Features such as the unfluted, four-columned Greek revival portico with triangular pediment and Colonial southern porch recessed on the second floor, the New England doorway, and mansard type of roof, the winding, inner stairways, large, high-ceilinged rooms and fireplaces combine several types of architecture.

It was built a century ago by William (Billy) Reynolds who died about 1890. Mr. Reynolds was a near relative of Frank Reynolds, former head of the Ohio Teachers Association. For many years it was the home of Mr. Easton, a well known writer, and was known in those days as a *"showplace"* and a favorite visiting place for people.

Several families have occupied this home. There is a legend that the head of one of these families went to the Boer War, and returned bringing with him an old colored man who became a familiar sight riding about the countryside on his horse, Easter. For some myserious reason, said to have been because he knew too much about what had become of a million dollars entrusted to his master by the Boer government for land investment, the old Negro disappeared. Years later what was believed to have been his body was unearthed from a cellar wall of the house. This incident and a suicide later occurring here, gave rise to the popular belief that the house is haunted, many claiming to have heard unearthly noises and to have witnessed strange happenings.

About ⅜ of a mile before reaching the house, a cluster of houses bordering a bend in the road, is passed. This settlement, Lincolnville, believed to have been named in honor of Abraham Lincoln, sprang up around a tanyard which, in its heydey, was a thriving industrial center of the region, where many settlers obtained their living.

The bark from the chestnut-oak trees, which are numerous here, was stripped or peeled in the early spring and seasoned. When thoroughly dried, it was crushed and mixed with water in large vats, ready for the tanning process. This industry flourished so that many hides were shipped in from a wide radius to be tanned. Tom Bragg, now of Kansas City, conducted, for a number of years, the business here which had been founded by his father.

Luxuriant bluegrass covers the tanyard site today, and nothing remains to mark the tanyard site except scattered parts of foundations scarcely visible to the eye. About 6 to 10 inhabitants reside in the tiny settlement.

Sinking Spring today is a farming community. It has a modern school plant accommodating grade and high school pupils, and a community building which is a combined gymnasium and assembly hall. It has a post office.

One by one, many descendants of the old pioneers of Sinking Spring are vanishing from the modern scene of the village. No more lovable character may be mentioned than the late Jennie McKeehan, postmistress, whose hobby was gathering church histories of the locality. When Frank Turley became seriously ill, she took over his chore of ringing the Methodist church bell to summon worshipers to Sunday School and church. Death took her two years ago just as she had finished ringing the bell. The research work she was attempting to assemble before the church should celebrate its 100th anniversary (1944) may be lost to posterity forever, but not the memory of her good deeds.

Sinking Spring has changed along with all the other towns and villages in Highland county. Times were, about 25 years ago, if a church or school needed fuel for the winter, the whole village turned out for a log rolling. The invitation to attend came from a prosperous farmer who had a great deal of timber on his land and did not mind contributing it. All day long the sound of axes and rumbling, creaking wagons filled the air. Women brought bulging baskets of fried chicken, home made cakes, and other good things and time was taken to eat, and play games, and sing such old refrains as these, that their forbears brought with them to Highland county:

"I'll have none of your weavily wheat,
  And I won't have any of your barley,
But I'll take some more of the good old rye,
  And make a cake for Charley."

"Oh, we'll shoot the buffalo,
  Oh, we'll shoot the buffalo,
And we'll rally through the canebreak
  And shoot the buffalo."

"Farewell to cold winters, due to white frost,
  Oh, I feel so very lonesome, since my old beau is lost,
But I'll sing and be as merry as the nightingale in May,
  But I can get another if he's gone far from me."

There are no log rollings and free lumber today. We are in another era.

CLAY TOWNSHIP
BUFORD
HOLLOWTOWN
STRASBURG
SICILY

BUFORD: Population, about 161; Altitude, 955 feet above sea level; Location, 15 miles southwest of Hillsboro on the Danville pike, on State Route 134, on the north fork of White Oak creek, in the western part of Clay township. Unincorporated.

Robert Lindsley platted Buford in August, 1834 and named it for his wife, daughter of Colonel Buford, a Kentuckian, who owned large tracts of land about Buford. The village was settled mostly by French, Irish, and English immigrants from North Carolina, Kentucky, and Virginia.

A Christian church was organized in 1835, members meeting in the home of Samuel Foreman. They later leased the Foreman district school which had been built in 1850. A Methodist church built in 1836 at the southern edge of Buford, passed into the hands of the Presbyterians in 1849. The Presbyterian church finally was abandoned and the church converted into a school house.

Many private burial lots were found near Buford long ago. When the settlers arrived they found a large Indian trail had been blazed through this part of the county, trending to Cincinnati, and northward. The unique society of Baldoons was organized in this township, a law requiring every member to drink intoxicating beverages without becoming drunk. There was a penalty for any omission.

An unusually large quantity of tools, axes, charcoal, pottery, and remains of kilns, of the moundbuilders were found throughout the township and villagers acquired prize collections of relics.

The chief industries of Buford are farming, lumbering, poultry raising, and manufacturing of feed. It has several stores, a modern grade and high school, a Christian and a Methodist church, saw mill, feed store, hatchery, and post office.

The story of Lydia House Ridings is representative of the lives of many settlers in and around Buford.

Lydia came with her young husband, John Duvall Ridings, a horse-and-buggy doctor and teacher, from Decatur, Illinois, to Buford, in 1873. She cried secretly, being homesick for two years until she became accustomed to Highland county.

Her father-in-law, Samuel Ridings, who lived at Hollowtown

about four miles away, was not only an undertaker, carpenter and blacksmith, but he had been a stanch abolitionist. His home had been a station on the underground railroad. He told Lydia how slaves were brought to his home hidden in the hay of wagon beds, in the night, and how he hid them and fed them until the next night when they were taken on to the next station.

Lydia's parents, Fielding and Nancy Todd House had moved to Illinois from Kentucky when Lydia was a small child. Her mother was a relative of Mary Todd, wife of Abraham Lincoln. The House family ardently admired their relative by marriage.

Lydia grew to love Highland county and made but two brief visits back to Illinois.

HOLLOWTOWN: Population, about 6; Altitude, 1,030 feet above sea level; Location, 11 miles southwest of Hillsboro on a crossroads about halfway between Danville and Buford on the Danville-Buford county highway, on the southeastern boundary line of Clay township. Unincorporated.

Hollowtown was never platted nor intended for a town. The settlement was named for Anthony Hollow who kept a candy store and whiskey shop some time in the early part of the 1800's. Isaac Jones kept a tavern here from 1834 to 1838.

A Dunkard church was established but when the store burned in 1921, it also was destroyed by fire. That same year a Christian church was built.

The post office established in the early part of Hollowtown's history, did not survive long, and the school was also abandoned. Grade and high school pupils attend school at Buford.

Hollowtown is a farming community.

STRASBURG: Population, about 6-8; Altitude, 980 feet above sea level; Location, about 15 miles southwest of Hillsboro on State Route 321 in the eastern part of Clay township. Unincorporated.

John Marconet, who emigrated to America in 1835 from France and came to Clay township in 1849, is believed to have named the place he chose for his home, Strasburg, in honor of a city in northeastern France. He opened a small store about 1850 and built a saw mill and flour mill in 1867. A small settlement formed around his establishments. When his mills both burned in 1861, he rebuilt the saw mill.

This is a farming community, served by rural mail delivery. School children attend school at Buford.

SICILY: Population, about 6-10; Altitude, 955 feet above sea level; Location, about 20 miles southwest of Hillsboro, on a county highway running south from Buford, in the southern part of Clay township. Unincorporated.

Sicily was platted for a town by John Newton Huggins, in June, 1848. He named it Sicily because of its close proximity to Sardinia, about four miles south, in Brown county. His platted town was near a Christian church which had been organized in 1837.

Then Harvey Scarborough opened a store and gradually 12 houses were clustered around it. A log school was opened on the Josiah Robbins farm with John B. Shelladay serving as the first teacher.

Sicily did not fulfill Mr. Huggins' hopes that it would become a sizable town and dwindled through the ensuing years until it can hardly be regarded as a hamlet.

The chief industry of the community is farming. Children attend school at Buford.

CONCORD TOWNSHIP
FAIRFAX
SUGAR TREE RIDGE

FAIRFAX: Population, about 62; 1,129 feet above sea level; Location, 11 miles south of Hillsboro on the intersection of State Route 137 and the West Union pike, on the line of Jackson and Concord townships, in Concord township. Unincorporated.

Benjamin Pulliam immigrated in 1833 to this part of Highland county and platted and named the village for his native Fairfax C. H., Virginia. Among the first settlers to arrive were John Dickey and John T. Wilson from Belfast, who established a general store on the northwest corner of the crossroads. The store later was used as a residence, but is now abandoned. Other early settlers were the Laforges, Lewises, Eylers, Naces, and Walkers, all Virginians.

The Methodist church was organized in 1856 and had the first coal oil lamps in this part of the country. The lamps were the gift of Mrs. D. S. Miller who brought them with her from Philadelphia. The century old chandelier in the church is still in use.

By 1880 the population had reached 50 or 60. The village contained a hotel, store, wagon and blacksmith shop, and the church.

Fairfax is situated in a farming community. Children attend school at Belfast. There is rural mail delivery service.

Fairfax View, on State Route 137 about ¼ mile west of Fairfax, reveals a panoramic view of deep, wide, picturesque valleys with the hills of Pike and Adams counties looming in the distance. This is considered one of the loveliest scenes in the county.

There is a state forest preserve about 1½ miles north of Fairfax on the Beatty farm on the West Union county highway where various species of evergreen trees are grown.

Small as Fairfax is, it produced many people of note. Among them was Edna Grey Rouse, one of the first women lawyers in Ohio; John T. Wilson, congressman, born in Belfast, whose *"nest egg"* for the fortune he accumulated, many claim, was laid in the store he kept at Fairfax; Benjamin Pulliam, who was a prominent church worker; Lewis Webster, who kept one of the largest and most complete general stores in Highland county; and Isaac Fenton Martin, one of the first Negroes in the county to secure a teacher's certificate.

The late Dan Webster, a native of Fairfax, who went to live in Dayton, wrote feelingly of the 90-year-old Fairfax Methodist Church as he remembered it as a boy.

"Fairfax church is redolent of the memories of a happy past," he said. *"Days when the Pulliams, LeForges and others of its first builders gave money made on hard-won farms, that the community might have a church.*

"Shouting had not gone out of style when I attended "big meeting" at Fairfax Church. Aunt Suseann Webster, Anna Griffith, Nancy Carlisle, Susan Roberds, Uncle "Wash" Stultz and others, with faces radiant with joy would tell of that home over there, and unforgettable the clear voice of Martha Cox as it rose in sheer happiness in some old church song.

"And Fairfax was always a friendly church, giving the Christian hand of fellowship to the two colored families who lived in the neighborhood — the Mortons and the Williamses. Uncle "Charley" Williams held office in the congregation and with his wife and family were faithful attendants.

"The only time the local cornet band was allowed within its sacred precincts was on Memorial Day, and at the funerals of Pearson Beatty and William Blair, soldiers of the Civil War.

"Of all the janitors the church had through its long years, the name of Aaron Roebuck stands out the most distinct. The stories related of him would make a book, and the best ones, when as a pillar of the church, the minister asked him to lead in prayer. From his position among the sinners occupying the rear seats he drawled: "No chance praying back here with all this devilment going on."

"In the old days it was the custom for farmers to bring their robes and buggy whips inside the church and place them in some back corner. One night Mr. Roebuck, annoyed by a youth and maid who persisted in leaning over to talk to the annoyance of preacher and congregation, calmly seized one of the buggy whips and brought it down with a resounding whack across the backs of the offenders. For the rest of the evening at least there was no more misbehavior.

"In the old days there was plenty to prophesy that should Fairfax church ever tumble down as it threatened to for so many years it would never be rebuilt. But an up and coming generation, led by their minister have shown the world it could be done."

SUGAR TREE RIDGE: Population, about 202; Altitude, 1113 feet above sea level; Location, 11 miles southwest of Hillsboro, in the northwest part of Concord township. Unincorporated.

John Bunn owned the land on which Sugar Tree Ridge was founded May 4, 1844. It was named for its situation upon a maple sugar tree ridge. The first settlers were Jonas Rotroff, Henry Nace, and St. Clair Ross who arrived in 1809. Mr. Ross, who came to the county in 1799, was one of our earliest settlers.

The first school was a log cabin with greased-paper windows, 70 odd rods southeast of the village. Samuel Hale was the first teacher.

James Mongor was the first merchant, opening a shoe and general store about 1813. Rachel Wilkin planted the first orchard in the township about 1811. A scattering of mills, tanneries, and a still followed. James Hetherington was the first postmaster of the post office established soon after 1840.

A Methodist church was organized about 1811 in the home of Rachel Wilkin and a frame church was built between 1836 and 1840. A Christian church was organized about 1868 in the school house and a church built a few years later. A New Light and a Presbyterian church were organized later.

The road cut through Sugar Tree Ridge to Winchester was known as the Whisky road because it had been cut by New Market citizens in order to reach the Hemphill distillery to obtain whiskey. This road is often referred to as Sugar Tree Ridge Drive. Designated as State Route 136, it leaves State Route 62 a short distance below New Market, and winds over pretty hills southward to Winchester, in Adams county.

By 1870, the population was 112. Ten years later, in 1880, it had dropped to about 80 and consisted of two churches, a school, post office, general store, wagon shop, blacksmith shop, and two hotels. These hotels are now residences.

Sugar Tree Ridge, familiarly called "the Ridge," is a farming community. It has a grade school. High school pupils go to school at Mowrystown. There are two churches, the Christian and the Methodist. A blind man operates a one man factory in his home, manufacturing a very fine grade of brooms.

Sugar Tree Ridge's most noted person was Albert Jeremiah Beveridge, author and statesman, who was born on a small farm near Sugar Tree Ridge, October 6, 1862.

DODSON TOWNSHIP

ALLENSBURG
DODSONVILLE
LYNCHBURG
WEBERTOWN

ALLENSBURG: Population, about 50; Altitude, 1024 feet above sea level; Location, 9 miles west of Hillsboro on State

Route 50, on the west branch of Dodson creek, in Dodson township. Unincorporated.

Allensburg was platted for a town, October 28, 1839, and was named in honor of Hon. William Allen, U. S. Senator from Ohio, by the owners of the land, Robert Pugh and Charles Henderson.

This is a farming community. Until recent years there was a one-room graded school but this building is now used for a church and children attend school at Lynchburg. There is one church, the Christian Union.

The Allensburg Auction Company conducts auction sales in the auction rooms here.

DODSONVILLE: Population, about 126; Altitude, 986 feet above sea level; Location, 11 miles west of Hillsboro on State Route 50, on the west branch of Dodson creek, in Dodson township. Unincorporated.

Daniel Shaffer, the proprietor, platted Dodsonville for a town April 29, 1839. The Shaffer families have been prominent in this part of the county ever since. L. L. Cartwright added to the town plat in 1839 and Daniel Shaffer made another addition March 1, 1845. The town was named in honor of Joshua Dodson, a Virginian, who surveyed and entered large tracts of land in the township in 1796 and 1797.

A Lutheran minister, John Surface, organized a Lutheran church in 1839. A Methodist church was established in 1839 and Greenbury Jones was the first minister. Two stores, three blacksmith shops, a steam saw mill and a one-room school completed the town.

The village today consists of 2 churches, 2 stores, a township hall and homes scattered along the rolling highway. Children attend school at Lynchburg. This is a farming community.

LYNCHBURG: Population, about 883; Altitude, 1009 feet above sea level; Location, 12 miles northwest of Hillsboro on State Route 135, on the left bank of East Fork of Little Miami river, in Dodson township. Incorporated.

A large and noted encampment of Indians under the leadership of the great Indian warrior, Tecumseh, occupied the site of Lynchburg until about 1806. Their camp extended from the mouth of Turtle creek to the first cemetery of the whites begun in 1817.

Near Lynchburg, in 1792, the first battle in the county took place between Indians and whites. Simon Kenton and a party of men were pursuing on horseback Indian marauders who had crossed the Ohio river into Kentucky, burned cabins of the white settlers and escaped northward with valuable horses they had stolen.

When Kenton's party reached what is now Lynchburg, they found that they were greatly outnumbered and began a retreat. The Indians followed and attacked them. In the battle that followed

U. S. 41 Through Sinking Spring

(Section of the Old Zane Trace, oldest road west of the Alleghenies).

The deepest natural gorge in Ohio is found at The Seven Caves.

Entering the McKimie Cave at The Seven Caves are Constance Fairley and Martha Judkins Ingle, representing two Highland County families.

Alexander McIntyre was captured and killed. For years, scarred, notched trees, remains of camp fires, and weapons, remained as evidences of the battle.

William Stewart owned the land on which Lynchburg was platted as a town, July 30, 1830, by Andrew Smith and Coleman Botts. It was named for their native Lynchburg, Virginia.

The first settler was Rev. William Hughey who built a house on High street. The next settler was Rev. Benson Goldsberry who built a house on Main street. About 1830, Andrew Smith established a saw and grist mill in the northwestern part of town. In 1832 William Harper started a tannery and a Mr. Coffman opened a blacksmith shop. In 1836, Judge John Duvall established a shoe shop and tannery and O. C. Collins opened the doors of the first tavern on Main street. Dr. Samuel J. Spees, the first physician, located in Lynchburg in 1834, and a little log school house was built in the southern part of town.

In 1857 the Bowen distillery was founded by Freiburg and Workum, of Cincinnati. It got its name from the Bowen Distillery in Kentucky which gave permission to brand the first 100 barrels of liquor with the Bowen brand.

The distillery, one of the largest in the country, covered 20 acres of ground. The capacity of 100 bushels of grain a day increased to 500 bushels. The distillery increased its output from 10 barrels of whisky a day to 225 barrels and at one time averaged 200,000 barrels annually. A large cooper shop was connected with it.

It ceased to operate in 1916, but later was wrecked and rebuilt under the new name of the Lynchburg Distillery Company. Plans for opening it failed, and the plant remains idle.

Lynchburg has a canning factory employing a number of people and canning tomatoes and corn in season.

The population in 1840 was 102; in 1880, it had reached 664, and by 1900, 763. It has 4 churches, two Christian, one Lutheran, and one Methodist; an excellent business district; a modern school plant accommodating grade and high school pupils; a post office; bank; newspaper. It is the trade center of the township. The chief industries are farming, canning, and milling.

Lynchburg has contributed much culturally and economically to the county and has given us many talented and prominent persons.

WEBERTOWN: Population, about 8-10; Altitude, 1000 feet above sea level; Location, on county highway west of Lynchburg, in the northwestern part of Dodson township. Unincorporated.

A Mr. Weber established a store here many years ago, and, together, with a few homes nearby, it formed a community known as Webertown.

This was never platted nor intended for a town. A mill was

built in 1825 by a Mr. Kilbreth who sold out to Benjamin and John Jenny who later sold to a Mr. Liggett. The mill was called Liggett's mill.

Children in this community attend school at Lynchburg. Residents attend church at neighboring communities. This is a farming community.

FAIRFIELD TOWNSHIP

BRIDGES
CENTERFIELD
EAST MONROE
HIGHLAND
HIGHLAND STATION
LEESBURG

BRIDGES: Population, about 7; Altitude, 889 feet above sea level; Location, about 8 miles northeast of Hillsboro on the East Monroe-Bridges county highway, on Hardin's creek, in Fairfield township. Unincorporated.

Bridges was never platted nor intended for a town. It was so named because each of four converging roads here has a bridge spanning the winding creek.

Waw-wil-a-way, famous Indian chief, once dwelled in harmony with his white brothers at the mouth of Hardin's creek where fishing was exceptionally good.

Shortly after 1804, a Friends church was built on a pretty knoll in this locality and flourishing woolen and grist mills were built along nearby Lees creek.

Bridges today consists of one house and a store, and the Hardin's creek Friends church. There is rural mail delivery service from Hillsboro and Leesburg. Children attend school at Leesburg. This is a farming community.

CENTERFIELD: Population, about 40-50; Altitude, 904 feet above sea level; Location, about 12 miles north of Hillsboro, on crossroads connecting with State Route 138 and State Route 28, on Rattlesnake creek, in Fairfield township. Unincorporated.

Centerfield was platted for a town by John M. Coombs, August 2, 1830. It was named because of its situation near the center of circling villages.

The first building constructed in Centerfield was the Dennison Tavern, a popular stage coach stop. Then a store, blacksmith shop, distillery, several mills, and a school were established. A Methodist church organized about 1½ miles northeast of the village and named "Zion Hill Methodist Church" was moved, in 1840, to

Greenfield where it was remodeled in 1876. A Friends church was established in 1877 in the western part of Centerfield. A brick Universalist church, next built, was later abandoned and used for a store and residence.

It was believed that Centerfield would become one of the large, prosperous towns of the county, until the railroad was built through Greenfield. Then Centerfield gradually declined.

Centerfield is situated in a good farming community. Children attend school at Leesburg. There is rural mail delivery service from Hillsboro and Leesburg.

EAST MONROE: Population, about 75; Altitude, 959 feet above sea level; Location, 13 miles northeast of Hillsboro on State Route 28 at the extreme end of Fairfield township, where Rattlesnake creek divides Fairfield township from Madison township. Unincorporated.

James Reece platted East Monroe for a town November 20, 1815. It is believed that he named it in honor of President James Monroe, popular at that time because of his "era of good feeling" term of presidency.

A post office was established in 1833, with Otho Dowden as the first postmaster. One of several grist mills built along the creek is still standing near the center of the village, where John Hay conducts a sorghum molasses mill and slaughter house. A Baptist church was organized in 1840 and in 1841, a Methodist church was built, and in 1887, rebuilt.

East Monroe Falls, south of the village, is known as the "Little Niagara Falls," of Highland county. Tumbling, hurrying water plunges 21 feet down into a deep basin and ripples southward along one of the loveliest, winding stretches of the county's scenery and prettiest hills in the county. Devil's Den, Cedar Cliffs, Sunfish Hole, Still Hole, and Sheep Pen Hole, are other pretty spots near East Monroe, along the creeks. East Monroe Park, a public picnic grounds, is south of the village. There is good fishing of small mouth bass, rock bass, and cat fish in Rattlesnake creek.

The abandoned two-room grade school is now being used for a residence and children attend school in nearby Leesburg. This is a farming community. There is a grain and feed elevator and coal office.

The B. and O. Fast Line No. 3, bound from Baltimore to St. Louis, passes through East Monroe once daily, with no stop.

HIGHLAND: Population, about 262; Altitude, 1,036 feet above sea level; Location, 10 miles north of Hillsboro on State Route 72 and intersected by State Route 28, on the crest of a rising hill on Lees creek, in the northwestern part of Fairfield township. Incorporated.

John Connor, who platted Highland in September, 1816, built the first home, naming it Lexington for Lexington, Kentucky. The name was changed later to Highland in honor of the county and because of its situation on high land. Most of the settlers came from Virginia, Kentucky, and the Carolinas.

David Terrell was the first merchant and the first postmaster.

The first Methodist church was built in 1837 on a lot donated for the purpose, now the site of the cemetery. When a storm destroyed the church in 1860, it was rebuilt on its present site. A Quaker church was organized a little later.

Jacob Jackson, the first Quaker minister in the township, lived just west of Highland. A Dunkard church was established south of Highland between Highland and Samantha.

Highland contained only 10 families in 1817. By 1840, it had reached 151. In 1870, it was 242.

HIGHLAND STATION: Population, about 15-20; Altitude, 1,085 feet; Location, about 10 miles north of Hillsboro on State Route 73. Unincorporated.

The brick school building in the northern part of town was rebuilt in 1875 on the site of the first school. A three-year high school course was offered, with A. J. Hixon the first superintendent. In recent years it became a first grade high school, offering a standard four-year course.

The industries of Highland are farming and milling. The Earl Mill, on Lees creek south of Highland, manufactures flour.

A Revolutionary trail marker designates a trail running northward, which Simon Kenton, frontiersman, blazed through here.

This is the home of Congressman James G. Polk.

Highland Station was never platted nor intended for a town. It is a settlement that sprang up near the railroad station about 1816 and was called Highland Station for the village of Highland about 1 mile north.

The B. and O. railroad passes through Highland Station. There are several homes scattered along the highway and a grain and feed elevator is near the railroad station.

Children attend school at Leesburg and residents attend neighboring churches.

LEESBURG: Population, 839; Altitude, 1,021 feet above sea level; Location, 10 miles north of Hillsboro on U. S. Route 62, and intersected by State Route 28, in Fairfield township.

The founding of Leesburg in the spring of 1802 by Nathaniel Pope, John Walters, John Howard and immigrants from Tennessee, has an interesting story.

Six years before, in the fall of 1796, Nathaniel Pope, prominent Virginia Quaker, set out with his family in search of a new home. They transported their household goods in a crude wagon and upon pack horses and walked and rode alternately.

By November they reached the falls of the Great Kanawha

where they wintered. When spring came, they struck out again, embarking in a boat Pope fashioned, and sailed to Gallipolis. Here they purchased necessities, using animal skins for money. They then continued their journey, Pope's eldest son and John Walters driving the horses and cattle through. At last they came to "Quaker Bottom," a fertile place up the north side of the river at the mouth of a small stream called Paddy's Run, about a mile above the mouth of the Guyandot. They tried to purchase land in this promising locality but failed to buy it for the price they wished to pay.

They pushed on, sending wagons, plows and heavy articles up the Scioto and Sunfish Hills to the Falls of Paint creek where they stopped for the winter. Pope sold most of his stock to General Massie in exchange for corn and land. The land was to be chosen from any of Massie's unsold lands in the Virginia Military District.

Pope spent the winter of 1801-1802 exploring the land for miles about and finally selected the land upon which Leesburg stands. That spring the Popes, Walters, Howards and the other immigrants moved on up to the place chosen. They found themselves surrounded by friendly Indian camps and bear ranges. The immigrants planted the first wheat sown in the township on the land.

They named the town Leesburg in honor of Leesburg, Virginia and General Lee, and the nearby creek was named Lee's creek.

Under a spreading elm tree near Pope's cabin, Indian chiefs held a council following the murder of Waw-wil-a-way; and 300 to 400 Indians assembled at the forks of Lees creek, in what was the last Indian uprising in southern Ohio. The noted Cooper Indian mound is located about 2 miles south of Leesburg.

Leesburg's growth was retarded at first because of a dispute as to the title of the land upon which it was laid out. This led to the platting of a "new" Leesburg adjoining, by "Gov." James Johnson, March 2, 1814, and many, fearing their location insecure, moved into the new part.

The Friends Church, the first place of worship established in the township, was built at the southern edge of the village in 1804. It was called Fairfield Quaker Meeting House, and a noted Quaker woman preacher named Bathsheba Lupton is credited with its founding. The story is that old and young settlers spent their Sundays in company with the Indians, indulging in sports with them. Bathsheba mounted her horse and rode from cabin to cabin, admonishing them, and charging them to keep the day holy. It is claimed that this brought about the organization of the church.

The first building was crude, built of logs, and covered with hewn slabs. A large hole in the middle of the church filled with charcoal, was the stove. This building was rebuilt later on. It became a popular place for state-wide Quaker meetings and people of all denominations came for the all-day meetings. Many famed Quaker preachers preached here and many noted Quakers lie buried in the large cemetery beside the red brick church.

Leesburg's first school was east of the village and Catherine Borum was the first teacher.

Isaac McPherson was Leesburg's first merchant, opening a little log cabin store. Then other stores, flour and woolen mills, churches, and a tavern followed. Samuel Sanders was appointed the first postmaster in 1816, but there is a claim that Harrison Radcliffe preceded him.

By 1840, the population was 298. By 1888 it had reached 513 and boasted of a thriving industry, the manufacturing of shoes. Grist and woolen mills prospered. In 1876 the Leesburg Bank was established.

The remains of the Davis Mill just north of Leesburg on U. S. Route 62, is all that remains of Leesburg's pioneer mills where men used to take their whole families to be measured and fitted for woolen articles of apparel.

Fine farm lands surround Leesburg. In addition to farming, milling, canning, lumbering, and manufacturing of gates, fences, etc., are other thriving industries.

Leesburg has a modern centralized grade and high school plant. There are four churches, the Methodist, Friends, Seventh Day Adventist, and Holiness Mission. Its newspaper, *"The Leesburg Citizen,"* is published and edited by Mack Sauer, well-known humorist and public speaker.

HAMER TOWNSHIP
DANVILLE
EAST DANVILLE

DANVILLE: Population, about 205; Altitude, 1,073 feet above sea level; Location, 8 miles southwest of Hillsboro on the Danville pike (county highway), in Hamer township. Unincorporated.

Daniel P. March platted Danville on April 14, 1835. The prospective town was named for him, but Danville was often referred to in olden times as Nevins for two Nevins brothers who were prominent in the early history of Danville. Robert Nevins was the first postmaster.

Before the platting of Danville, about 1800, a group of Irishmen settled on the banks of a stream nearby. They called their settlement Smoky Row from a name that had been given to it by Indians because of the smoke from sugar camps along the creek.

Danville is credited with burning the first bricks in the county, in 1816, on the Eakins farm. The bricks were widely used in making chimneys.

A Christian church was built west of Danville in 1835. A Methodist church was established in 1842, but it had been organized earlier. The history of a Lutheran church which occupied the site of a grist mill, has been obscured by time. The population by 1870 had reached 147.

In its most flourishing days, Danville had 3 stores, 1 hotel, 1 shoe shop, 1 harness shop, 1 cooper shop, 1 wagon shop, 2 churches, and a school. Today, Danville consists of a store and filling station, 2 churches, a stone quarry, a $9,000 automatic telephone exchange and residences. Farming and quarrying are the chief industries.

There is a Christian church at the western edge of the village and an abandoned German Reform church at the eastern edge. Mail is delivered by rural mail delivery from Hillsboro. Grade pupils attend school at Danville and high school pupils attend school at Hillsboro.

EAST DANVILLE: Known also as Winkle. In pioneer days named Straight Out; Population, about 150; Altitude, 1,048 feet above sea level; Location, 9 miles southwest of Hillsboro and about 1 mile east of Danville, in the southeastern part of Hamer township. The Norfolk and Western railroad passes through East Danville, running from Hillsboro to Sardinia, one round trip daily. Unincorporated.

East Danville was first named Straight Out because it is "straight out" from Danville. It was never platted nor intended for a town and its history is dim. John DeHaas kept a grocery and dry-goods store many unknown years ago and a cluster of houses near it was the result. When a post office was established the hamlet was named East Danville and Winkle Post Office. The name Winkle was derived from the Winkle families, prominent residents.

East Danville's chief industries are farming and lumbering. It has 2 general stores, 1 garage, 2 feed mills, and 1 saw mill. Its one-room grade school was abandoned recently and pupils attend school at Hillsboro. Its one church, the United Brethren, was formerly called Stevens Chapel before it was removed to East Danville.

JACKSON TOWNSHIP
BELFAST
NORTH UNION

BELFAST: Population, about 303; Altitude, 858 feet above sea level; Location, 11 miles southeast of Hillsboro on Brush creek, intersected by State Route 137 and State Route 73. Unincorporated.

James Storer, Jonathan Weaver, and Lancelot Brown platted Belfast for a town on March 19, 1834, on a part of survey Number

2,409 entered by Robert Powell and Number 1,321 entered by William Johnson. It was named for Belfast, Ireland.

When a post office was established between 1836 and 1840 it was discovered that there was a Belfast post office near Milford, in Clermont county, so the name was changed to Bell Post office. Later it was renamed Belfast. J. Wallace Blair was the first post master. The first merchant was a Mr. Smith.

The Methodist church was organized about 1815 in Samuel Clark's home but a church building was not built until 1836. A Presbyterian church was organized about 1835 and meetings were held in James Storer's home north of Belfast. About 1839 a log Presbyterian church was organized at the north edge of Belfast.

Benjamin Massie, brother of the noted Gen. Nathaniel Massie, was the first teacher in the first log school which was built about 1806 in Brown's woods. Until then the boys had been sent to West Union in Adams county for the few short winter months of school. Girls stayed at home.

About ¾ of a mile northwest of Belfast above the forks of Brush creek, near a large, partially explored Indian mound, occurred the second and last battle between Indians and whites in Highland county. John McNary, a border soldier from Kentucky, with a party of about 50 men, were homeward bound from near Lynchburg where they had been sent to recover and bury bodies of whites who might have been killed there. They had stopped to rest and breakfast when surprised by the Indians. Although greatly outnumbered, they made a successful retreat and reached Manchester on the Ohio river in safety.

Here, in Belfast was born, April 16, 1811, John T. Wilson, son of Sarah Haigh and Spencer W. Wilson, who became a capitalist and philanthropist of Adams county. He was one of the first to apply for a teacher's certificate at Hillsboro when the Ohio Legislature passed the free-school law, and he taught a four-months term of school at North Union where he received a salary of $12.00 per month and paid $3.00 per month board.

There is a conflicting account as to how he got his start on the road to wealth, some authorities claiming that it was when he and John Dickey went to Fairfax and established a general store. Others claim that with his share of his birthplace in Belfast, $300.00, he began his career of capitalist when he started a store at Tranquillity, in Adams county. He was instrumental in organizing the 70th Ohio Infantry and, as Captain, led his company into the battle of Shiloh.

He was appointed Senator of the 7th Senatorial District of Ohio in 1863, and reelected in 1865. He was elected Congressman in 1866, reelected in 1868, and again in 1870.

On March 6, 1882, he gave Adams county $50,000 toward the erection of a children's home. By his last will and testament he gave this children's home an endowment of $35,000 in money and $15,000

TOWNSHIPS — THEIR TOWNS, VILLAGES AND HAMLETS

in farming lands. He also gave $5,000 to the erection of a soldiers' monument to the memory of the Adams county soldiers who had died or been killed during the Civil War. He gave $150,000 to the Adams county comimssioners to be spent in the support of the poor. He made numerous other generous bequests.

He died October 6, 1891, at the age of 85 years and was buried in the United Presbyterian cemetery at Tranquillity.

The family of Elgar Brown, direct descendants of Benjamin Franklin, resided in Belfast until recent years. The 200-year-old book, *"Journal of the Life, Labours, Travels, Etc., of Thomas Chalkley,"* printed and bound by Franklin, is owned by the family. The journalist, Thomas Chalkley, gave a vivid day by day account of his persecution as a Quaker youth in England and his subsequent escape to America.

The chief industry of Belfast is farming, but there is also some lumber and feed manufacturing. It is within a few miles of the famous Serpent Mound. It has a modern grade and high school plant.

The entrance to Belfast from Hillsboro is exceptionally beautiful, a deep, wide vista to the west rivaled only by practically the same view seen at a different angle at Fairfax (Fairfax View). There is good fishing in Brush creek.

NORTH UNION: Sometimes called Uniontown; Population, about 20; Altitude, 1,002 feet; Located about 14 miles southeast of Hillsboro in the northeast corner of Jackson township, on the Marshall-North Union county road. Can be reached via Marshall or Belfast. Unincorporated.

The hamlet consists of about 5 houses and a small store. Its history is obscure and not much is known about it except that Obediah Countryman platted it on land he owned, June 3, 1848, on a part of John Mark's survey. Thomas Berryman, Justice of the Peace, recorded the plat on January 27, 1849.

North Union has no churches. Residents attend neighboring churches and children go to school at Belfast. This is a farming community.

LIBERTY TOWNSHIP
HILLSBORO
HOAGLAND CROSSING

HILLSBORO: Population, 4,713, 1944 census: Altitude, 753 feet above sea level; Location, near the center of Highland county on the dividing ridge between the Miami and Scioto rivers, upon seven hills. Intersected by U. S. 50 and U. S. 62 and State Routes 73, 124, and 138; 62 miles south of Columbus, 57 miles east of Cincinnati, and 40 miles west of Chillicothe.

Hillsboro has beeen referred to as the *"hilly city,"* and the *"city of hills."* The literal meaning of it is *"hilly town."* There is no official record of its naming, but David Hays, the young director selected by the legislature to pick the site, named it. Popular belief favors the idea that he named it in honor of Captain Billy Hill, a popular and esteemed citizen, although it is also conceded that he might have so named it simply because it is a *"hilly town."*

In 1807 when Hillsboro became the county seat, military companies were being formed throughout the county. One of the first to be formed was a rifle company. George W. Barrere was chosen captain. The men wore white hunting shirts as part of their uniforms. When the War of 1812 occurred, the entire company and Captain Barrere volunteered for service. One of these soldiers, William A. Trimble, was appointed Major in the 26th U. S. Infantry and, following an outstanding record in the Maumee River Campaign, was promoted to the rank of Colonel.

An old newspaper carried the following account of the history of the military activities of Hillsboro:

"Several other communities followed Captain Barrere's lead until Highland county had five well drilled military organizations. There was a general muster of the militia of the county in September, 1808, out at Capt. Billy Hill's on Clear Creek. Hillsboro's wide streets were full of logs and the adjacent grounds had not been cleared save for a few potato patches. The militia was ordered to Hill's "cow pasture."

"Capt. Barrere, who was appointed Adjutant for the occasion, formed all the companies into columns. His men in his own company were described as spotless as to uniforms but some were clad in their frontier garb, others in the full dress of their Revolutionary fathers. All had swords, the old long broad swords of the Revolution, many of which had seen service in that conflict.

"When all was ready, a flourish of drums at one end of the line announced the approach of the Commander, Major Anthony Franklin of Sinking Spring. He was mounted on a fine bay horse and uniformed in a blue coat of Revolutionary cut, buff leather breeches and top boots, a long sword, and a cocked hat with a black ostrich plume. This uniform included the sword that had been worn by Major Franklin's father at the surrender of Cornwallis at Yorktown. James A. Trimble carried the sword that his father had used as a weapon of offense and defense at the bloody battle of the "Point." All day long the men drilled.

"When the Mexican War occurred, the infantry company was enlisted and called into service. David Irick was Captain, Jackson Kennipe, 1st Lieutenant, and Samuel D. Stewart, 2nd Lieutenant. These officers were from Hillsboro. Stewart proved himself a hero in this war and for his bravery Congress voted him a gold sword and

he was promoted to the rank of Lieutenant in the regular army of the United States.

"In the War of the Rebellion, Highland county contributed Company I of the 24th Ohio Infantry; Company K to the 12th Regiment O.V.I.; Company H to the 27th O.V.I.; Company A to the 48th Regiment; and Company E to the 50th Regiment. The 50th and 60th Regiments contained a number of Highland county men as did the 73rd, 65th, 81st and 88th. To the 88th Regiment, Highland county contributed several companies under the command of Captains W. H. Glenn, D. M. Barrett, and Joseph Mullenix. The 175th Regiment of O.N.G. was enlisted in Hillsboro in the fall of 1864 and saw great service at the battles of Franklin and Nashville. Company H of the 1st Ohio Cavalry was from Highland county and Martin Buck became Major of the Regiment. The 2nd and 4th Cavalry also contained many men from this section.

"The Cavalry Regiment with which Highland county was most closely associated was the 11th, organized by Col. William O. Collins in the fall of 1861. This regiment served mainly on the western plains and among Indians and in their wild encounters Lieut. Caspar Collins, only son of the colonel, lost his life.

"The county also made contributions to the 1st Regiment of Ohio Heavy Artillery."

About the time of the Civil War when political lines were viciously sharp, platforms on sawhorses were erected in the court house yard at Hillsboro and speakers orated to large gatherings. Samuel Pike, a local newspaper man, it is recalled, was often one of the speakers. His son, Corporal James Pike, ranger, scout, spy, soldier, printer, and adventurer, not only was the author of *"Scout and Ranger,"* but he was one of the unsung heroes of the Civil War.

One day a speaker was called for a statement he had made and when he refused to argue the question he was ordered to come down off the platform. This he refused to do, whereupon a scuffle ensued which resulted in the platform being upset and a free for all fight.

The 60th Volunteer Infantry was recruited from Highland county for the Civil War. The recruits encamped at the eastern edge of town.

Years later some of these veterans would gather in the office of Dr. William M. Hoyt to talk over Civil War days. In this group were Judge S. F. Steele, Judge H. M. Huggins, J. J. Pugsley, and Judge G. B. Gardner.

Dr. Hoyt's young son, Maurice (now Dr. Maurice Hoyt) used to listen in on the true tales they spun. One of these tales was when the young soldiers, encamped east of town, were issued beef so tough they could not eat it. They decided to hold services and bury it. Will Steele, son of Rev. Steele, pastor of the Presbyterian church, and a member of the Infantry, preached the sermon. He chose for his text, *"She was old and full of years and not years of corn."*

"I remember clearly that a well with a pump was at each corner of the court yard in those days," Dr. Maurice Hoyt said. "A big quart copper cup was chained to the pump and one pump had a spout that ran out to a watering trough. There was a fence around the courtyard and hitching posts for horses.

"The sheriff's residence faced Main Street then, on the west end of the court house lot. The jail was back of the residence and back of the jail was the work house where rock was kept. The rock was hauled out to fix the streets. On bad days the prisoners worked indoors. On good days, with ball and chain attached to each one, they were marched out to the stone quarry to dig rock. They used two hammers, a long one to break the big rock up into pieces about the size of grape fruit, and small hammers to pound the rocks into pieces small enough to go through a two inch ring."

When the Spanish War came about, Hillsboro and Highland county sent one company, Company F of the 2nd Regiment O.V.I. Officers were Captain Quinn Bowles, 1st Lieutenant Arthur Jenkins, and 2nd Lieutenant John Gorman who died in Hillsboro the next day after reaching home on furlough. The greater part of the men in this company were from Hillsboro and Greenfield.

About 800 men from Highland county served in World War I. Eleven from Hillsboro were killed and 13 died from other causes. Captain Earle V. Miller commanded the Hillsboro company, the title of which was Company D (Machine Gun Company) 147th Regiment 37th (Buckeye) Division. The title of the Greenfield Company was Company G 166th Regiment (Rainbow) Division, with Captain Don Caldwell in command.

Words can not estimate or describe just how much Highland county gave to the service of her country during World War II. There were 2,754 Highland county men in the armed forces. Although 103 of these men made the supreme sacrifice and several others were injured permanently, a true estimate of the sacrifice of this tiny bit of America to the greatest conflict of them all can not be made.

Highland county men served in every corner of the world, in romantically-named spots which often belied their names. They fought on land, on sea, and in the air. The exact number in each branch of service is not known.

The county's highest ranking Navy officer during the war was Vice Admiral John J. Ballentine of Hillsboro, who played an important role in the Navy's share of the fight against Japan in the Pacific.

On this side of the hemisphere illustrating the widespread activity of local soldiers, Lt. General John Edwin Hull of Greenfield, the county's highest ranking Army officer, served as chief of operations. He was with Roosevelt at Casablanca in 1943 and at Yalta in

1945; he was with Truman at Potsdam last summer when the final ultimatum was issued to Japan.

Among other county war heroes was Colonel John Blount, of Hillsboro, Pacific veteran and former regimental commander of Ohio's famed 147th Infantry Division.

But war has not always occupied the Highland county scene.

If you had been a child of the long ago in Hillsboro, you would have heard chilling and fascinating tales of experiences with Indians and wild animals as you sat in your homespun clothes at eventide before a sparkling wood fire in a huge fireplace. You would have hung breathless on the last word of the incredible tales and you would have found yourself lost in fanciful reflection about your ancestors. You would have been awed as the immensity of the universe dawned upon you. Like the story my grandfather told me about his grandfather back in Virginia:

David Morgan, a Virginian, and of Scotch-Irish descent, was *"a famed Indian fighter,"* according to Virginia historical records.

Returning to his cabin in the wilderness one day in company with two small sons, he found the cabin smoldering in ruins and the rest of his family murdered and lying about on the ground. One brawny fellow was cavorting about the circle of yelling Indians, with my great great grandmother's apron tied about his waist and her long honey-colored hair in his flourishing fist. Infuriated, my great great grandfather, it is claimed, attacked the savages single-handed and after a fierce and bloody battle, killed them all. The Virginia legend goes on to state that he skinned the savage who had slain his wife and that powder pouches were made out of his tough hide.

Outside in the long, purpling twilight, you might have heard an ox cart creaking its rough way homeward, or the loud voice of a benighted drover urging his flock of cattle, sheep, or hogs through the dusty main street of town. You would have shuddered perhaps at the howl of a wolf in the distance. The night would have been pitch dark save for the intermittent lantern light of a straggler; as deep and mysterious as the future looming upon you.

But years have a sly way of slipping past; and if you had been a young girl 90-100 years ago, your spare time not only would have been devoted to packing your hope chest with linens and quilts, but you would have delighted in *"tripping the light fantastic toe"* at the town dances. You would have worn a long *"ball dress"* made out of fashionable pink or blue silk, with a full skirt and waist. Pink or blue ribbon would have adorned your left shoulder, made into a rosette with flowing streamers. Your hair would have been braided into 7 or 8 strands about your head with rosebuds fastened in your hair with a gold or silver ornament. You would have descended the wide curving stairway in one of the best homes in Hillsboro and stepped joyously out onto the dance floor with your partner under the brilliant lights of chandeliers.

If you had been a housewife in that time you would have been a great home lover and had all kinds of pet superstitions such as, when moving into a new house you always took the oldest broom you possessed with you on account of it being bad luck to take a new one; and the pulverized lining of a sun-dried chicken gizzard taken in a tumbler of water was a common cure all for any kind of sickness. You would have spent hours weaving, knitting, sewing, quilting, or cooking for your large family.

If you had been a man of 1840, and musically inclined, you no doubt would have belonged to the first brass band organized in Highland county. The time you went in the delegation sent by Hillsboro to Columbus when General Harrison was to speak at a big mass meeting, was something always to talk about. You sat in the yellow bandwagon drawn by four prancing horses and followed by horsemen with provisions. Then came Colonel Armsted Doggett with his log cabin on wheels, and after that many voters in wagons. Do you remember how it rained all the way and you were feeling depressed; and just as you entered Columbus some one shouted, *"Play Hail to the Chief?"* Well, the Hillsboro band was the only one of 14 visiting bands that could play the tune. Your spirits rose with your pride and the rain was ignored.

Climbing up the years to about 60 years ago, when the days of the carriages with the fringes on top were at hand, you might have been a guest in the elegant Gardner home on South High street, when the Judge's young daughter, Grace, just home from travel and study in Europe, gave a recital. Her clothes, plumed hats, parasols, and fans were gorgeous creations. Her whirlwind courtship and brief marriage with a prominent attorney, Ulric Sloane, formed a love story for the book.

Miss Gardner opened a studio in Cincinnati where she found success and prominence in the musical world as a teacher of voice and a composer. In her waning years she returned to Hillsboro accompanied by an intimate woman friend, a Dr. Edmiston.

Dr. Edmiston was short and tubby and wore a man's hat and coat and carried a man's cane. She puffed big cigars in public and swore as roundly as any man. One of her hobby's was needlework and she was meticulous about the colors she chose for embroidering. She was conceded to be very intellectual however, and folks said that the men doctors were just jealous of her. She claimed to have invented a secret process that would take nicotine out of tobacco but she died without divulging her secret.

Both women died in poverty. The lovely Gardner home and its beautiful furnishings and keepsakes were sold at public auction that the once feted darling of Hillsboro might be provided for in the Methodist Home for the Aged in Cincinnati.

Sixty years ago you might have followed the band all the way to the town celebrations at Eagle Spring, owned by my grandfather, Wesley Copes, now the James Hogsett farm, one mile south on the New Market pike. This land was once favored by David Hays for the site for Hillsboro. A favorite gathering place for young and old, Eagle Spring offered many amusements. There, in the summer, was a band stand for the Hillsboro Band decked out in splendid uniforms; a platform for dancing; and a pretty lake (they called it *"the pond"*) for boat riding in summer and ice skating in winter. In the spring there were two large sugar camps where maple sugar was boiled down in huge-iron pots in the open and you could have all you wanted for maple sugar fudge or taffy; and there was no rationing.

Before the coming of the movies you might have attended a lantern show at a schoolhouse or church. Colored slides were put in the lantern and the pictures reflected on a screen. A lecturer explained the slides and for variety a pretty young girl usually sang when the slides depicting a popular song of the day were shown.

Forty or fifty years ago, Circus Day was the most eagerly anticipated day of the springtime. Big name circuses played Hillsboro like John Robinson's big three ring show. Advance men billed the town and fortunate ones obtained *"comps,"* (complimentary tickets). You couldn't sleep all night for listening for the train's low whistle before dawn that meant the train was pulling in. You were one of the town *"kids"* who threw your clothes on and ran breathlessly down the street maybe to clamber up the side of a freight train on the siding where you could look down upon the unloading, which in itself was a big show. Everyone came to town and the streets were lined with people waiting for the parade, and people standing on tops of flat roofs, or sitting in window sills of upstairs windows, all waiting for the parade. The young fry of the town sold lemonade at stands on the street corners.

The big elephants with signs of leading merchants on their sides, (*"V. E. Morgan, the West End grocer,"* one sign read), the clowns running alongside the parade and keeping folks in an uproar with their antics, the pretty ladies in glittering costumes gracefully riding beautiful horses, the colorful band wagon and the bandmen in equally colorful uniforms, the cages with the animals, and last of all the calliope followed by admiring town youngsters. It was more like an enormous county fair that day.

Perhaps you will remember the day a small circus played Hillsboro on the commons on East South street, facing Johnson street, when a lion broke out of its cage, killed a pretty Shetland pony, and made for the street. Everyone flew for home and indoors, scarcely daring to breathe until the word was put out that the animal had been shot.

Then there were the minstrel shows and stock companies, playing at Bell's Opera House for a number of seasons about 35 years ago. Many of you will recall the curtain with the painted realistic scene of fierce and stalwart Indians standing erect on a high cliff looking down at a valley where cattle grazed beside a stream. One Indian was pointing out a settler's cabin in the distance. This awed you, but while you were engaged in staring at it, the orchestra struck up a popular piece and the show was ready to start.

You may remember the Shannon Stock Company best of all. Mrs. Shannon whom everyone familiarly called *"Ma Shannon"* emerged from behind the stage by way of a side door, descended into the orchestra pit and, seating herself at the piano, her ringed fingers rippled over the keys. The Shannons' daughter, Hazel, was always the heroine in the gripping melodramas and their son, Harry, Jr., played comedy roles and between acts did a song and dance number. *"Pa Shannon"* was the manager.

Many young Hillsboro hopefuls formed stock companies of their own and put on original melodramas in attics. The price of admission was 10 new common pins. One attic in Hillsboro still has the cast of characters scrawled in childish writing on a wall.

When Chautauquas came into vogue, a favorite spot for the pitching of the big tent was on the Webster school grounds. They were the big events of the summer season. Waving of handkerchiefs by the audience before the program began was called the *"Chautauqua salute."* Some nationally known artists played to Hillsboro audiences.

We could go on and on with stories of the people of Hillsboro to illustrate its history. Stories that bring smiles like the one where the old gentleman on East Main street washed his wig and left it on a window sill to dry. Birds made off with it and when the gentleman found it, it had been made into a bird's nest and young birds were nesting in it. Or stories of pride where folks tell about their ancestors being related to presidents of the United States, or to signers of the Declaration of Independence.

We would not have Hillsboro too perfect, nor yet too imperfect, only intensely human like the other towns and villages in the county. Like the rest of Highland county, the history as a whole of Hillsboro, county seat, has been good. May her future be as auspicious as her past and present!

HOAGLAND CROSSING: Population, about 25; Location, four miles west of Hillsboro on U. S. Route 50, near a small branch of Rocky Fork creek and intersected by the B. and O. railroad, in Liberty township. Unincorporated.

Hoagland Crossing was never platted nor intended for a town. It was named for a Hoagland family, people who settled here at an unknown date. It is a farming community.

The two-room school was abandoned a number of years ago. Children attend school at Hillsboro.

MADISON TOWNSHIP
GREENFIELD

GREENFIELD: Population, 4,228, 1944 census; Altitude, 912 feet above sea level; Location, 18 miles northeast of Hillsboro on U. S. Route 138, in the northeastern part of Highland county and Madison township, on the west bank of Paint creek, two miles from the Fayette county line; Intersected by State Routes 70, 28, 138 and 41. Incorporated.

General Duncan McArthur and his party of surveyors were laying off the College township road from Athens to Oxford in 1799 when General McArthur came upon a level green plain. The natural beauty of the place inspired him to select it as part of his share of the Virginia Military District. He planned to pattern a town on the plain, then a part of Ross county, similar to General Massie's Chillicothe and to name it for his boyhood home, Greenfield, in Erie county, Pennsylvania. It was not until 1802, however, that the plat of the town was recorded.

General McArthur hoped that this town would become a county seat when new counties were being formed. He donated a square for a court house and jail and a plot for a cemetery. His dream could not be realized because Greenfield was not near the center of Highland county when it was carved out, and a county seat must always be centrally located.

The first permanent settlers arrived in 1800. Job Wright, an eccentric North Carolinian, and inventor of a hair sieve used by the townspeople, was the first resident. His cabin stood on the site of the Harper Hotel. His first neighbors were friendly and peaceful Indians encamped on the west bank of Paint creek, near town.

Other first arrivals were John Coffey, Lewis Lutteral, Samuel Schooley, Joseph Parmer, James Curry, James Milligan, William Bell and Hugh Smart.

Hugh Smart, a public benefactor, and Charles Bell, *"the town scales of Greenfield,"* used to go together to Philadelphia, a journey requiring from six to seven weeks, to buy dry goods, iron, nails, steel, glassware, and other heavy goods which were transported to Greenfield by wagons and boats.

Mr. Bell, a natural and brilliant mathematician, could accurately calculate difficult problems mentally and was known far and near because of this.

Mr. Smart served as associate judge of the Common Pleas Court of Highland county, State Senator, stock holder and leader in the Marietta and Cincinnati railroad through Greenfield, benefactor of the Baptist church, builder of the first two-story brick house and also of a brick building for a grain elevator and grocery where the Peoples National Bank is situated.

Judge Mooney was Greenfield's first teacher. The school, made of light poles covered with rough clapboards, was built in 1810 and was situated on what is now the corner of Washington and North streets. Judge Mooney had taught previous to this, in 1803, in a log building just outside the town.

In 1811 a post office and popular tavern, *"The Traveller's Rest,"* were established. Ginseng, ashes, salt, and skins which had been used in place of real money were succeeded by real currency.

A temperance movement called the Murphy Temperance Movement marked the years 1829-1830 when prominent citizens attempted by means of meetings and moral suasion to convert people to the idea of temperance. The movement met with strenuous opposition, although pledges were signed in 1829 and for the next two or three years. An outgrowth of this was a raid upon the saloons in 1864. The women who led the movement were sued for destroying liquor containers. The third temperance movement in Greenfield occurred January 13, 1874, following the *"Mother"* Thompson Crusade in Hillsboro. These were the most exciting events in the history of Greenfield.

In 1875 the city building was constructed, the result of the organization 20 years earlier of a band of young men called the Shanghai Council. The purpose of the organization was municipal reform.

The first newspaper was the Paint Valley Spectator, 1844, edited by John Wright, a *"botanic and steam doctor,"* who believed in, and practiced, the use of herbs and steaming as a cure all for ailments.

Two brothers, Dr. Alexander Dunlap and Dr. Milton Dunlap, achieved fame when they performed the first surgical operation of ovarotomy in Ohio, an operation which helped to revolutionize surgery.

Dr. Alexander Dunlap was a member of the International Medical Congress in Philadelphia in 1876, vice-president of the American Medical Association in 1877, and a contributor to the literature of the medical profession.

Dr. Milton Dunlap attended 5,500 births during his practice of 55 years, and in 1890, when he died, four at whose births he had attended were pallbearers at his funeral. His daughter, the late Mrs. E. B. Watt, recalling the pioneer days of Greenfield, said:

"On days of special celebrations, the young men and boys of the village would gather at the public square and build hugh bonfires. In those days fireworks such as we have now were not known and "fireballs" were used. These were padded balls of cotton dipped in turpentine and ignited. The lads would throw them up and down the street. They looked like comets.

"I recall how we children (there were seven of us) used to help Pa get ready to make a call. He would first ask for his leggings,— wide cloth strips that he wound about his legs. Then he would take

his saddle-bags, go outside where his horse was waiting, mount, and go jogging off down the road. I still remember how we used to tie up the horse's tail."

Mrs. Watt said that the death rate among the younger people due to tuberculosis, was very high; that she and her sisters used to raid her father's medicine cabinet for small empty containers which they would fill with milk they took from cows pasturing in a field that is now a part of the Greenfield cemetery.

The same year that the brothers performed the surgical operation, the noted Greenfield Seminary was founded with Rev. J. G. Blair as its first teacher. The old seminary still stands on the pad factory grounds. Rev. Blair later moved to West Virginia where he became president of the Fairmont Normal School and editor of the West Virginia Educational Journal. Greenfield's first high school course was established in 1871 with Miss Kate Dwyer as principal.

The Methodist church was organized in 1804, the Presbyterian church in 1820, the Baptist church in 1829, and the African Methodist in 1843. The Catholic church was organized between 1840 and 1850, meeting in homes until 1854 when Archbishop Purcell appointed Rev. John B. O'Donoghue, of Fayetteville, to serve Greenfield; and in 1858 a stone church on South Second street was dedicated. The Church of Christ was organized in 1896 and in 1910 the United Brethren Society was formed.

Rev. Samuel Crothers, Presbyterian minister from 1820 to 1863, was one of Greenfield's most noted ministers. He was author of *"The Gospel of the Jubilee,"* and *"The Life of Abraham."* He died in Oswego, Illinois, in 1858.

Rev. John McClain, grandfather of Edward Lee McClain, was another noted minister. For fifty years he served the Greenfield Methodist church as its minister.

On the southeast corner of East Jefferson and Second streets is the site of the Knott Tavern, kept by Francis Knott, first man to be publicly whipped in Highland county. He was convicted by a jury of stealing two guineas near Leesburg in 1808 and was given 11 lashes on the bare back. This old territorial whipping law, framed in 1787, was repealed in 1815.

By 1880 the population had reached 2,104. The school census in 1888 was 745, 95 of which were colored.

Prior to and during the first World War, Price's Premier Band, directed by Prof. Ralph W. Price, was one of the most famous bands in southern Ohio. Prof. Price was the composer of *"Western World," "The Stadium," "Marching Men,"* and other military music; also sacred choir music.

Another band attaining note was a negro band, the Butler Cornet Band, often referred to as Hackley's Pepper Boxes. This band captured first prize in a band contest held at Chillicothe.

Greenfield is the birthplace of Otway Curry, poet, lawyer, and editor, who was born in a one-room log cabin on what is now the corner of First and South streets, on March 26, 1804. He was the son of Colonel James Curry, an officer in the Revolution and State representative of Ohio in 1812. Col. Curry's cabin home contained an excellent library which was visited by persons for miles around.

Otway Curry began writing poetry when a lad. He was 11 when the family moved to Marysville. His poems were published in the leading magazines of the day and in Coggershall's *"Poets and Poetry of the West."* He also composed songs.

He was editor of the *"Hesperian,"* a magazine, and of the Chillicothe Scioto Gazette; also of the *"Xenia Torchlight."* He was president of the Ohio Editorial Association. The Twentieth Century Club of Greenfield grew out of the Otway Curry Literary Club.

His poem, *"The Lost Pleiad,"* which appeared in McGuffey's Sixth Reader has been described by critics as *"sublime in conception, dignified in execution, and rates wth the classics."* It is his best remembered poem.

Another Greenfield man of note was Admiral Irvin who was born two miles west of Greenfield in 1870, the son of Henry and Anna Irvin. Admiral Irvin entered the U. S. Naval Academy at Annapolis, Maryland at the age of 18 and he did not retire until after 46 years of service. He was the only American naval officer wounded in the Battle of Manila Bay when, as Ensign of the BALTIMORE, he and six of his gun crew were injured when a Spanish shell struck the turret.

Major H. C. Blackburn, a famous criminal lawyer, was known throughout southern Ohio.

Prominent in the political life of the county and state today is the Honorable Albert Daniels who served two terms as Representative to the General Assembly for Highland county. He was mayor of Greenfield for two years, commander of the Department of Ohio of the D.A.V., National District Committeeman; and at the present time is our State senator.

Although Greenfield lies in a rich farming district of which it is the center, it early identified itself as an industrial center of the county. Ever since Job Wright invented his hair sieve, it seems that unwittingly he set a pace that was to endure.

T. F. Browder invented the Browder Life-Save Net; Fred Patterson founded the Greenfield Bus Body Company, makers of the Patterson-Greenfield automobile; James A. Harps founded the Harps Manufacturing Company, specializing in the Never-Fail Oil Can; Edward Lee McClain invented a horse collar pad and later improved it by adding a steel hook which was easily adjusted and eliminated frightening the animal. This culminated in the establishing of the American Pad and Textile Company, the largest of its kind in the world. Mr. McClain's greatest achievement was his gift of the county's costliest and most beautiful school plant to the village of Greenfield.

Once Greenfield was noted for the raising of fine Shetland ponies. One of the best county fairs in Ohio was held from the 1860's to the 1880's on the Greenfield Fair Grounds. Later Chautauquas were held on the grounds.

An amusement park flourished at the Island Grove Mill and mill dam, site of the first mill built in Greenfield, about 1894. People came from miles away for a day's outing which consisted of dances, picnics, Sunday School gatherings, band concerts, camp meetings, balloon ascensions, and boxing matches. The place was located about one-half mile north on U. S. 70, on Paint creek, along the D. T. and I. railroad.

More recent industries of Greenfield are the United States Shoe Corporation and the Blue Rock, Inc. Quarries. The latter industry, located about three miles north of Greenfield on State Route 73, was organized in 1929. It has a capacity of 759 tons daily and ships material to Michigan, Indiana, Kentucky, West Virginia, and eight counties in Ohio. Its products are crushed limestone, agricultural limestone, limestone sand, building rock, chicken grit, and washed concrete stone.

Bert Leaming who, at the age of 71, returned to Greenfield for a visit in 1941, came back to a modern town electrically lighted and with paved streets. Many years ago, as lamp lighter, he used to carry a five-foot ladder on his rounds and clean the wicks, fuel, and light 150 lanterns mounted on seven-foot poles to illuminate the village streets.

At midnight he would retrace his steps and extinguish the lamps except on moonlight nights when he slept *"right on through."*

Sometimes he would borrow his father's horse and ride from pole to pole to light or put out the lanterns to relieve himself of carrying the ladder and climbing up and down.

Leaming's day as lamp lighter ended when Greenfield acquired its water and light plant in the early 1890's and began using electric lights in 1893-94. He left Greenfield and went to Columbus where he became a cabinet maker.

Greenfield, like all the other places in Highland county, is packed with human interest stories and the thrilling record of the accomplishments of its people.

Highland county may well be proud of her *"green field"* of the Indian legend.

MARSHALL TOWNSHIP
HARRIETT
MARSHALL

HARRIETT: Population, about 40 or 50; Altitude, 992 feet above sea level; Location, 10 miles southeast of Marshall on a bend of a county highway, 2 miles south of Marshall, in Marshall township. Unincorporated.

Harriett was first named Cravensville in honor of Benjamin Cravens, an early settler, but the Post Office Department changed the name to Harriett because another Cravensville already existed in Ohio. It was also known for years as Squashtown because of a mammouth squash which grew in the center of the hamlet and was displayed on a front-yard fence.

Harriett was never platted as a town. Like Topsy in *"Uncle Tom's Cabin,"* somehow it *"just grew,"* and its history is obscure.

One of the most unusual churches in the county, the Mennonite Brethren in Christ Church was organized a number of years before a church was built in 1905. It retains its foot washing rituals and is the only church of its denomination in the county.

Harriett once had a small frame one-room school and was noted for its production of good teachers. Henry G. Williams, a well-known educator who became president of Wilmington College in Clinton county, was a product of this tiny country school. There is no school in Harriett today and children attend school at nearby Marshall.

Interspersing a small number of residences are a store, a garage and blacksmith shop, and the church.

MARSHALL: Population, about 119; Altitude, 1,013 feet above sea level; Location, 8 miles southeast of Hillsboro on State Route 124, and intersected by a county-township road leading to Carmel, on an elevation near the central part of Marshall township. Unincorporated.

Marshall was platted as a town by William Simmons, June 17, 1817 and first named West Liberty with the nick name of Slabtown. In 1836 the name was changed to Marshall by permission of the State Legislature, the name Marshall originating out of admiration for John Marshall (1755-1835), Chief Justice of the United States, and an authority on the interpretation of the Constitution.

Bigger Head and family from Barren county, Kentucky, arrived at what was to become the site of Marshall, about 1800. The first sermon was delivered in the township in his home in June, 1802, by Rev. David Young, a traveling Methodist preacher. Bigger Head's house was a temporary fort for the settlers in this community when a false alarm was spread that the Indians were uprising following the murder of Captain Herrod and Chief Waw-wil-away. Indians returned to this community to hunt and fish for some time after they had been relocated on western reservations. In 1837, land owned by William and Sarah Head and John and Susan Butters was added to the village proper.

A frame Methodist church built in Marshall about 1840 was replaced by a brick building in 1855. A Presbyterian church was organized in 1851 in a meeting house; and in 1864 a Christian Union church was organized and a frame church built in 1866.

A post office was established in 1844 and Matthew Sypherd was the first postmaster. Another post office was established on the Turkey road nearby and named Turkey Post Office. Both post offices were abandoned and Marshall is served by rural mail delivery out of Hillsboro.

The first store was opened by Edward Burns about 1822. Several tanneries flourished in Marshall's early history. Thomas Dick, Marshall's first teacher, kept an underground railroad station for slaves journeying northward from the Ohio river. His son, C. G. Dick, was the first white child born in the township. C. G. Dick's son, Thomas H. Dick, who died a few years ago, at the age of 95, and whose home near Marshall had been a station on the underground railroad, remembered clearly incidents of those days when he was a child.

"Father was an ardent abolitionist and our home was a haven for runaway slaves. He never turned one away and I recall him many times starting with a small, weary, frightened group of them toward Rocky Fork and Paint creeks to what is now U. S. Route 50. He always took our horse, "Baldy Mare" along for the women to ride. When anyone was heard to say, "There goes Campbell Dick's Baldy Mare," that meant Father was known to be escorting his dusky friends to the next station."

Many of the slaves, Mr. Dick recalls, usually came from the Wickersham home a few miles away in Sinking Spring, on the old Zane trace, where they had been hidden in the fields near the house to await a favorable time for removal. Beyond the Dick's, to the north, were three other important stations, the Moses Tumbleson home, the Jonathan Van Pelt home, and the Richard Lucas home on Churn creek.

Mr. Dick says that many of the slaves harbored in their home were intelligent persons. One, a large, fleshy Negro, always carried his Bible which he treasured and he spent his time reading it while sitting safely beside a calaboose. (A calaboose was a secret closet built in the walls of the upper story of the house for the purpose of hiding slaves.) Another Negro was an eccentric, sorely crippled fellow who was well-armed and who lingered for several days as though loath, for some reason, to leave.

A railroad projected from Hillsboro to a short distance below Marshall was abandoned before completion, but it had been the intention of extending it to the coal fields at Jackson. It was hoped that it would open up this part of Ohio and stimulate the growth of towns along the way.

Dens of huge rattlesnakes are said to have infested the hollows along the sloping road into Marshall from Hillsboro, in the early days.

A little Marshall girl named Ann once tied a cow to the pulpit of the Methodist church in Marshall in the spirit of fun, many years ago, and incurred the displeasure of the townspeople. She later became a prominent Highland county teacher.

Marshall's chief industry today is farming. It has three churches, the Methodist, Presbyterian, and Christian Unon; one store and filling station. A modern school plant for grade and high school pupils stands on the lot where May and Katie Madden's father, John Madden, kept a blacksmith shop many years ago.

This was the birthplace of Dusty (Thurman) Miller's beloved *"Uncle Bill,"* whose life story he tells in his book, *"Uncle Bill,"* published at Wilmington in 1943.

"Uncle Bill" was born William Hampton Miller in a farmhouse near Marshall, April 2, 1863. His father was Dr. John Mortimer Miller and his mother was Mary Louisa Thurman Miller. His grandfather, Aaron Miller, was a Virginian, and one of seven brothers all with Bible names, who migrated to Ohio in 1832.

Uncle Bill began teaching school in Pike county at the age of 16. He taught other schools later in Adams, Highland, Warren, and Clinton counties. He was married to Emma Davis, February, 1885. He studied law and was admitted to the bar in 1895, serving as prosecuting attorney of Clinton county 1899-1904 when he resigned to become assistant attorney general of Ohio. He became noted for his trying of riot cases in Springfield and Newark. In 1912 he served as special counsel in the federal department of justice and in 1913 formed the firm of Miller, Thompson, and Dunbar. He was general counsel for the Pullman company until his death which occurred at his Highland county farm home, Sunrise Acres.

Another distinguished Marshall citizen was Judge Oliver Hughes who was born at Marshall December 3, 1863, the son of John L. and Elizabeth Carlisle Hughes. His wife was the former Miss Elizabeth Watts.

Judge Hughes was appointed adjutant general of the State of Ohio by Governor Pattison. He was appointed a member of the Railroad Commission by Governor Harris and reappointed by Governer Harmon and Governor Cox, serving until December 15, 1915 when he resigned. He also served on the Public Utilities Commission of Ohio. His enormous old brick residence stands on an eminence overlooking the village.

NEW MARKET
NEW MARKET
SHACKLETON

NEW MARKET: Population, about 126; Altitude, 1,137 feet above sea level; Location, 6 miles southwest of Hillsboro, on U. S. Route 62, in the south central part of New Market township. Unincorporated.

New Market was the first county seat of Highland county; and it is the oldest village.

Henry Massie, younger brother of General Nathaniel Massie, had come from Virginia shortly after the founding of Manchester, and had been engaged by his brother as an assistant surveyor. While his brother was busy with the settlement of Chillicothe, in 1796, Henry explored and surveyed lands on the headwaters of Brushcreek. In the spring of 1797 he came upon the tract of land upon which New Market is situated and was so impressed by the attractive lay of the land that he decided to found a town. This town, he was confident, would outshine Chillicothe in Ross county.

His small party consisting of himself, Oliver Ross and his 15-year-old daughter, Rebecca, Robert Huston, and unknown others, camped near the site of the proposed town while it was being surveyed and platted. It was planned after Philadelphia, the plat covering 400 acres. Copies of the plat were sent to Massie's friends in Maysville, Manchester, and Chillicothe, with alluring descriptions, with the result of a tide of immigration this way. By the fall of 1799, six or seven cabins had been built.

Here, in this land of plenty, where bear, venison, wild turkeys and smaller game abounded, William Wishart kept a tavern in his cabin. He held the first state office held by a Highland countian, that of Justice of the Peace, an office highly respected. He also was postmaster when a weekly pack-mail line between Chillicothe and Cincinnati was innovated.

The Ross and Huston families, Jonathan Berryman, Jacob Barnes, George Barrere, David Hays, and a Mr. McCafferty were among the first New Market citizens.

George Barrere and family who arrived in the spring of 1802, came from Anderson's Prairie in Clinton county where they had immigrated from Kentucky. Purchasing a house from Jacob Eversole, Mr. Barrere opened a tavern on the post road. This house was of hewed logs, with a cabin roof, and had one room. Mr. Barrere improved his property by adding another room and a sort of attic reached by a ladder. Barrere's Tavern, opposite Wishart's cabin, was the most popular inn round about.

Jonathan Berryman, who selected his home south of the town

plat of New Market, had brought with him from New Jersey a careful selection of apple and peach seeds. He lost no time in planting the apple seeds, walking to Manchester for manure from the cow yards there, and carrying it home in sacks on his back to bed the seeds in. His Learing apple orchard bore abundant fruit as did the peach trees he planted. He also began the cultivation of bees. When Wishart quit his commission as postmaster of New Market Berryman was appointed his successor and continued his position for 20 years.

Highland county's first tanyard was established in New Market by John Compton from Kentucky, in 1803. That same year Michael Stroup, the unusual hatter, and Polly Walker were married. Polly had come with her mother and stepfather, Joseph Myers from the Falls of Paint, to New Market, in 1801. Polly was one of 14 children in the home.

That autumn Rebecca Ross, who had come to New Market as keeper of the camp for her father and the surveyors under Massie, was married to George Parkinson.

The first storekeeper in New Market was Adam Barngruber, from Kentucky, who arrived from Kentucky in 1805, with a four horse wagon and team. With him was a Dutchman named Fritz Miller. It was about this time that James B. Finley the *"New Market devil,"* became a member of the Methodist church and started on his career as itinerant evangelist. His father, Robert W. Finley was a teacher of Latin, Greek, and Hebrew in his cabin school.

This was *"the year of nuts,"* when a remarkable abundance of nuts thickly scattered the land of New Market and surrounding territory; the time when weary trips were made to the Scioto salt works for precious salt; the period in which bark-colored linsey, wool hats and cow skin shoes were superseded by the leather hunting shirt and breeches, moccasins, and coonskin hat.

On May 16, 1805, the first special court held in the county was held at New Market. The three associate judges elected by the legislature, Richard Evans, John Davidson, and Jonathan Berryman, presided, with David Hays clerk pro tem. Court was held in the woods with the judges seated on a long puncheon. There were many interruptions. One man on horseback rode into the *"court-room,"* brandishing a bottle of whiskey under the judges' noses, and invited them to drink with him. Five or six fights took place while court was in session. Dan Evans, Highland county's first sheriff, maintained order with great difficulty.

George Barrere was elected Senator and John Gossett, Representative, to the State Legislature.

Removal of the county seat to a more central location by an act of legislature, was favored by some, but there was strenuous opposition by many. John Kerr, who owned large tracts of land about the town, had sold lots to people with the assurance that New

Market was central and permanent. As *"leader and defender of the people's rights,"* he demanded that the citizens raise money and erect public buildings for the county at their own expense. This, he said, would solve the problem.

"The great knocking down," described elsewhere was the result. Commissioners appointed by the legislature under the directorship of young David Hays, set about to select a new site. After some deliberation, the town site of Hillsboro was selected. Early in 1807 New Market ceased to be the county seat.

The first churches were the camp meetings in the woods, the ministers itinerant evangelists of different faiths. Then the Baptists, Methodists, and Presbyterians met in the homes of the pioneers and organized the churches. The Presbyterians held church meetings in the first log school until they built their church in 1840. The Methodists, who organized soon after 1800, built their church in 1853. In 1837, 16 Baptists met under an apple tree to constitute the Baptist church.

By 1840, the population of New Market was 212. By 1870 it had decreased to 143.

Not much of the old New Market remains today. The large brick Grant McConnaughey residence in the southern part of the village was once the *"Ohio Tavern."* At the northern edge was the *"New Market Inn."*

The well opposite the school building, which was once the first jail in the county, has been filled in. Here during the day prisoners were incarcerated but at night they were taken by officers to their homes for safe keeping.

At *"God's Garden,"* a scenic spot two miles southeast of New Market, are found boulders left by the glacier. Indian relics were found in abundance until recent years.

New Market is a farming community. There is a modern grade school. High school pupils attend school at Hillsboro.

SHACKLETON: Population, about 10; Location, about 5 miles west of Hillsboro on the Danville road.

Shackleton was never platted nor intended for a town. A Mr. Shackleton settled here at an unknown date and a settlement grew up around his residence and blacksmith shop. It was believed that the proximity of the railroad nearby might result in the development of a village or town but the dream was never realized.

PAINT TOWNSHIP
BOSTON
NEW PETERSBURG
RAINSBORO

BOSTON: Population, about 105; Altitude, 1,038 feet above sea level; Location, 6 miles east of Hillsboro on U. S. Route 50, in Paint township. Unincorporated.

Boston was platted November 7, 1840 by Robert Moore, Noah Glasscock, and Abraham Pennington, and it is believed that they named it for Boston, Mass.

When a post office was established the name was changed to Dallas Post Office to differentiate it from Owensville, Ohio Post Office which at that time was called Boston Post Office, too. Later the name, Dallas, was changed back to Boston. The first merchant was Joseph Glasscock.

Boston has a two-room grade school. High school pupils attend school at Hillsboro. There is a Methodist church. A Christian church, erected at the south edge of the hamlet was abandoned and torn down leaving only an old cemetery to mark the spot. Boston is a farming community.

It is within a short driving distance to the Seven Caves.

RAINSBORO: Population, about 252; Altitude, 969 feet above sea level; Location, 10 miles east of Hillsboro on U. S. Route 50, in Paint township. Incorporated.

Rainsboro was platted by its proprietors, George Rains, Garrett Cope (or Copes), and David Davis, October 15, 1830, and named for the Rains family. Although Aaron Rains sold a few groceries such as tea, sugar, coffee, and spices in his house, the first merchant was Henry W. Spargur who opened a store in 1832. He was also appointed the postmaster when a post office was established in 1832. By 1840 the population was 115.

The early settlers of Rainsboro were from Virginia, New Jersey, North Carolina, and Pennsylvania. Near Rainsboro was born United States Senator Joseph Benson Foraker who served two terms as Governor of Ohio. In a corner store room of Rainsboro, now a restaurant, a notorious outlaw, Robert McKimie, established a dry goods store with money he had stolen in a stage coach hold up in the Black Hills.

Near Rainsboro is an old three-story building known as Barrett's Mills, on a small branch which empties into Rocky Fork creek. It was built in 1805 by Jesse Baldwin. Mr. Baldwin built a combination saw-mill, grist-mill, and a carding and fulling mill, to which the woolen-mill was added in 1820. In later years the property passed into the hands of Dr. Boyd, a grandfather of the late Col. L. B. Boyd of Hillsboro, who enlarged and improved the mill. Dr. Boyd sold the mill to David M. Barrett in 1860. The mill was in continuous operation until after the Civil War and was not completely abandoned until about 45 years ago.

The old dam, which originally was about 20 feet high, was built out of rocks quarried by hand and placed on the dam by hand. Traces of the mill race which connected the dam and the mill still exist. While in operation a gate was installed but at night when the mill ceased operation for the day, it was closed. A wooden trestle supported the runway to the mill and the gears on the outside of the wheel were hand made.

George L. Garrett, who was reared in this neighborhood, wore suits tailored from cloth in these mills, when he was a boy. He described the beautiful blankets woven there and the huge 20-foot overshot waterwheel slowly turning under the weight of the flow of water. It is claimed that Joseph B. Foraker worked in this mill in his youth. The mill, now used for a tobacco shed, contains some of the original machinery and the sign *"Woolen Mills"* still adorns the front of the building.

The story of the Spargur families of the Rainsboro and New Petersburg localities is representative of the many interesting family histories of Highland county.

Mrs. Margaret Spargur Swadley, former postmistress of Rainsboro and mother of Ruth Hughes Carroll (Mrs. Charles Carroll) of Hillsboro, traced and wrote the history of the Spargur families. She said that until she investigated the only thing she knew about the Spargurs was that they had come from Mount Airy, North Carolina.

Mrs. Swadley said:

A man by the name of Wolfspargur obtained a land grant in Lancaster county, Pennsylvania, in 1734, and in 1744 was naturalized under the name of John Wolfspargur. Seven persons whose names were entered in the Certificate were foreigners and of the people called Quakers, who only affirmed as they had some scruples about taking the oath; as did our great grandmother, Christiana, whose maiden name was Frey.

It is interesting to note that the Freys came to America in 1734 as recorded in the Moravian records. Everything indicates that both families came over at the same time from Alsace. They spoke the German language. The records of the Reformed Church at Campbellstown, Pennsylvania, show they were among the pillars of the church. This ancestor's record carries eligibility to membership in the D.A.R. He was probably too old to fight but he gave assistance to the Revolution. This John Wolfspargur was the father of John Wolfspargur who was born in 1754 in North Carolina and died in Ohio in 1840, buried at upper Quaker Cemetery.

I have brought you from the Wolf Mountains in Alsace through Pennsylvania, Virginia, to North Carolina.

They lived among the Moravians in North Carolina and many strange entries are made in the Diary of the Moravians and kept in the Archives at Winston-Salem. They read as follows:

One, Anne Barbara Frey, who was born in Alsace, April 5, 1696, married in her twentieth year. She had twelve children. She is my great great great great grandmother. The Savior granted her desire that she might be spared a long and painful illness, and that she might be taken quickly, which happened on January 9, 1768 in the forenoon. Only a couple of hours previously she had been spinning when she was taken with a severe chill and great pain in the chest. The last verse she had been singing was, *"I am melted unto tears when I sing of Jesus' death."* Her age was 71 years.

In Volume 111, page 110, of the Moravians Records, Valentine Frey, son of A. B. and our great great great grandfather, on February 23, 1776 with others signed the oath of allegiance to the colonies, gave up his gun and refreshed Captain Fornes and his company with food and drink.

One more entry in the Moravian records, April 28, 1777, states thus:

We went to Christian Frey's, (Christian was a brother of Valentine Frey and our great great uncle), and they told us what danger they had been in. Four rascals had broken into their house and behaved in a murderous fashion, and if their dear Savior had not protected them their lives would not have been safe.

With a large stone they broke the paneling out of the cupboard and with a sword cut the wood around the locks taking all the money and whatever else they wished.

After Christian had received another cut on the head he tried to get out of the house, but was given a blow on the chest with a gun by the guard at the door so that he became faint. Finally he escaped from them and raised an alarm when they fired after him, but God so ordered it that he was not hit. Poor Sarah, who had hidden behind the door, sank to her knees when she heard the shot, and when the rascals had left, she was happy to find her husband still living. Here appears a comment by W. M. Creasy: *"It would be interesting to know where John Wolfspargur was all this time."*

We have the record of another ancestor, Peter Binckele, born in the village of Guckensburg in Canton Bern, Switzerland, March 2, 1704. He was our great great great grandfather. In his sixth year he had to seek support from outsiders, so great was his poverty. In his 13th year his mother moved to Alsace. In the year 1736 he came to America and settled at Philadelphia. In 1748 his wife died after a married life of about 24 years, blessed with 14 children. In 1749 he married Maria Margaretha Schmell, and in his second marriage God gave him nine children, making 23 in all.

Leaving these entries we pick up the wanderings of the Spargurs.

Our ancestor, John W. Spargur who came from North Carolina in 1833 owned large tracts of land there and many transactions are recorded. The name he used until 1802 was John Wolfenberger, then it changed to John W. Spargur. The circumstances which caused the changing of the name is thus related: Shortly after John Wolfenberger moved to North Carolina, the sheriff of the county in which he resided, was sent through the county, as was the custom in those days, to impanel a jury. Wolfenberger was among those elected by the sheriff. He wrote the name, John W. Spargur. The name was adopted by Mr. Wolfenberger from that time forth.

John W. Spargur, as he now wrote his name, was the father of nine children. Hannah, Nancy, Sallie, William, and John married and remained in North Carolina. Reuben never married. In the fall of 1804, Joseph and Reuben Spargur, two of the sons, emigrated from North Carolina and settled in the present county of Highland, southwest of the town of New Petersburg, where Joseph made the necessary improvements for the temporary comfort of himself, aged 25, his wife, Rachel, aged 18, and John W. Jr., aged 19 months.

Joseph was a millwright by trade and followed his profession when he could get employment. He built Worley's mill near New Petersburg, and had occasion to be away from home quite frequently. The Indians were passing almost daily, which alarmed Rachel very much. At night when Joseph happened to be away with his work, she always barricaded the cabin in the best manner she could, and armed with two loaded rifles and an ax, and butcher knife, and her dog close, did she feel sufficiently secure enough to sleep.

In 1815 the brothers sold their mill and Reuben went back to North Carolina, while Joseph packed his goods and moved, cutting a road through the forest as he went to the Rocky Fork of Paint creek. There he built a saw mill, a grist mill, and a wool-carding and fulling mill. He also built a substantial brick dwelling house, yet in use and occupied at this date, 1937, by H. D. Beaver, his great grandson and family. He was Orpha Upp's grandfather.

Joseph W. Spargur was the father of 18 children, all reared to manhood and womanhood. All were present at the death of their father who died in 1845, aged 64 years.

Phillip Spargur, a brother of Joseph, came from North Carolina in 1809 and settled on a large tract of land near the present site of New Petersburg. He brought with him his wife and 10 children. Aunt Nancy Redkey was his granddaughter.

In 1833, Henry W. Spargur, another brother, came from North Carolina and settled in the home now cocupied by Carl Phillips. He and his bride and his venerable father made the entire trip on horseback. What hopes, what fears, what hardships that couple suffered! They overcame all obstacles and lived to ripe old age raising a Christian, law-abiding family of 12 children, thus making 40 children in all for the three brothers, Joseph, Phillip, and Henry.

When the three families would happen to get together on the same day they would have a reunion of their very own. So in 1875, while my Uncle Joe Spargur was visiting with Aunt Nancy Redkey, they planned a reunion. It was not only for the Spargurs but for all who wished to come. The first year was quite a success but grew until in 1886, the crowd was estimated at 5,000 to 6,000 people. They came in road wagons, in buggies, on horseback, and on foot. Not a single automobile!

Dinners were spread on the grass in the shade of the trees. What fun to see how gracefully some of the women sat down on the ground! We had a very high class band that came from Greenfield in a four-horse band wagon painted red, with gold stripings, the men in uniforms, and the horses with red plumes in their bridles. We did not see anything like that in those days only at county fairs and at the Spargur reunion.

The date was always the Saturday or Sunday nearest the 20th of August since that is the anniversary of Joseph W. Spargur's arrival in the Northwest Territory, August 20, 1804.

Thus from Europe to America — from 1696 to 1937 — we have the Spargurs; and it is fitting that at this time, we note their prestige throughout the centuries and honor their memory.

The Spargur Reunion Grounds were situated at the western edge of Rainsboro. From 1906 to 1929 this was also where the Highland County Agricultural Society Fair was held.

PAINT P. O.: About 13 miles east of Hillsboro on U. S. 50, near the junction of Rocky Fork and Paint creeks, a post office and general store were established in the 1800's. The Hope families were among the first settlers and the general store was operated by the Hopes. Hulitt Hope was the last proprietor of this store.

A hotel, started in 1877 by A. J. Pummell, was under his management until 1881 when it was taken over by Edward Hope.

The history of this locality is closely interwoven with adjoining Ross county, when mills, forges, and distilleries dotted the creek banks.

There are summer cottages along the Caves road and good fishing waters.

NEW PETERSBURG: Population, about 239; Altitude, 956 feet above sea level; Location, 10 miles northeast of Hillsboro and 3 miles east of Rainsboro, in Paint township.

New Petersburg was platted June 19, 1817 by Peter Weaver, the proprietor, and named for him. The majority of the first settlers were Virginians.

The settlement thrived so rapidly that by 1830 it was the trading center for the eastern part of the county with a population of 227, and with stores, churches, schools, the Union Academy, and two taverns. John Hulitt and Enoch Overman were co-owners of the first store. By 1840, the population had increased to 278.

The first school building costing $69.00 was built on Philip Spargur's farm and Abner Thornton was hired to teach at a salary of $11.00 a month.

New Petersburg was incorporated as a town by an act of the Legislature, February 4, 1848. When a railroad was projected through this part of the county it was expected to intersect New Petersburg, but the citizens were disappointed. Naturally the impetus was given Greenfield when the railroad intersected it, just when it was believed that New Petersburg would grow into a large railroad town.

Family settlements marked early New Petersburg. Among them were the Lucas and Cowgill settlements. Six Lucas brothers and their families immigrated from Pennsylvania and constituted what was known as the Lucas settlement. Henry Cowgill and his large family from Virginia were so well known for their hospitality and their prominence in church and civic affairs that their home became known as the Cowgill settlement.

The last of the full-blooded Indians of Highland county are believed to have lived on the Philip Rhodes farm near New Petersburg, where they remained unmolested on land provided for them by Mr. Rhodes until they were offered horses in exchange for their land, and, accepting, departed for a western reserve.

About one mile north is Sally Carson's creek which empties into Rattlesnake creek, named for a pioneer New Petersburg girl whose story was never preserved. Near this branch was an Indian burial ground, the graves hemmed by small bits of stones, all now obliterated.

About 4 miles east is John McMullen's noted Deer Park, where once a large salt lick attracted numerous deer and Indians. A beaten Indian trail once wound through a gap between rock banks and cliffs, and under one cliff was a famed bears' den.

New Petersburg is a farming community and manufactures feed and fertilizer. It has 2 churches, the Methodist and Presbyterian. Its modern brick school house accommodates grade pupils, and high school pupils attend school at Greenfield. There is no post office but New Petersburg has rural mail delivery service.

PENN TOWNSHIP
CAREYTOWN
SAMANTHA

CAREYTOWN: Population, about 25; 1,155 feet above sea level; Location, about 10 miles north of Hillsboro on a crossroads connecting with U. S. Route 50 and U. S. Route 62.

Careytown was never platted as a town. It was named in honor of the family of Charles Newton Carey, son of David McPherson Carey whose father, Samuel Carey, was born in Virginia. About 1840, Charles bought 33½ acres of land from his father and when his father died, in 1885, he purchased the interest of the other heirs.

Careytown residents attend neighborhood churches and children attend grade and high school at New Vienna, in Clinton county. There are no stores.

Close to Careytown is a place of special interest, the Gist Settlement, referred to as Darktown on county atlasses, on a road extending from the highway through Careytown to U. S. Route 73.

Settled between 1815 and 1820 by emancipated slaves of Samuel Gist, a fabulously wealthy English benefactor, the few living descendants dwell on 208 acres of fine farm land, purchased for them by appointed trustees. This land must never be sold but is to remain in the possession of these Negroes forever. There is one church in the settlement, the Carthaginia Baptist church, an abandoned frame school house, and an interesting old cemetery where the freed slaves were buried. There are no stores.

SAMANTHA: Population, about 100; Altitude, 1,124 feet above sea level; Location, 6 miles north of Hillsboro on U. S. Route 62. Unincorporated.

David Kinzer, the owner and proprietor of this land, platted a town on it in 1945 and gave it the name of Beeson's Crossroads. He recorded the plat, July 31, 1845.

Tradition says the settlers were not satisfied with the name and decided to rename it in honor of the first girl to enter the crossroads store. A young girl by the name of Samantha came riding into the settlement on horseback and up to the store, hence the name, Samantha.

Samantha is an agricultural community. It has two churches, the Methodist and Friends; a centralized graded school with high school pupils attending school at Leesburg and Hillsboro; a township meeting house; and two stores.

SALEM TOWNSHIP
PRICETOWN
PULSE (HARWOOD)

PRICETOWN: Population, about 110; Altitude, 1,003 feet above sea level; Location, 12 miles southwest of Hillsboro on the Danville-Pricetown road on White Oak creek, in Salem township. Unincorporated.

Pricetown was platted for a town April 13, 1847 by Elijah, David, and Jane Faris, and Alexander Murphy. It was named in honor of Judge J. W. Price, of Hillsboro, a man greatly admired by the proprietors.

Before its platting, however, a number of settlements had been made, a saw and grist mill had been erected about 1830 by J. B. Faris, and a Universalist church established north of town. Abraham Welty opened the first store in the township in 1838 and a carding mill a year later. Aaron Eyler kept a tannery between 1844 and 1856.

The same year that Pricetown was platted, a temperance crusade against three liquor sellers, John Hastings, Sr., Thomas Cannon, and Anthony Hess, resulted in the curtailing of the sale of liquor.

Alexander Murphy built a flour mill west of town in 1849. In 1856 the Christian church was organized in the school house and a church built in 1857.

It is claimed that Pricetown and other parts of the township produced more school teachers than any other township in Highland county.

The industries of Pricetown are farming and milling. There is an elementary grade school and high school pupils attend school at Lynchburg. Mail is brought by rural free delivery since there is no post office.

An interesting place is Fort Salem, an unexplored Indian mound at the southwest edge of Pricetown where the legend has been handed down of a child named Lydia Osborne who was lost and wandered along White Oak creek in this vicinity. A scrap of her dress and places where she is believed to have slept were found. This was in the fall of 1802 when deer and wolves prowled about and were troublesome to the settlers.

Pricetown has given many important persons to Highland county and the United States. The most famous is Charles Gossett, son of the late Mr. and Mrs. Wyatt H. Gossett, who became governor of the state of Idaho.

Another resident of the Pricetown community who has had a very interesting life is Ira Gossett Hawk, son of W. H. and Grace Gossett Hawk, who resides on a 133 acre farm known as *"Plainview."*

At the age of 11 Gossett was struck with infantile paralysis and for nearly a year he lay on his back with his leg in a cast. With the aid of braces and crutches he learned to walk again. He was operated on again two years later and his leg sealed in a cast for the fifth time.

With the idea of a *"pleasant pastime,"* Gossett started publication of *"The Salem Echo,"* running off his first issue on April 8, 1938. The circulation grew until it numbered almost 2,000 subscribers in all 48 states and several foreign countries. A few months ago the paper suspended publication after having won, consistently, honors as the best junior newspaper in the United States.

Gossett, who was a graduate of Wilmington College this year, was forced to abandon his career as editor of *"The Salem Echo,"* because of his many activities.

PULSE (HARWOOD): Population, about 8; Altitude, 988 feet above sea level; Location, 14 miles west of Hillsboro on a crossroads in Salem township.

When a small settlement formed around the church which was built here in 1880, it was called Harwood Methodist Chapel for the first minister of the church, a Rev. Harwood. When a post office was established it then became known as Pulse for the Pulse families.

All that remains of this settlement is the abandoned post office, the church, and two or three houses near the crossroads. This is a farming community.

Small and insignificant as it may seem, Pulse is rich in local Americana. Elizabeth Gossett Cochran's story is representative of this. Mrs. Cochran will celebrate her 95th birthday on November 29th of this year.

Her grandparents were a Mr. and Mrs. Rader who immigrated to Highland county from Pennsylvania. They settled near Harwood in a little cabin in a clearing. Years later, Mrs. Rader's request was carried out to bury her when she died beneath an old cherry tree she loved across the road from her first Highland county home.

Mrs. Cochran's parents, Laura and Joseph Gossett, were both natives of the Pulse community. They were the parents of eight children, three boys and five girls. Elizabeth is the sole survivor of this family.

Her childhood home was made of logs, hued from native timber. Across the road from this cabin was another small log house in which they made their flannels and linens for all their clothing. Obtaining the rolls from the factory at Hillsboro, Aunt Lib, as she came to be familiarly called, would spin and make the flax thread and wind it on the rolls. The flannel was dyed various shades by means of home-made dyes. Most of her dresses were red and blue barred, her favorite design.

Mrs. Cochran was the mother of six children, four of whom are living. She has 12 grandchildren and 15 great grandchildren. She makes her home with her daughter, Mrs. Verda Belle Savage, and her granddaughter, Mrs. John Dole, near Buford.

UNION TOWNSHIP
FAIRVIEW
RUSSELL
SHARPSVILLE
WILLETTSVILLE

FAIRVIEW: Population, about 37; Altitude, 1,026 feet above sea level; Location, 6 miles west of Hillsboro on State Route 50, in Union township. Unincorporated.

Jonah Van Pelt, Justice of the Peace, platted Fairview on land he owned, March 21, 1845. He recorded the plat March 22. The name Fairview is believed to have been derived from its literal meaning, *"fair view."*

Fairview is a farming community and the Wilkin Flour Mill manufactures flour. Children attend school at Hillsboro.

The Church of Christ, Fairview's one church, was built in 1856. The Barnes cemetery at the western edge of the hamlet developed out of the Barnes family burial plot begun in 1807. It is now a tri-township cemetery,—Union, Dodson, and Hamer.

RUSSELL: Population, about 40; Altitude, 1,054 feet above sea level; Location, 7 miles northeast of Hillsboro, on county road one mile east of U. S. Route 50 at Fairview. Unincorporated.

Russell was the name given this part of Highland county in honor of a family by the name of Russell, January 4, 1854. The land belonged to Asa R. Butler.

A Methodist church established in 1830 was called Oldaker Chapel in honor of Isaac Oldaker who was instrumental in the reorganization and rebuilding of the church.

The B. and O. railroad runs through this hamlet which consists of little more than a store, residences, and the church. A two-room grade school beside this church was abandoned in recent years. Children attend school at Lynchburg.

Here, until his death in 1935 lived Dr. Benjamin Granger, who had been a surgeon in the Civil War, and who was one of the last of the county's *"old fashioned country doctors."*

SHARPSVILLE: Population, about 25; Altitude, 1,077 feet above sea level; Location, 7 miles northwest of Hillsboro on the Willettsville pike, a county road. Unincorporated.

Sharpsville was never platted for a town and received its name from a family named Sharp. An unknown number of years ago, a small store and a Methodist church were established.

The chief industries are farming and quarrying. Sharpsville children attend school at Lynchburg.

WILLETTSVILLE: Population, about 50; Altitude, 1,111 feet above sea level; Location, 6 miles northwest of Hillsboro, on the Willettsville pike, a county road, in Union township. Unincorporated.

Willettsville was named for the purpose of securing a post office in the township. It was named in honor of John Willett who bought the Baylis Shepherd store building and opened up a store in it. The post office was in the store and the first post master was Alfred Johnson. It was a connecting link on the mail route from Hillsboro to Lebanon.

Children attend school at Lynchburg. Residents attend church at Mt. Olive, Dunn's Chapel, and Sharpsville.

The chief industries are farming and quarrying. The American Asphalt Rock Co., a large quarry, is operated close to Willettsville.

A Baptist church once stood beside a cemetery near Willettsville on the Anderson State road. It was believed to have been built about 1812. George McDaniel was one of its first ministers. The congregation scattered, finally the building itself deteriorated and disappeared, and all that remains to mark the spot is the old cemetery.

WASHINGTON TOWNSHIP
BERRYSVILLE
FOLSOM
PROSPECT

BERRYSVILLE: Population, about 75; 1,045 feet above sea level; Location, 6 miles southeast of Hillsboro on State Route 73, in Washington township. Unincorporated.

Berrysville was platted as a town in March, 1846, by Amos Sergeant and named for the Berryman family which was quite prominent in the history of Highland county. A number of homes had been established in the township prior to the founding of Berrysville.

The first house was built by Newton Allen and the first store by Enos West. In 1847 or 1848 a post office was established with Bruden Smith as postmaster. Zimri Mancher was the first mail carrier through the township, carrying mail from Hillsboro to Youngstown, by pack horse. A small horse mill was erected in 1830 and a saw and grist mill nearby, in 1849.

A Baptist church was organized about 1856 and meetings held in the school house until a church was built about 1859. A New Light church, date of founding unknown, was purchased by the Christian Union church after its organization in 1869. The population of Berrysville by 1870 had reached 78.

Berrysville has one church and a store. Its school was abandoned and children attend grade and high school at Belfast. Auction sales of used furniture have been held of late in the school house.

The chief industry is farming. The hamlet is served by rural mail delivery.

FOLSOM: Population, 15 or 20; Altitude, 1,083 feet above sea level; Location, about 8 miles south of Hillsboro on the West Union road, in Washington township. Unincorporated.

Folsom was never platted for a town and little is known of its history. It was named for Frances Folsom, wife of President Grover Cleveland, and for the purpose of securing a post office. It is situated in a rugged, rather isolated part of Highland county, and the approach to it from Hillsboro is up a very steep, long winding hill.

The Burnett Methodist church was erected in 1885. A two-room graded school was abandoned in recent years and children attend school at Hillsboro.

Folsom consists of a store and oil station, 5 or 6 houses, and the church. It has rural mail delivery service from Hillsboro, the post office having been abandoned.

PROSPECT: Population, about 5 or 6; Altitude, 1,100 feet above sea level; Location, 5 miles southeast of Hillsboro, and intersected by township highway running east and west. Unincorporated.

Prospect was never intended for a town, nor even platted as one. Settlers in this locality attended the first regular meetings of Methodists in Highland county at the home of James Fitzpatrick in the autumn of 1805, and organized the Prospect Methodist church. Origin of name Prospect is unknown. The first frame church was replaced in 1855 by a brick building. Peter Cartwright and James Quinn, famous circuit ministers, ministered to the settlers when they made their horseback journeys through the Prospect wilderness. A large cemetery adjoins the church grounds.

A feed mill and residence are at the crossroads. Prospect lies in a farming community. Children attend school at Belfast.

WHITEOAK TOWNSHIP
MOWRYSTOWN
TAYLORSVILLE

MOWRYSTOWN: Population, about 427; Altitude, 988 feet above sea level; Location, 14 miles southwest of Hillsboro, on the east fork of White Oak creek, in the southern part of Whiteoak township, intersected by State Route 321. The N. and W. railroad runs through Mowrystown, serving it with freight and passenger service. Incorporated.

Mowrystown was just a pioneer settlement until May 29, 1829, when Samuel Bell platted it for a town and named it in honor of Squire Abe Mowry, a highly esteemed resident. The first settler was Captain Andrew Badgley who had established his home near Mowrystown soon after 1800.

About 1810 a man named Sloan organized a Methodist church near Mowrystown and it was known as *"Sloan's Church."* George Barngrover built a grist mill about 1812 and several distilleries were opened. The first store was established in 1830 and a post office about 1832 with Joseph Bell as postmaster. A Temperance society was formed in 1834, the second in the county. James B. Finley was the first school teacher.

French Protestants who had fled the persecution in France began to arrive in the spring of 1834. They organized the Presbyterian and Baptist churches. Presbyterian meetings were first held in an unfinished log building which Rev. James Gilland, the traveling minister from Brown county, called the Moccasin Church because men attending services dressed in hunting shirts and carried hunting knives.

A United Brethren church was organized about 1842 in the school house and a church built in 1855. The first tavern was built by Peyton Hough about 1835. In 1865 a steam mill was built by Weaver and Riley. The population, in 1870, was 414.

Emily Grand-Girard, a native of France, went from Mowrystown in her early teens to enter the Oakland Seminary in Hillsboro. When her ability was disclosed, she was employed to teach the French language in the school. Later she opened the Highland Institute at Hillsboro. There is an Emily Grand-Girard memorial window at the First Presbyterian Church in Hillsboro to honor her. Descendants of the Grand-Girard family live in Circleville.

Mowrystown has 3 churches, the United Brethren, the Presbyterian, and Christian. It has a flour mill, brick and tile company, a modern school plant for grades and high school, and a small business district. The chief industry is farming.

Several Indian mounds are 3 miles east of Mowrystown, and the quaint cemetery of the first French settlers is of unusual interest.

Diehl Park, in Mowrystown, is a delightful place for boating, swimming, and picnicking.

TAYLORSVILLE: Population, 10-15; Altitude, 1,004 feet above sea level; Location, 10 miles southwest of Hillsboro on the east side of the east fork of White Oak creek, on a county highway near Mowrystown. The Norfolk and Western railroad passes through Taylorsville, a flag stop. Unincorporated.

Isaiah Roberts platted Taylorsville on November 20, 1846 on a part of the land he owned and named it in honor of a family named Taylor. Mr. Roberts was the postmaster of the post office established in 1849 which was named New Corwin Post Office. He and a Mr. Stringham kept the first store. There was a grist mill, saw mill, hotel, and blacksmith shop.

A United Brethren church was organized a long time after the founding of Taylorsville, but no church was ever built, the services being held in the school house. In 1901 the Union Chapel was built between Taylorsville and East Danville.

The late Wilbur J. Carr, of Taylorsville, was one of Highland county's most famous sons. He became an international diplomat.

CHAPTER EIGHT

SOME INTERESTING PEOPLE
of Past and Present

JUST what is an interesting person? This is a matter of rather personal opinion, because all worthwhile people are interesting. Highland county is full of them. It would be impossible to include a sketch of so many in the space of this small book. Perhaps some day some one will write a book of biographical sketches.

Some people consider those who do unusual things as the most interesting. Today we look back upon some of the people of long ago and regard them as *"odd."* In many instances these people were not only considered interesting then, but they were looked upon as remarkable. For instance the water witch, or the would be inventor.

Highland county has had a number of *"water witches,"* men who, with a peach or willow or some other supposed magical stick from a tree came to your farm to locate your best supplies of water. A water witch walked along with his stick to the ground in front of him. When he reached a spot where a good supply of water flowed beneath, the stick was said to bend and point to it. *"Witching water"* was not uncommon at all, and in some localities is still believed in.

Then ever so often through the years there rose a man who believed he had invented *"perpetual motion."* One of these was Zeno Wilcox who advertised as follows in the Cincinnati Gazette, December 12, 1840:

"After several years of close investigation I have succeeded in discovering the principles on which is founded perpetual motion, which fact I am prepared to prove both by actual experiment and sound philosophy."

Zeno took his idea from the 10th chapter of Ezekiel in the Bible which is about a wheel within a wheel. He made his model out of wood and it resembled a miniature ferris wheel. Taking it to Portsmouth he had it molded in iron and set in a wooden frame. As the wheels turned over they were supposed to gain power and keep turning perpetually. Zeno's invention now rests motionless in the basement of the Ohio Historical and Archaeological Museum at Columbus.

Zeno got another idea from the Bible about sheep. He believed that it was wrong to enclose sheep by fences and whenever a settler missed his sheep and found them at last wandering freely about the community he knew that Zeno had passed by. Zeno worked for a long time on a rat trap which would catch a rat and then reset itself. Relatives say that he lost his mind over this and died in or about 1857.

Just as the water witch and Zeno are interesting in their way, for one reason or another, other personalities stand out all along the way in Highland county history. The influence of some is felt in both state and national affairs.

In listing impartially a representative few of them, all are hereby honored.

THE PAST:

ALBERT JEREMIAH BEVERIDGE

ALBERT JEREMIAH BEVERIDGE, author and statesman, was born on a small farm near Sugartree Ridge, October 6, 1862, the son of Thomas H. and Frances Parkinson Beveridge.

When Thomas Beveridge lost his property in 1865 he moved his family to a farm in Illinois. Povery heeled them and they lived a life of privation and hardship.

Young Albert was a plow boy at the age of 12, a railroad hand with a section gang at 14, and a logger and teamster at 15. However, he managed to enter high school when he was not quite 16. Ambition led him to borrow fifty dollars from a friend and with this he entered Asbury College (Depew University) at Greencastle, Indiana in the fall of 1881. He graduated in 1885. He won many interstate oratorical honors and prizes during his college days and these enabled him to pay for two years of college.

By the time Mr. Beveridge was admitted to the bar in 1887 he had become known throughout the state of Indiana as a political orator. He was married in 1887 to Katherine Langsdale of Greencastle. His wife died in 1900 and he was married to Catherine Eddy of Chicago in 1907.

He was elected to the United States Senate in 1899 when he was 36 years old, one of the youngest members ever to be elected. In 1905 he was reelected. During the 12 years he held this office the Progressive Party rose to prominence and he was one of the Senate *"insurgents"* of the original Progressive Republicans. He supported many Roosevelt policies and took a strong stand against child labor. His speech on this amendment occupied the greater parts of three days and made a notable contribution to the controversy. He was defeated for a third term, the original Republicans and the Democrats banding against him. He never again held public office.

He served as temporary chairman in the Progressive National Convention in Chicago in 1912 and is remembered for his *"Pass*

Prosperity Around" address. He was nominated as a candidate for governor and for United States senator twice successively but was defeated.

He was more successful as a writer than as a politician. Eager to get his information first hand he traveled to the Philippines to make a personal investigation of the Philippine problem. He made a trip to Siberia and Russia during the Japanese and Russian conflict and from his observations wrote *"The Russian Advance,"* published in 1903.

Other books were, *"The Young Man and the World,"* 1905; *"The Bible as Good Reading,"* 1906; *"Meaning of the Times,"* 1907; *"What is Back of the War,"* 1915, while serving as a war correspondent in Germany. He was regarded in America as pro-German and this made him unpopular.

His greatest talent lay in biographies and his biography of Chief Justice John Marshall gained wide approval among leading critics and scholars. In this book he gave an historical and political interpretation of the Supreme Court and portrayed Marshall's part in giving this court its place in the history of America. The first two volumes of *"The Life of John Marshall"* appeared in 1916, the second two in 1919.

Beveridge then began the task of writing a similar biography of Lincoln in four volumes, but had only completed two of them when he died April 27, 1927.

CHARLES WILLING BYRD

CHARLES WILLING BYRD, acting governor of Ohio, was born at Westover, Charles City county, Virginia, in July, 1770. He received his education in the schools of Philadelphia, afterwards studying law with his uncle, William Nelson, professor of law in William and Mary College. He was appointed attorney and land agent to Kentucky by Robert Morris and came to that state in 1795.

In 1799, when William Henry Harrison resigned as Secretary of the Northwest Territory, Byrd was appointed to fill his position. He took the oath of office from Governor St. Clair. Byrd became acting governor of Ohio in 1802 when St. Clair was removed from office by President Jefferson. He served until 1803 when Edward Tiffin was elected governor of Ohio. He was a member of the Convention that framed the first Constitution for Ohio. In 1803 he was appointed judge of the supreme court of the United States for the district of Ohio, by President Jefferson. At that time he was 32 years old.

Mr. Byrd lived in Cincinnati for a few years possibly on Fifth street, reputed to have been called Byrd street in his honor. He moved his family to Buckeye Station in 1807, two miles east of Manchester, on the Ohio river. Buckeye Station had been built by Nathaniel Massie, his brother-in-law, in 1797.

Byrd was married twice. His first wife was a Miss Head of Kentucky. When she died, he moved to West Union, Adams county, Here he was married to a Mrs. Miles from Massachusetts, and lived in West Union until 1822.

Mr. Byrd rode to the courts at Chillicothe over Zane's Trace through Sinking Spring. He liked the place so well, especially the water from the *"sinking spring"*, that he purchased the land on which the spring was located and lived there until his death.

He had eight children. His fourth son, Samuel Otway Byrd, who died at the age of 45 in 1869, was at one time a member of the legislature of Ohio.

When Byrd died in 1828 he was survived by his wife and several children. Mrs. Byrd later remarried and had two sons by her third husband, but when she died she was buried next to the grave of Mr. Byrd and her headstone was marked, *"Hannah, wife of C. W. Byrd."*

On Sunday, October 19, 1941, a dedication program took place at Sinking Spring when a marker was placed at his grave and unveiled with appropriate ceremonies. A display of Governor Byrd material was in the octagon school house. The Governor Byrd residence (private) still stands beside the spring.

WILBUR JOHN CARR

WILBUR JOHN CARR, international diplomat, was born at Taylorsville, Ohio, October 31, 1870, son of Edward Livingston and Catherine Fender Carr. He has one brother, Alva Lee Carr, and this brother resides at Taylorsville.

Graduate of Commercial College of Kentucky University, Lexington, in 1889; took a stenographic course at Oswego, N. Y., and obtained a position at Peeksville, N. Y. He was next appointed through a Civil Service examination to the State Department at Washington, D. C. Since a knowledge of law was one of the requisites of his position, he attended law school at night at Georgetown University, graduating with LL.B., in 1894; LL.M., Columbian (now George Washington) University, 1899; LL.D., George Washington University, 1925; Hillsdale College, 1927, where he was conferred the highest degree of law.

He married Edith Adele, daughter of Ezra Lafayette and Lottie M. Koon, January 20, 1917. In 1897 he married Mamie Crane. He had no children.

Clerk of Department of State, 1902-07; Chief Clerk, Department of State, 1907-09; Representative of the Department of State on

United States Board of Jamestown Exposition, 1907; International Congress Tuberculosis, 1908; Seattle Exposition, 1909; Director Consular Service, November 30, 1909-24; Assistant Secretary of State, July 1, 1924; Minister to Czechoslovakia and sent by the Government on secret missions in World War I. As international diplomat, he was sent to foreign countries by the United States prior to World War II.

Member American Society International Law, Ohio Society, Council on Foreign Relations, National Research Council, Contributor Encyclopedia Americana, American Journal International Law, etc.

From early childhood, Mr. Carr was ambitious. His habit of seeing how high he could carve his name on trees on the Carr home place was symbolic of this.

In failing health, Mr. Carr retired from active service in 1939. He died at Johns Hopkins Hospital, Baltimore, Md., June 27, 1942.

His nearest living relatives are his brother Alva; four nieces, Mamie Flint (Mrs. Kenneth) Middleton, Ethel Yochum (Mrs. Carl), Fairfax, near Mariemont, Eleanor Carr, a teacher at Sharonville, and Virginia Carr, a nurse at Dayton; also one nephew, Wilbur Edward Carr, Taylorsville.

CHARLES H. COLLINS

CHARLES H. COLLINS, attorney, traveler, and author, born April 15, 1832 at Maysville, Kentucky, the son of General Richard and Mary Ann Armstrong Collins. General Collins was an eminent attorney and legislator of Ohio and Kentucky, the son of the Rev. John Collins of New Jersey, a pioneer Methodist preacher whose biography was written by Judge John McClean of the United States Supreme Court. The Collins family is of Scotch-Irish ancestry.

Charles H. Collins' boyhood days were spent in Maysville. In 1850 he moved to Horse Shoe Bend near Batavia in Clermont county, where he kept a country store for two years. His beautiful Southern-Colonial estate on the East Fork of the Little Miami river is now known as Marclarada Farm, the owners, Mr. and Mrs. Clarence J. Heiby.

He went to Cincinnati March 1, 1852, and worked in a dry goods establishment until the following October when he took up the study of law under his brother-in-law, Thomas J. Gallagher. He was admitted to the Bar at Batavia, May 11, 1854 and began the practice of law there. He was elected Prosecuting Attorney of Clermont county.

On November 29, 1855 he was married to Mary E. Tice of Bethel, Ohio. They had five children: John; Nellie; Richard; Frank A.; George. Two are living, George of Los Angeles, and

Frank, of Hillsboro, a retired attorney.

In 1858 Attorney Collins went to Waverly, Missouri where he was elected mayor April 3, 1860. In 1864 he left Missouri and came to Hillsboro where he resided until his death December 28, 1904 at the age of 72 years.

Mr. Collins was one of the best known lawyers in southern Ohio. He was an extensive traveler and visited nearly every foreign country. He was the author of a number of books, both prose and poetry. Among his best known publications were: *"Highland Hills to an Emperor's Tomb; "Echoes from Highland Hills;" "The New Year Comes, My Lady;" "Here and There;" "Past and Present;" "Wibbleton to Wobbleton"* (a play); *"Our Common Schools."*

LILLIE ANN FARIS

LILLIE ANN FARIS, author and teacher, was born in Lynchburg, Ohio, November 13, 1868, the daughter of Uriah Thompson Faris and Naomi Dean Faris. She graduated from the Lynchburg High School at the age of 14 years. She taught her first school at Sharpsville, Ohio and 12 of her 40 pupils were about the same age as their teacher.

After teaching two terms in the Cloverdale school and two terms in the Zink school, both one-room schools, Miss Faris was given the position of first grade teacher in the Lynchburg school at a salary of $30 a month.

She was chosen City Training Teacher for the schools in Marietta, Ohio. Later she became first grade Critic Teacher in the College of Education at Ohio University, which position she relinquished of her own volition to accept an editorial position with the Standard Publishing Company of Cincinnati.

Miss Faris returned to Ohio University in 1920 where she contacted hundreds of teachers from different states, many from Ohio.

She traveled and lectured on educational and religious work in almost every county in Ohio and in 43 of the 48 states.

In 1924 she secured leave of absence from the Training School in order to give her entire attention to the publication of supplementary readers entitled, *"The Standard Bible Story Readers,"* which have enjoyed a popular reception in all countries and islands where the English language is spoken.

One of her most recent books was *"Lights Aglow,"* designed for teachers and mothers of the pre-school child. Another, *"The Primary Teacher and Leader,"* is a training book, used widely in training classes in Sunday School work.

Each year, at Easter time, she invited the primary grades and the teachers of the Lynchburg schools to her home opposite the school. A special program pertaining to the Easter season was presented.

Miss Faris died at her home March 6, 1945.

JOSEPH BENSON FORAKER

JOSEPH BENSON FORAKER, governor of Ohio, son of Henry and Mary Reece Foraker, was born near Rainsboro in Paint township, July 5, 1846. His boyhood was spent at his home on Rocky Fork creek.

When the Civil War broke out he was only fifteen years old. One year later he enlisted in the 89th Ohio Volunteer Infantry and thus began a noteworthy military career. In turn he became orderly sergeant, second and first lieutenant, and then captain. He was in the battles of Missionary Ridge, Kennesaw Mountain, and Lookout Mountain and was with Sherman on his famous march to the sea. He had a brilliant war record.

After being mustered out of service he attended South Salem Academy, then Ohio Wesleyan University at Delaware, and graduated in law in the first graduating class of Cornell University, Ithaca, New York, in 1869. He was a founder and a member of Phi Kappa fraternity.

Beginning his law practice in Cincinnati he practiced law until he was appointed supervisor of congressional elections. He was elected judge of the superior court in 1879; governor of Ohio in 1886; and reelected governor in 1888.

Then he resumed his law practice and continued in this until 1897 when he became United States senator from Ohio, succeeding Calvin S. Bryce.

In 1886, 1890, and 1900 he was chairman of the Ohio Republican state conventions; Delegate-at-large from Ohio to the Republican national conventions in 1884, 1888, 1892, 1900, and 1904, when at this latter date he became leader of the party's conservative faction. He presented John Sherman's name for presidency in 1884 and 1888; and William McKinley's in 1896 and 1900.

He was married to Miss Julia Bundy of Jackson, Ohio, October 4, 1870. They had four children.

Following his retirement from active political life, Governor Foraker spent the remainder of his life at his home in Walnut Hills, Cincinnati. He died May 10, 1917.

HUGH STUART FULLERTON

HUGH STUART FULLERTON, son of Hugh Stuart and Mary Alice Fullerton, was born in Hillsboro, September 10, 1873. He attended grade school and high school at Hillsboro and was a student at

Ohio State University from 1891 to 1893. He began writing for the newspapers at Hillsboro at the age of 15. He was married to Edith Zollars of Fort Wayne, Indiana, August 8, 1900. They had one daughter, Dorothy Zollars Fullerton (Mrs. Lloyd S. Burns) and one son, Hugh S. Fullerton, Jr., Englewood, N. J.

Recognized as an authority on baseball and one of the great baseball writers of all time, his biggest scoop was his expose of the *"Black Sox"* scandal in 1919. He was convinced the series between the Chicago White Sox and the Cincinnati Reds was crooked because the results did not coincide with predictions of a system which he had devised for *"doping"* results of baseball games.

The system operated with unbelievable accuracy and after Cincinnati won the series Mr. Fullerton, then with the New York Evening World, wrote a series of articles and late in the 1920 season the prosecution of the scandal began.

While a student at Ohio State and shortly thereafter he played briefly in organized baseball at Olean, N. Y., Lynchburg, Va., and Newcastle, Pa. He was an organizer of the Baseball Writers Association of America.

Hugh was affectionately known to many Highland county friends as *"Ching."* Many of his articles appeared in nationally known magazines as the Saturday Evening Post, featuring noted persons from his native county. His descriptions of Highland county were inimitable and endeared him to people who did not know him. Perhaps no other person has brought more favorable publicity to this county than Mr. Fullerton. He had a brilliant mind and a gift for story telling.

He was a writer on the Cincinnati Tribune; Cincinnati Enquirer; a baseball writer on the Chicago Tribune from 1894 to 1917; New York Evening World, 1918 to 1919; New York Mail, 1919 to 1921; with the Liberty Magazine, 1923 to 1928; and sports writer for the Columbus Dispatch.

He was the author of *"Touching Second,"* (with J. J. Evers), *"Shasta Boys Team," "Cascade College," "Tales of the Turf," "The Movement of the Tribes,"* and a number of articles and short stories.

He died, at the age of 72, in a Dunedin, Florida hospital, December 27, 1945 and his body was brought to Hillsboro and laid to rest in the Hillsboro cemetery. He had spent the last five winters of his life in New Port Richey, near Clearwater.

ROY ASA HAYNES

ROY ASA HAYNES, federal prohibition commissioner, was born at Hillsboro, Ohio, August 31, 1881, the son of Charles Elliott and

May West Haynes.

He attended Western Reserve University from 1903-1904. On September 9, 1903 he married Katherine Logan Mason, of Lancaster, Kentucky.

In 1908 he became editor of the Dispatch at Hillsboro, continuing in that capacity for a number of years. In 1921-27 he was appointed federal prohibition commissioner by Presidents Harding and Coolidge. Before his appointment he had been an active worker in prohibition campaigns.

He was: president of the Economy Fire Insurance Company for several years; twice delegate to the General conference of the M. E. Church heading lay delegation from the West Ohio Conference; author of *"Prohibition Inside Out"* (1923). He was a Republican, Methodist, Mason, and Woodman.

DUNCAN McARTHUR

DUNCAN MCARTHUR, founder of Greenfield and governor of Ohio in 1831, was born in Dutchess county, New York in 1772, of Scotch parentage. When a child the McArthur family emigrated to Pennsylvania.

He was 18 years old when he enlisted in Harmar's army and participated in a campaign against the Indians north of the Ohio river. Reenlisting in 1792, his record was such at the battle of Captiva that when the captain, William Enoch, was killed, he was made captain. At that time he was but 20 years old.

When his term of enlistment expired, he went to work at the salt works at Maysville, Kentucky, leaving in 1793 to assist General Nathaniel Massie in making a survey of the valley of the Scioto and to take part in a military expedition against the Indians. His part was to patrol the Kentucky side of the Ohio river and give the alarm to the settlers when the Indians crossed the river. That fall he rejoined Massie and was made his assistant surveyor. He assisted General Massie in laying out Chillicothe.

In 1797, accompanied by William Rodgers, James Manary, Joseph Clark, Thomas McDonald, and Michael Thomas, General McArthur crossed Paint creek and came upon the meadowland that was to become the site of Greenfield.

In 1805 he was elected to the State Legislature. In 1808 he was elected major general of the State militia. After the outbreak of the War of 1812, he was given the commission of colonel of Ohio volunteers. He accompanied Hull to Detroit as second in command. In the fall of 1812 he was elected to Congress; and the following March he was commissioned brigadier general of the army. He was again elected to the Legislature in 1815. The next year he was commissioned to negotiate treaties with the Indians.

In 1817 he was reelected to the Legislature and was chosen speaker. He was elected governor of Ohio in 1831.

When his term as governor expired he retired from public life, going to Fruit Hill, his estate near Chillicothe, Ohio where he died in 1840.

EDWARD LEE McCLAIN

EDWARD LEE McCLAIN, philanthropist and benefactor, was born in Greenfield, Ohio, May 30, 1861, the son of William Page and Margaret Ann Parkinson McClain. He was educated in the schools of Greenfield. On December 17, 1885 he was married to Lulu Theodosia Johnson of Oakley, Cincinnati. Their children are: Edward Lee McClain, Jr., of Hood River, Oregon, and Los Angeles, Calif.; Helen St. Clair McClain (Mrs. Robert S. Young) of Cleveland Heights, Ohio; Donald Schofield McClain of Atlanta, Georgia.

Mr. McClain when a youth of fifteen began his active business career in the harness shop of his father. He conceived the idea of a horse collar pad for the general trade and invented one. He later improved it by adding a spring steel hook which was easily adjusted and eliminated frightening the animal. He began the manufacture of the pads November 1, 1881, thus founding the American Pad and Textile Company, the largest of its kind in the world.

In 1903, near Cartersville, Georgia, he founded a model cotton mill and a village named Atco. This village was the first cotton mill village in the South where cottages were designed with unusual regard for the comfort and welfare of the employees, "*where streets and sidewalks, laws and parks, were part of well-laid plans, where a regular church building was provided exclusively for Divine service, a large and beautiful brick building for school purposes, with rooms for lodge meetings and a hall for moving pictures and local entertainment, a kindergarten, swimming pool and playgrounds centrally located.*"

In 1915 he gave to his native Greenfield the McClain High School, Vocational Building, athletic field, and the school cottages. The combined cost of the three buildings comprising the school plant without grounds and equipment was nine hundred and fifty thousand dollars.

Mr. McClain supervised numerous industries such as: The American Pad and Textile Co., Greenfield, Ohio, and Evansville, Indiana; The Sand Mixing Co., New York, N. Y.; The National Lumber and Box Co., Detroit, Mich.; The Crescent Manufacturing Co., Louisville, Ky.; The Wellston Rich Run Coal Co., Wellston, Ohio.

Mr. McClain's grandfather was the Rev. John McClain, who was pastor of the Methodist Episcopal Church for fifty years in Greenfield, and his great grandfather was the Rev. Peter McClain,

thus making in all members of four generations of McClains who have been continuously associated with Greenfield since 1857.
He died May 2, 1934, in Greenfield, Ohio.

OLIVER NEWTON SAMS

OLIVER NEWTON SAMS, bank director and attorney, son of Andrew J. and Ruth A. Bell Sams, was born October 19, 1862 near McCoppin's Mill on Rocky Fork creek.

He attended the National Normal University at Lebanon, Ohio, where he received the B.A. degree in 1886. Two years later, March 20, 1888 he was married to Mary E. George of Rainsboro, Ohio. They had three children: Ralph of Louisville, Ky. and Heber, both deceased; and Sarah Ruth (Mrs. Conrad Ottelin) of Cleveland, O.

He was admitted to the Ohio bar in 1887 and practiced law in Hillsboro from 1888 to 1907. Then he became president of the Merchants National Bank of Hillsboro. Later he became director of the Federal Reserve Bank of Cleveland.

He was: prosecuting attorney for Highland county for six years; delegate to the Democratic National Convention at St. Louis, 1904; president of the Ohio State Bankers Association, 1915-16; a member of the executive council of the American Bankers Association.

He served in many important civic affairs of Hillsboro, was a trustee of Wilmington College, and a delegate to the General Conference of the M. E. Church at Baltimore in 1908. He belonged to the Masonic Lodge (32, K.T.).

Trustees of Holbrook College at Manchester in 1936 established a $3,000.00 scholarship in his memory. The National Normal University at Lebanon of which Mr. Sams was a graduate, merged with Holbrook a number of years ago.

SAMUEL PARSONS SCOTT

SAMUEL PARSONS SCOTT, lawyer and author, authority on Spanish law, was born July 8, 1846 in Highland county. His parents were William and Elizabeth Jane Parsons Scott.

He graduated from Miami University in 1866 with the degree of A.B., the youngest member of the class, and its valedictorian. He received the degree of A.M. from Miami, in 1887. On October 10, 1895, he married Elizabeth Woodbridge Smart of Paint, Ohio.

After being admitted to the bar in 1868 he engaged in the active practice of law at Leavenworth, Kansas, and San Francisco, California until 1875.

He was a member of: the Comparative Law Bureau of American Bar Association; editor of the Spanish department of the Compartive Law Bureau of American Bar Association for 20 years; a life member of the Royal Academy of Arts and the Royal Meteorological Society, London, England; member of Alpha Delta Phi and Phi Beta Kappa.

He was author of "Through Spain," 1886, and, "History of the Moorish Empire in Europe," 1904. He was translator and editor of many works of ancient Spanish law. Among these works were: The Forum Judicum, 1910; Las Siete Partidas, 1912; El Fuero Viejo de Castilla; El Fuero Real; Las Leyas del Estilo; El Ordenamiento de Alcala; Las Leyas Nuevas; El Ordenamiento de las Tafurereas; Las Leyes de Toro; Leyes para los Adelantados Mayores, 1913; El Codigo Penal de Espana, 1914; Corpus Juris Civilis.

He belonged to: Societe Academique d' Histoire Internationale (Paris); Academie Latine des Sciences, Arts et Belles Lettres (Paris); Societe de La Renaissance Nationale (Paris); American Bar Association; American Society International Law; International Law Association.

He died at Hillsboro, May 30, 1929.

WILLIAM HENRY TAYLOR SHADE

WILLIAM HENRY TAYLOR SHADE was born at Centerville, Ohio, January 16, 1864, the son of the Rev. John W. and Sofronia Vance Shade, and named for his uncles. His father was a Methodist preacher. He was married to Frances McKeehan of Hillsboro in 1912. They had no children.

Mr. Shade was one of the most talented persons produced by Highland county. Musician, composer, author, poet, editor and band leader, he was unusually gifted.

He lived for a time in New York where he was employed by Hearst's and wrote feature stories of theatrical life for the Telegraph.

Reminiscing on his 80th birthday, Mr. Shade said:

"I guess I worked on every daily paper in Chicago that wasn't printed in a foreign language, the Tribune, Chronicle, Mail, Record, Examiner, Dispatch and Inter Ocean, to mention a few that I can name offhand.

"In St. Louis I was a reporter on the Post-Dispatch and for a while editor of its semi-weekly farm edition.

"I was music and drama editor of the Kansas City Journal in 1888 and of the Cincinnati Tribune in 1893. I also at the same time was financial and commercial editor of the Tribune. You are quite right, I earned all they paid me.

"I'll bet I've been city editor of more small city dailies than anybody living, among them the Canadaigua (N. Y.) Messenger, the Lima (Ohio) News, the Middletown (Ohio) Journal, the Vicks-

burg (Miss.) *Evening Post*, the Chattanooga *Commercial*, the Belvidere (Ill.) *Northwestern* and the Port Huron (Mich.) *Times*. Hope I'm not overlooking any.

And in the way of a vacation I edited and published a country weekly of my own in Iowa for 15 years.

"It was something to have interviewed people like Clara Barton, Nat Goodwin, Capt. Paul Boyton, Bancroft, the historian, and Jeff Davis. And it was something to have played for Joseph Jefferson, Modjeska, Janauschek, and Keene.

In the minstrel business I traveled with practically all the big ones, Baird's, Haverly's, Primrose's, and Cleveland's. From the orchestra of the latter I graduated into advance work, more specifically press agentry.

"For eight different seasons I was with Liberati's Band and Opera Company in the various capacities of trumpeter, trombonist, saxophonist, secretary and press agent. And also had some experiences as a really-truly stage actor.

On the circus line I was with all kinds of them, big and little railroad shows, steamboat shows that chugged up and down bayous little wider than Clear Creek and wagon shows that at first glance might easily have been mistaken for gypsy caravans.

"It was something to have played with musicians like Liberati, Bellstedt, Vonterno and Barnhouse, and to have enjoyed the personal friendship of P. S. Gilmore and Victor Herbert who honored me with a personal invitation to hear the first performance of a new composition and seemed particularly anxious to know how I liked it."

Friends of Mr. Shade attest to his versatility, recalling that he would take a composition he liked and overnight write the scores for every instrument in his orchestra or band. His "*Aristo Band*" of Hillsboro women was a triumph in local musical achievement.

Hugh Fullerton said of him that he was all genius that isn't always understood.

His book of poems, "*Buckeyeland and Bohemia*," is a classic of local Americana.

He died at Reseda, California, April 20, 1945, at the age of 81.

DAVID SINTON

DAVID SINTON, industrialist and philanthropist, was born in Armagh county, Ireland, of an English father, John Sinton, a linen weaver, and a Scottish mother, who was a McDonnell. The name Sinton was originally Swinton. The Sintons were of the Quaker faith.

When David was three years old, the family emigrated to the United States and settled in Pittsburgh, Pennsylvania, where the father kept a small store. Ten years later, when David was 13 years old, they moved to Sinking Spring, Ohio. Here David was employed as a clerk and his wages were $4.00 a month and his board.

Two years later he went to Cincinnati, Ohio, but soon returned to Sinking Spring where he remained until he had saved a small sum of money. With this money he went to Cincinnati where he established a small commission business.

Then he went to Washington C. H. where he managed a dry goods establishment until the James Rogers & Co., of Hanging Rock hired him as manager of the *"landing and river"* business. He next went to Lawrence county where he was manager of Union Furnace owned by John Sparks Company, becoming a partner two years later. It was here that he learned the iron business and laid the foundation for the immense fortune he accumulated. He bought large quantities of pig iron cheap and sold it at a profit of 700 or 800 percent, having foreseen that iron would increase in price.

He moved to Cincinnati in 1849 and established an office for the sale of his iron products. From then on he became actively identified with the history of Cincinnati as a capitalist and philanthropist.

The Sinton building was one of several fine edifices erected and owned by him. He purchased the Grand Opera House in 1862, paying over $200,000 for it. One of his philanthropies was a gift of $33,000 to the Young Men's Christian Association.

His wife was Jane Ellison of Manchester, Ohio. They had two children, Edward, and Annie who married Charles P. Taft.

A life size statue of David Sinton is at the entrance of the Art Museum in Eden Park in Walnut Hills, Cincinnati.

ALLEN TRIMBLE

ALLEN TRIMBLE, governor of Ohio, was the oldest son of Captain James and Jane Allen Trimble, Virginians, who emigrated to Kentucky in 1784. He was born in 1783. When eleven months old his parents went to live near Lexington, Kentucky.

When the father died, the mother brought her family consisting of 8 children to Highland county where they owned extensive land grants. Allen, then a young man, became the head of the family.

Allen and his two brothers, William A. and Carey A., took active parts in the War of 1812. Allen was elected colonel of one of the regiments which was raised immediately after the surrender of Hull.

In 1816 Mr. Trimble was elected to the legislature from Highland county and in 1817 he was elected to the senate. In 1818 he was elected speaker of the senate.

When his brother, William, a United States senator, died in

1821 he was elected to fill the vacancy. It was during this service that he influenced the early adoption of the common school system and was instrumental in penitentiary reform.

He was elected to the general assembly in 1824 as one of the canal fund commissioners authorized to negotiate the first loan of the State for canal purposes.

In 1826 he was elected governor of the State and was re-elected in 1828. At the close of his second executive term in 1830 he retired from public life. He died at Hillsboro, his home for more than 60 years, in February, 1870.

His first wife was Margaret McDowell whom he married in 1806 in Woodford county, Kentucky. To this union were born two sons, Joseph and Madison. After her death he married Rachel Woodrow in 1811. Their three children were Carey A., William H., and Eliza Jane who became the nationally known *"Mother"* Thompson.

MARY McARTHUR THOMPSON TUTTLE

MARY MCARTHUR THOMPSON TUTTLE, portrait and landscape painter and writer, was born at Hillsboro, Ohio, November 5, 1849, the daughter of J. H. and Eliza Jane Trimble Thompson. She received her education in the Hillsboro College, graduating with an A.B. degree in 1867. She studied art in Cincinnati and went to Europe to study art, and French and German literatures and languages.

On July 5, 1875 she was married to Professor Herbert Tuttle, Berlin correspondent of the London Daily News for eight years and professor of international law. When they came to the United States, he was professor of European history in Cornell University. He died in 1894.

Attaining much recognition for her art, especially landscapes and portraits, she achieved distinction for her two portraits of her mother, the famous *"Mother"* Thompson. One of these portraits is in the Crusade Memorial Room in the Presbyterian Church of Hillsboro. The other was on exhibition at the World's W.C.T.U. Convention in Berlin. She painted two portraits of her husband, one for the University of Vermont, his alma mater, and the other for Cornell University.

Mrs. Tuttle gave lectures on color as pictorial art and industrial art, and other relative subjects. She assembled and cared for and edited hundreds of papers belonging to her grandfather, Governor Allen.Trimble, and her mother, and this collection was given over into the custody of the Western Reserve Historical Society, Cleveland, Ohio, a few years before Mrs. Tuttle's death in 1916. She is listed in "Who's Who Among American Women."

THE PRESENT:

JOHN J. BALLENTINE

REAR ADMIRAL JOHN J. BALLENTINE, was born in Hillsboro, Oct. 4, 1896, son of George M. and Ora Eakins Ballentine. After graduating from Hillsboro High School, Admiral Ballentine entered the U. S. Navy Academy at Annapolis and graduated in the class of 1918. He served on the U. S. S. Nebraska during World War I. He has the Victory Medal, Yangste Service Medal, and the Second Nicaraguan Campaign Medal.

He received on the same day in ceremonies at Pearl Harbor on June 8, the Legion of Merit and the Silver Star Medal. Admiral C. W. Nimitz, Commander in Chief of the Pacific Fleet and Pacific Ocean Areas, made the presentations. Admiral Ballentine received the awards for gallantry, meritorious service and intrepidity in action as the commanding officer of an aircraft carrier during actions in the Central and South Pacific, during World War II.

Admiral Ballentine is Highland county's highest ranking officer in the Navy. Stationed in General Headquarters of the Supreme Command of the Allied Powers as the Naval Liaison Officer for the Commander-in-Chief, U. S. Pacific Fleet at Tokyo. He was present at the official surrender of Japan.

His wife was the former Miss Catherine Shields, of Yorktown, Va. They have one son, Bally, Jr.

NORMAN B. BEECHER

NORMAN B. BEECHER, born in Hillsboro, Ohio, July 22, 1877, the son of George B. and Nannie O'Hara Beecher, the great grandson of Rev. Lyman Beecher, and the grand-nephew of Henry Ward Beecher, and of Harriet Beecher Stowe.

Educated in the public and private schools of Hillsboro. Graduated from Phillips Academy, Andover, Mass., 1893; B.A., Yale University, 1898; member of Phi Beta Kappa Society; L.L.B. Harvard University, 1901; editor Harvard Law Review.

Enrolled as private in Battery A of the First Regiment of Connecticut Volunteers May 4, 1898, discharged from the service of the United States October 25, 1898.

Admitted to practice law in New York, 1901. Member of law firms of Robinson Biddle and Ward, Robinson Biddle and Benedict, and Burlington Montgomery and Beecher in New York City.

Served as General Counsel of the Oil Division, United States Fuel Administration during World War I in Washington D. C. Served as Special Admiralty Counsel of U. S. Shipping Board, Washington D. C. 1920-23. Delegate of the United States to International Maritime Conference held in Brussels, Belgium, 1922 and 1923.

Married in 1922 to Miss Miriam E. Woolley of Woodbury, N. J. They have three children. Now residing in Clearwater, Florida.

MILTON ARTHUR CANIFF

MILTON ARTHUR CANIFF, Highland county's most famous son of today, was born in Hillsboro, Ohio, February 28, 1907, the son of John and Elizabeth Burton Caniff. His father was a printer on the Hillsboro Gazette and he would take his family to a warmer climate during the winter season.

Milton's first "job" was that of messenger for the Western Union in Hillsboro when he was about eight years old. The Caniff family lived in Redlands, California the winter that Milton was nine, and Milton became a newsboy and an extra in the movies.

In 1919 when the father came back from service with the Ohio National Guards (which became the 37th Division), he took his family to Dayton. Milton completed grammar school and high school at Dayton. He was an active Boy Scout in his school days.

Milton was office boy in the Dayton Journal's art department while yet in high school and received an offer of a job on the Miami, Florida *"Daily News,"* owned by James M. Cox of Dayton. He accepted this job for the summer of 1925, the year he graduated from Stivers High School.

He majored in fine arts at Ohio State University. During his college days he was a member of Sigma Chi, Sphinx, Toastmaster, Scarlet Mask, Student Council, and was a cheer leader. He was art editor of the Makio and Sundial and his cartoons appeared in issues of the Ohio State Lantern. He graduated in Arts in 1930.

Milton then went to work on the art staff of the Columbus Dispatch, his first full time job. His variety of talents was allowed full play, and his mastery of heavy blacks became a characteristic of his work. His portrayal of the arrival of the first Highland Countians at Sinking Spring on the frontispiece of this book is an example.

In the meantime he had considered the theater as a profession for he had played bit parts in Hollywood films and worked in amateur theatricals and stock companies. The late Billy Ireland, cartoonist for the Columbus Dispatch, said to him, *"Stick to your ink pots, kid, actors don't eat regularly,"* and Milton stuck to his art.

Billy Ireland, Noel Sickles, Roy Crane and Russell Patterson are credited by Milton with having influenced his career the most.

When the Associated Press offered Milton a job in 1932 he left Columbus for New York. He drew *"Dickie Dare,"* an adventure strip and *"The Gay Thirties,"* a human interest panel, for the Associated Press.

Two years later Captain Joseph M. Patterson, publisher of the New York Daily News, was seeking a comic strip with the Orient as the locale, for the Chicago Tribune-New York Daily News Syndicate. He had been impressed with Milton's work and offered him the job.

In an effort to achieve authenticity, Milton did extensive research on China. He filled his studio with a large collection of books relating to the Orient and Oriental objects. The now famous comic adventure strip, *"Terry and the Pirates,"* was created, which proved to be just what his employer had asked, *"a strip based on a blood-and-thunder formula, carrying a juvenile angle, and packed with plenty of comedy, sex, and suspense."*

Authorities say, *"Terry and the Pirates showed the full-scale Japanese invasion of China and the Japanese attack on the United States well in advance of their actual occurrence."*

On September 25, 1936, *"Terry and the Pirates"* was broadcast over the radio. The comic strip appears in 83 newspapers over the world. In story and picture form it was reproduced in big-little books which enjoyed great popularity.

Milton has the happy faculty of making his characters real and living in real worlds. His characters are all taken from life. He draws with his left hand, writes with his right. People write to his comic strip characters and an enormous amount of fan mail from all over the world pours in to him.

"Male Call," another strip with another set of characters was another of Milton's creations. Besides many other contributions he made to the war effort, he illustrated the Army's *"Pocket Guide to the Orient,"* an official hand book distributed to all United States soldiers in the Orient.

John Paul Adams who wrote Milton Caniff's biography recently, calls him,*"Milton Caniff, Rembrandt of the Comic-Strips."* He says, *"Many people do not know that Disney and Caniff have been hung in the Metropolitan Museum of Art. Caniff personifies the most popular art of his time. He is one of the most articulate of the comic-strip artists."*

In October, Milton will begin a new strip for the Marshall Field Enterprises of Chicago, for which he will be paid $100,000 a year. Unnamed at the present time the strip will have a foreign locale. *"Terry and the Pirates,"* the property of the Tribune-News Syndicate, will be given over to another cartoonist to portray.

Milton was listed in *"Who's Who in America, 1942-43"* and *"Who's Who in American Art, 1940-41."* His success story has appeared in many magazines. During the early part of the depression preceding the late war, Milton encountered many discouragements but nothing deterred his progress and his determination to succeed.

He was married to the former Esther Parsons of his high school days, in 1930. They live in a beautiful home forty miles up the Hudson from New York.

CHARLES GOSSETT

CHARLES GOSSETT, son of Wyatt H. and Margaret Finnegan Gossett of Pricetown, was born at Pricetown, September, 1888, and is Pricetown's most famous son.

When a boy he worked on farms in the Pricetown neighborhood until he was 18 years old. Then he went west with Jim Moberly where he worked on a farm in the state of Washington for two years.

He then took up the work of bridge construction and two years later homesteaded in Idaho where he remained for four years.

In 1920 all but one brother of the immediate family died, all being stricken during the *"black flu"* epidemic. His mother, three brothers, a sister-in-law, and niece were victims of the epidemic.

Mr. Gossett's rise to fame in Idaho came because of his untiring efforts and work with irrigation systems. Through him this method of farming was introduced to Idaho. Not only does he own a large farm, specializing in the raising of fine *"Idaho potatoes,"* and a flock of several thousand sheep at Nampa, Idaho, but he is co-owner of a farm near Pricetown.

He was elected to the office of governor of the state of Idaho in November, 1944. He had served previously as lieutenant-governor and two terms as representative to congress from his home district in Idaho. He is a Democrat.

In 1945 he resigned his governorship to fill out the unexpired term of United States senator William E. Borah. He ran for nomination to this office a few months later, but was defeated.

Mr. Gossett was married to Clara Fleming. They have three sons, Wyatt, Jr., Robert, and Elmer. Robert is an ensign in the U. S. Navy.

He has many relatives in Highland county. Among them are two aunts, Mrs. W. P. Roberts and Mrs. R. W. Pratt of Hillsboro; a nephew, Leroy Gossett of Tipp City; and a niece, Mrs. Miller Purdy of Buford.

FRANK RAYMOND HARRIS

FRANK RAYMOND HARRIS, Greenfield's *"skylarking pedagogue,"* educator and speaker, was born in Greenfield, April 19, 1880, the son of David M. and Sarah Schrock Harris. He was the great grandnephew of General Duncan McArthur.

Graduating from the Greenfield high school in 1897 and from Ohio Wesleyan University in 1902 with the degree of A.B., he served as principal of the Greenfield High School and 14 years as superintendent of the Edward Lee McClain High School, the total years of service 33 years. In the meanwhile he attended Harvard University for one year, receiving the M.A. degree, taught Latin for one year in the Male High School at Louisville, studied at the Universities of Chicago, Wisconsin, and Cornell. He worked with the late Edward Lee McClain in the building and development of the $2,000,000 school plant.

Mr. Harris has traveled in every state in the Union, every province in Canada, every nation in Europe, every country in South America except Paraguay, Mexico, the West Indies, the South Sea Islands, Hawaii, Australia, China, Japan, the Philippines, Northern Africa, the Near East and the Far East—as far north as the northern tip of Greenland and as far south as Tasmania.

Mr. Harris's first trip across the Atlantic (1900) was made on a cattle boat with Texas steers and Iowa cows. His last trip (1936) was on the mighty Leviathan which he describes as a "giant silver shuttle." Before the late war he had planned an 11,000 mile Odyssey from London to Cape Town and return.

During 1935 and 1936 he traveled some 35,000 miles along the skyways of the world, and his ambition has always been to some day encircle the globe by air.

DR. SAMUEL GALLOWAY HIBBEN

DR. SAMUEL GALLOWAY HIBBEN, one of the great lighting experts of the nation, was born at Hillsboro, Ohio, June 6, 1888, the son of Joseph M. and Harriett Martin Hibben. He was married to Ruth Rittenhouse in 1922 and they had four children: Eleanor R.; Stuart G.; Barry C.; Craig R. His father conducted the Hibben Dry Goods Store at Hillsboro, the oldest store of its kind west of the Alleghenies.

Dr. Hibben was educated in the schools of Hillsboro, with college work as Case School Applied Science, Cleveland; Carnegie Institute of Technology, Pittsburgh; and University of Paris. In college he specialized in illumination, particularly the design of glassware and lighting recommendations of all types.

He designed the lighting of the Washington Monument; the Holland Vehicular Tunnels; Statue of Liberty; Endless Caverns in Virginia; Virginia Bridge; Century of Progress Exposition, Chicago, and many important buildings in America. He also designed the illumination for the New York World's Fair of 1939, besides devoting much time to lectures, technical articles, and studies of special uses of lighting including underwater illumination, insect trapping, plant growth, air sterilization, food treatments and special laboratories of the Westinghouse Lamp Division, Bloomfield, N. J. He is Director of Applied Lighting, Westinghouse Lamp Division at Bloomfield.

JOSEPH HIESTAND

JOSEPH HIESTAND, born on a farm near Hillsboro, November 28, 1906, son of Harry and Ella Gabriel Hiestand, graduated from Hillsboro High School in 1925 and started his shooting career about 1929. He has been called *"Joe, the farmer boy,"* and *"Joe, the Hillsboro plow-follower."* Winner of 10 national crowns in 1935 and 1936, 6 of which were won in the Grand American shoot, Joe held the title of the world's outstanding trapshooter in 1936.

In 1931 he won Ohio State Championship Singles; in 1932, success in Florida shoots; in 1934, Grand American Handicap at Vandalia, six championships, with high over entire field; in 1935, North American Clay Target Championship in Singles and Doubles, high over entire field by new world's record score of 880 out of 900. In 1936 he repeated these championships which had never been done before. Joseph broke his own record and made a new world's record of 881 out of 900.

The North American was won with 198 out of 200; the National Doubles, 96 in 100; Class AA with a perfect score, 200 in 200; the All Around with 881 in 900, and the Over All, 16-yard with 595 in 600.

Joseph was a member of World's Squad Record which broke 499 out of 500 at York and Delaware. He was captain of All American Trap Shooting Team, 1934 and 1935. He has shot in all the states in the Union except Maine, Arizona, and North Dakota.

1938 found Joseph hanging up a total of 966 consecutive hits at the Grand American Trapshoot held at Vandalia. This was a world record. He won high-over-all honors with a mark of 881x900 during the week, tying the record previously held by him.

In 1939, Joe, world's acknowledged champion trap shot, won all of the coveted titles at the state meet held at Columbus, Ohio. His unbroken string of broken targets ran better than 1,700. He received another title, *"The Buckeye Bullet."*

The Associated Press story from New York following his phenominal success in 1939 described him thus:

"He's quick, and watching him, you get the idea. He stands on the firing line poised, relaxed. A white cap tops his black dome. A lightweight red sweater, trousers that are just another pair of trousers, and black and white sports shoes compete his costume. There is a rhythmic flexing of his right knee, and he chews gum in 2-4 time as he waits his turn.

"When it comes he draws a bead over the trap, softly calls out something that sounds like "whua," the boys pull a lever, and the disk pops out of sight. It is then you get the meaning of his friends' contention that "he's quick." The target zooms out of the trap with no sense of direction and seems to dodge and sidestep."

In August, 1942, Joseph was commissioned Captain and stationed at Spence Field, Fort Moultrie, Georgia, in charge of ground ranges for the Air Force gunners training school. Here he trained men on skeet ranges, and became assistant commandant of cadets at Fort Moultrie before being transferred to Buckingham Field, near Ft. Myers, Florida, in 1943. Joe won his wings here, and was put in charge of the primary gunnery ranges. In September of this same year, he was made director of all ground activities and was commanding officer for the range squadron of seventeen officers and 200 enlisted men.

He was married to Miss Mary Custer in 1938. They have three children, James Edwin, Linda Joe, and Marilyn Ruth. Their permanent address is Hillsboro.

ESTELLE HUNTINGTON HUGGINS

ESTELLE HUNTINGTON HUGGINS was born in Green township, Brown county, August 28, 1867, the youngest child of James Edward Huggins and Arethusa Diboll Huggins. She received her education in a small district school. Her talent for art was discovered early in life by her mother who gave her encouragement.

In the fall and winter of 1893-4 she attended the Methodist College for women in Hillsboro for the purpose of studying drawing and painting. She attended the Columbus Art School in the fall and winter of 1897 and 1898, graduating June 10, 1890.

In August, 1891, she and her sister, Catherine, who had made a study of photography, entered the photographic business in London, Ohio. Estelle attended the Art Students League in New York City through the fall, winter and spring terms of 1896, 1897 and 1898, returning each summer to resume work in the gallery.

In 1899 she opened a studio in New York City where she achieved success, articles concerning her studio and reproductions of her work appearing in the Cities publications. Her studio was a center for art students, artists, musicians, and literary people. Among her customers were Miss Ann Morgan; Mrs. J. Gould; Mr. and Mrs. Albert Payson Terhune; Mrs. Dean Howells; Mr. and Mrs. MacDowell; Henry Twatchman; William Chase; Douglas Volk; John Alexander.

There were intervals during her stay in New York in which she spent a summer in Maine, one in Boston, and a few weeks at the Lyme Summer School in Connecticut. She made a trip to

Europe in 1906 where she studied and visited leading art galleries.

Miss Huggins closed her studio in New York in 1917 and returned to her home in Leesburg. Her studio, *"The Country Studio"* has been the inspiration for much of her best known works.

Her paintings were displayed at the Columbus State Fair in 1936; and in 1937 there was an exhibition of her works at the Southern Hotel in Columbus.

Her most noted canvasses are: *"The Sunfish Hills;" Winter on Lees Creek;" "Highland Roads in Winter;" "Covered Bridge on the Washington Road;" "Whiteoak Creek, a Memory of Childhood."*

Some of her best portraits are: *"Mr. and Mrs. Chester Bryan;" "Aunt of Mrs. Albert Payson Terhune;" "Harold, son of Mrs. Sweezey, of Englewood, N. J., Resting;" "Mr. Theodore Schroeder;"* and *"James Edward Huggins, Reading."*

LT. GENERAL JOHN EDWIN HULL

LT. GENERAL JOHN EDWIN HULL was born May 26, 1895 about 4½ miles from Greenfield, the youngest of nine children (six boys, three girls) born to Mary and Joseph Hull. Graduated from Greenfield High School in 1913. Attended Miami University at Oxford, Ohio. Left the University to enlist in the first officers' training school at Ft. Benjamin Harrison, Ind. His diploma was forwarded to him.

Stayed with the army through the peace between two world wars. He was a lieutenant colonel when the United States entered World War II. Made full colonel December 24, 1941; brigadier general, June, 1942; major general January, 1943; lieutenant general June, 1945.

Acted as Chief of Operations of the War Department General Staff during World War II. Assigned to Hawaii as commanding general of the U. S. Army in the middle Pacific. He is Highland county's highest ranking officer in the Army.

Mrs. Hull was the former Lucille Davis of Middleport, Ohio.

DR. PHILIP C. JEANS

DR. PHILIP CHARLES JEANS was born at Hillsboro, Ohio, January 3, 1883, the son of Frank Hibben Jeans and Anna Mary Stafford Jeans. He married Grace Whittier Cushing and they had one son, Robert Philip Jeans.

Dr. Jeans received an AB degree from the University of Kansas, 1904; MD at Johns Hopkins University, 1909. He received training in hospitals in Baltimore, Md., Hartford, Conn., and Boston, Mass., before going to St. Louis Children's Hospital and Washington University Medical School. In the latter institution he progressed from instructor to associate professor, leaving this position in 1924 to take a position as professor at the University of Iowa. His various teaching titles were in pediatrics.

Now a professor of pediatrics, Dr. Jeans is in charge of the medical division of the Children's Hospital of the University of Iowa. He has published some 50 scientific papers and two books on medical subjects.

He belongs to the following national societies: American Pediatric Society (member of its council); American Institute of Nutrition; Society for Experimental Biology and Medicine; Society for Pediatric Research; Society for Research in Child Development. He also is a member and vice chairman of the Council on Foods of the American Medical Association (their seal is on your box of Wheaties).

WILLIAM H. McSURELY

WILLIAM HARVEY McSURELY, born January 27, 1865, in Oxford. Butler county, Ohio, was the son of Rev. William Jasper (D.D.) and Hulda Taylor McSurely. He came with his parents from Loveland, Ohio to Hillsboro in 1869 or 1870.

His first schooling was under Miss Jenny Weaver, sister of Dr. Patrick Weaver, a well known person. Miss Weaver had a kindergarden class in which were enrolled Irvin Smith, Tom and Noble Shawe, Charlie Lilley, John Wallace Evans, Will Kibler, and others. Then for a time he went to the Institute presided over by Miss Emily Grand-Girard; then to the public school on Walnut street, to a Miss Fenner—on from room to room until he *"landed in Professor Ed Smith's room along with a number of other boys."*

He went to Wooster College in 1881 and graduated in 1886; read law in Judge Frank Steele's office in Hillsboro for a year, and has always remembered his kindness and understanding of legal principles. He would go to Judge Steele's office every night for examination on the day's work. This training, he said, was the most valuable training in law that he ever received.

In the summer of 1887 he went to Chicago where he was employed as an office boy with Norton, Burley & Howell at a salary of $4 a week, which was increased the following January to $7.50.

Mary Elizabeth Cadman of Chicago became his wife October 18, 1892. They had two children: Marion (Mrs. Alfred Schnoor); and William Cadman.

Mr. McSurely was admitted to the Illinois bar March 29, 1889.

He was a member of the Illinois General Assembly, 5th Senatorial District, 1905-6; elected judge Superior Court of Cook county, Ill., April, 1907; chief justice Superior Court, 1911-12; appointed to Appellate Court, First Dist., Ill., 1912; presiding justice Appellate

Court.

Judge McSurely is a Presbyterian, a member of the Chicago Historical Society, Ohio Society, Art Institute, Sigma Chi, Phi Beta Kappa. He belongs to the following clubs: Union League (Pres. 1913-14), University, Flossmore Country, Law.

His home is in Chicago, Ill.

DR. HUGH M. PARSHALL

HUGH MAYNARD PARSHALL, son of Leslie and Flo Eubanks Parshall, was born at New Petersburg, Ohio, December 21, 1898. The Parshall family moved to Hillsboro and Hugh attended the Hillsboro schools.

One of the leading drivers of harness horses in the country, his name appears in all the daily papers when there are Grand Circuit races. He is a veterinarian and breeder of fine race horses and began training and driving trotting horses in 1920.

In 1936 he was credited with 67 wins, only 14 of which were dashes, the others being regular races.

Dr. Parshall raced 19 head at both Grand Circuit and half-mile track meets. Jane Azoff was the leading winner, winning 10 races. McElwyn Abbe came second with 8 races, and Calumet Epson with 7.

The second division of the Parshall stable with Harry Craig in charge, won 43 races. Of these only 11 were dashes. Muscletone, developed and raced by Dr. Parshall before he was sold for export to Italy held the European trotting record for the kilometer. He won at the Crois Laroche track near Paris in 1:13 1-5, a rate of 1:57¾ for our mile. The previous European record was 1:14 3-10, held by Sam Williams, another American trotter, raced by Walter Coy before he was sold for export to France.

In 1939 Dr. Parshall had a record behind him of having won more harness races in the past 13 years than any other driver in the country. His horse, Peter Astra, won the biggest harness race in the world, the $40,000 Hambletonian.

Dr. Parshall was married to Eulah Duncan. They have three sons: Hugh Nolan (Buddy) and Melvin and Marvin, twins. The family home is at Urbana.

CAPT. HARRY LANGLEY PENCE

CAPTAIN HARRY LANGLEY PENCE, United States Navy, was born at Sardinia, Brown county, Ohio, September 23, 1882, the son of Ellis and Margaret Luella Langley Pence, natives of Hillsboro. He was married to Ruth Montgomery of Montclair, New Jersey, in the Little Church Around the Corner, New York City, January 19, 1924.

He has one daughter, Margaret Langley Pence who was born in Newport, Rhode Island, January 6, 1926.

His forbears on the Pence side helped to comprise one of the parties that formed the third settlement in the Northwest Territory, landing about 1796 in the general vicinity of what is now Manchester, Ohio.

Captain Pence was educated in the public schools of Hillsboro where he graduated from the Hillsboro High School in 1901. While in high school he participated in the formation and development of the Cadet Corps. His family moved to Columbus, Ohio in 1901 where he completed one year at Ohio State University. Then the family returned to Hillsboro to live.

During the summer of 1901 he was appointed as a Midshipman to United States Naval Academy at Annapolis, Maryland, by Senator J. B. Foraker of Ohio. He entered the Naval Academy September 24, 1902 and graduated as a Passed Midshipman in February, 1906.

From ensign in 1908 he became lieutenant (junior grade) in 1911; Lieutenant in 1911; Lieutenant Commander July 1, 1917; Temporary Commander July 1, 1918; Commander in 1921; Captain, April 1, 1931.

He received the following decorations: Navy Cross—World War; Mexican Campaign—1914; Victory Medal—World War; Nicaraguan Campaign (2nd); Commander Nichan Iftakhar (Tunisian-French).

He belongs to the following clubs: Chevy Chase, Washington D. C.; Army and Navy, Manila, P. I.; New York Yacht Club, New York City; Mason, Scottish Rite, 32, Commandery and Shrine.

JAMES GOULD POLK

JAMES GOULD POLK was born October 6, 1896, the son of William Alexander and Amy Isyphena Ockerman. He was married March 26, 1921 to Mary Smith. Their children are: Martha Jane; Helen Ruth; William Alexander; Lois May.

He graduated from Ohio State University in 1918 with a B.S. in Agriculture and from Wittenberg College in 1923 with an M.A. degree. From 1919-20 he was a teacher of science, athletic director and principal of the high school at New Vienna. From 1920-1922 he was the superintendent of the schools of New Vienna. He was engaged in farming from 1922-1923, becoming principal of the Hillsboro High School at Hillsboro from 1923-1928 after which time he retired to his farm to take up farming again. He was a member of the 72nd and 73rd Congress from the 6th Ohio District, 1931-1935.

CONGRESSMEN FROM HIGHLAND COUNTY —

NELSON BARRERE, 1850-51, 32nd Congress
JONAS R. EMRIE, 1855-56, 34th Congress
JOHN A. SMITH, 1869-70, 41st Congress
JOHN A. SMITH, 1871-72, 42nd Congress
JOSEPH J. McDOWELL, 1834-44, 28th Congress
JOSEPH J. McDOWELL, 1845-46, 29th Congress
HENRY L. DICKEY, 1877-78, 45th Congress
HENRY L. DICKEY, 1879-80, 46th Congress
ALPHONSO HART, 1883-84, 48th Congress
JACOB J. PUGSLEY, 1887-88, 50th Congress
JACOB J. PUGSLEY, 1889-90, 51st Congress

UNITED STATES SENATORS —

ALBERT J. BEVERIDGE (born on border of Adams and Highland counties, O., served from Indiana), 1889-1905, 1905-1911
JOSEPH B. FORAKER (born in Highland county), 1897-1909
WILLIAM A. TRIMBLE, 1819-21

TABLE OF POPULATION

1800	3,492 (estimated)
1810	5,766
1820	12,308
1830	16,345
1840	22,269
1850	25,781
1860	27,773
1870	29,133
1880	30,281
1890	29,048
1900	30,982
1910	28,711
1920	27,610
1930	25,416
1940	27,099
1944	25,018

The greatest gain in population was from 1810 to 1820, when the population more than doubled itself. In 1900 the peak was reached. Since then there was a steady decline until 1940. From 1940 to 1944, Highland county's decrease in population was 2,081, with an estimated population of 25,018 in February, 1944.

The population for 1800 was estimated by taking the list of free male inhabitants in the four then existing townships of New Market (143), Liberty (232), Fairfield (303), and Brushcreek (98) and multiplying the total by 4½, thus making a total of 3,492. All other populations given in table above were given according to Federal census (except 1944).

BIBLIOGRAPHY

A

Adams, John Paul, *"Milton Caniff, Rembrandt of the Comic-Strips."*
Atwater, Caleb, *"A History of the State of Ohio, National and Civil."* Glezen and Shepherd, Cincinnati, Ohio, 1838.
Autobiography and Correspondence of Allen Trimble, Governor of Ohio, with genealogy of the family. Reprinted from the *"Old Northwest"* Genealogical Society, 1909.
Auginbaugh, B.A., *"Know Ohio"* (Revised) Columbus, O., 1939.
American Home Magazine, March, 1938.
Appleton's Cyclopedia of American Biography by James Grant Wilson and John Fisk, N. Y. 1887.

B

Bancroft's Works, Vol. XXV, p. 715, *"Colorado and Wyoming."*
Banks, L. A.—Heroic Personalities.
Barrere, Granville, A Toast to Hugh Fullerton.
Bayhan, Frank.
Berry, Thomas E.
Biographical Cyclopedia of the State of Ohio.

C

Columbia University Press, *"Caspar Collins."*
Caspar Tribune Herald, Caspar, Wyoming, 1934.
Collins, Frank, Att., Hillsboro, Ohio, 40 old family scrap books.
Cherrington, H. E.—The Evolution of Prohibition in the U. S.
Capital Gallery of the Official Portraits of the Governors of Ohio—compiled by the Ohio Newspapers Artists Ass'n, 1905.
Cincinnati Gazette, 1840.

D

Amelia Newby DeVault's grandfather's diary.
Dunlap, Arthur Beardsley, *"Historical Sketch of the Greenfield Schools,"* The Dragon, Souvenir Edition, 1915.
Doggett, Henry S., *"A Sketch of the Life and Professional Services of Isaac Sams, for 50 Years a Distinguished Teacher,"* Pub. by Peter G. Thomson, Cincinnati, Ohio, 1888.
Dickens, Charles, *"American Notes."* London, 1842.
Drake, Benjamin, *"Life of Tecumseh."*
Dispatch, The, Hillsboro, Ohio, numerous articles.
Dispatch, The Columbus, Columbus, Ohio, numerous issues.
Ditty, R. M., Sketch of Highland county, 1895.
"Dictionary of American Biography" by Allen Johnson, N. Y., 1929.

E

Early Homes of Ohio by Garrett and Massie, 1936.

F

Firestone, Clark B., "*Into the Ohio Wilderness.*"
Ford, W. H.
Fullerton, Hugh.
Fehlandt, "*A Century of Drink Reform in the U. S.*"

G

Galbreath, Charles B., History of Ohio, 5 Volumes
Geological Survey of Ohio, Report of the
Geology and Palaeontology. Columbus, Ohio, Nevins and Myers, State Printers, 1874.

H

Henkle, Rev. Paul, "*Rev. Paul Henkle's Journal*" 1806, pp. 184-186 in Vol. 23 of the Ohio Archaeological and Historical Society.

Howe, Henry and Son, "*Historical Collections of Ohio, an Encyclopedia of the State,*" Vol. II and III. Publishers, Henry Howe and Son, Columbus, 1891.

Howe, Henry, "*Historical Collections of Ohio,*" publisher, Henry Howe, Cincinnati, Ohio, 1851.

Hatcher, Harlan, "*The Buckeye Country,*" H. C. Kinsey & Co., Inc., New York, 1941.

Harris, Oliver, Diary of Life in Highland County, New Market, 1798-1845.

J

Jenkins, Warren, "*The Ohio Gazetteer and Traveller's Guide, Together with an Appendix or General Register,*" pub. by Isaac N. Whiting, Columbus, 1841.

K

King, Rufus, "*Ohio; First Fruits of the Ordinance of 1787,*" Boston and New York, 1888.

M

Martzolff, "*Fifty Stories from Ohio History,*" Ohio Teacher Publishing Co., Columbus, Ohio, 1924.

Monica, Sister, O.S.U., Ph. D., "*The Cross in the Wilderness,*" St. Martin's, Ohio, 1922.

Mother Stewart, "*Memories of the Crusade.*"

N

Newberry, *"Newberry's Geological Survey,"* 1871.
News-Herald, The, Hillsboro, Ohio, numerous issues.

O

Ohio Archaeological and Historical Quarterly, Columbus, Ohio.
"Ohio Indian Trails" by Frank N. Wilcox, The Gates Press, Cleveland, 1934.
Ohio Labor Statistics, 1880.

P

Presbyterian Church, History of, Francis J. Malzard, 1940
Press-Gazette, The, Hillsboro, Ohio, numerous issues.

R

"Representative Men of Ohio, 1904-1908," by James K. Mercer, Columbus, Ohio. Fred J. Herr Press.

S

Scott, Daniel, Esq., *"A History of the Early Settlement of Highland County, Ohio,"* Publishers, The Hillsboro Gazette, Hillsboro, Ohio, 1890.
Stout, Wilbur, State Geologist, Orton Hall, Columbus, Ohio.
Shetrone, Dr. Henry C., *"The Importance of Ft. Hill Historically and as a Recreation Center,"* 1938, address; also, *"The Moundbuilder,"* New York, 1930.
Shade, William Henry Taylor Shade, *"Buckeyeland and Bohemia,"* The Lyle Printing Co., Hillsboro, Ohio, 1895.
Spring, Agnes Wright, *"Caspar Collins—The Life and Exploits of an Indian Fighter of the Sixties."*
Scudder, Horace E., *"American Commonwealths."*
Swadley, Mrs. Margaret, *"A Brief History of the Spargur Family,"* Hillsboro, 1937.

T

Trollope, Frances, *"The Domestic Manners of the Americans,"* London, 1832.
Times, The Greenfield, Greenfield, Ohio, numerous issues.
Thompson, Eliza Jane Trimble, Her Two Daughters and Frances Willard. Hillsboro Crusade and Family Records. Second Edition, Cincinnati, Ohio, Jennings and Graham, 1906.
Temperance Crusade, A Brief History of the, by G. Herbert Broomhall, Hillsboro, Ohio, 1942.
Times-Star.

Thompson, *"History of Highland County,"* (1878).
Trimble-Thompson Scrapbook, O. S. U. Museum.

U

"Uncle Bill" by Dusty Miller.

W

Williams Bros., *"History of Ross and Highland Counties, Ohio,"* Williams Bros., Published by W. W. Williams, Printer, Cleveland, Ohio, 1880.

"Who's Who in the Buckeye State," by C. S. Van Tassel, Toledo, O.

"Who's Who in America," by Albert Nelson Marquis. The A. N. Marquis Co., Chicago, 1936-1937.

INDEX

— A —

Allen, Newton—200
Allen, William—161
Allensburg—161, 162
Ambrose, Rev. William—80
Anderson, Richard C.—83
Anderson State Road—83
Antioch College—80
Appleseed, Johnny—55, 153
Auburn Methodist Church—147

— B —

Badgley, Andrew—201
Baldwin, Jesse—190
Ballentine, John J.—174, 218
Baltimore and Ohio Railroad—86
Banking, (See Oliver Newton Sams)
Barnes, Jacob—187
Barngrover, George—201
Barngruber, Adam—188
Barr—20
Barrere, George—49, 51, 85, 172, 187
Barrere, Nelson—229
Barrett, David M.—173, 190
Barrett's Mill—190, 191
Battise,—20
Battle of Belfast—20, 21
Battle of Lynchburg—18-20, 162, 163
Beecher, Norman B.—218-219
Beals, Thomas—41
Beatty, Pearson—160
Belfast—169, 170, 171
Bell, C. S.—55, 56, 86
Bell, Charles—179
Bell, Joseph—201
Bell, Virginia—56
Bell, William—179
Belpre and Cincinnati Railroad—86
Berryman, Eli—47
Berryman family—200
Berryman, Jonathan—47, 55, 187, 188
Berryman, Thomas—171
Berrysville—200
Between-the-logs, Chief—27
Beveridge, Albert Jeremiah—161, 204-205, 229
Black, John B.—143, 144
Blackburn, H. C.—182
Black Snake—20
Blair, Rev. J. G.—181
Blair, J. Wallace—170

Bloom, Christopher—52
Blount, John—175
Boone, Daniel—1, 26
Borum, Catherine—168
Boston—189, 190
Botts, Coleman—163
Bowen Distillery—163
Bowles, Quinton—174
Boyce, Robert—83, 84
Boyd, L. B.—190
Bragg, Tom—156
Bridges—164
Brouse, Frank—11
Browder, T. F.—182
Brown, Elgar—171
Brown families—147
Brown, Lancelot—169
Buck, Martin—173
Building a cabin—33
Buford—157-158
Buford, Colonel—157
Bullard, John and James—136-138
Bunn, John—161
Burk, William—76
Butler, Asa R.—199
Butler, Bess—153
Butler Cornet Band—181
Butler, Leonard—153
Butters, John and Susan—185
Byrd, Charles Willing—205-206

— C —

Caldwell, Don—174
Caley, George—50, 83, 84
Campton, John—52, 188
Caniff, Milton Arthur—219-221
Cannon, Thomas—197
Carey, Charles Newton—195
Carey, David McPherson—185
Carey families—147
Carey, Zimri—148
Careytown—195-196
Carlisle—145
Carlisle, James—55
Carlisle, Nancy—160
Carlisle, Samuel B.—55, 144
Carmel—151
Carr, Wilbur John—202, 206-207
Cartwright, Peter—75, 76, 201
Celeron—1
Centerfield—164-165
Chautauquas—178

Chinskau—20
Cincinnati and Eastern Railroad—86
Clark, George Rogers—1
Clark, Joseph—83
Clark, Samuel—176
Cochran, Elizabeth Gossett—28, 198
Clouser, Charlotte, Simon and
   Susanna—146, 147
Coffey, John—179
Coffman—163
Collins, Caspar—94-99, 173
Collins, Charles H.—207-208
Collins, O. C.—163
Collins, William O.—173
Columbus and Maysville Railroad—86
Connor, John—165
Cooke, William Bridge—6
Coombs, John M.—164
Cooper Mound—13, 14, 167
Cope, Garrett—190
Copes, Wesley—177
Corn huskings—33
Cornstalk—26, 27
Countryman, Obediah—171
Courting—35-40
Cowgill settlements—195
Cravens, Benjamin—184
Crawford, Noble—61
Crawford, Col. William—26
Crockett, Davy—85, 86
Crothers, Rev. Samuel—181
Crusade Church—79
Crusaders (See "Mother" Thompson)
Cummings, Ferris—155
Curry, James—179
Curry, Otway—181, 182

— D —

Daniels, Albert—16, 182
Danville—168, 169
Davidson, John—49, 52, 188
Davis, David—190
Davis, Edwin H.—12
Deer Park—195
DeHaas—169
Devault, Amelia Newby—138, 139
Dick, C. G.—25
Dick home, Marshall—145
Dick, Thomas—25
Dick, Thomas H.—185
Dickey, John—170
Dickey, Henry L.—229
Diehl, Park—202
Dittey, Robert M.—31, 73
Dodson, Joshua—162
Dodsonville—162
Doggett, Prof. Henry—65, 68
Donalson, Israel—26

Dowden, Otho—165
Dunlap, Dr. Alexander—180
Dunlap, Mary L.—65
Dunlap, Dr. Milton—180
Duvall, John—163
Dwyer, Kate—181

— E —

Eakins, Joseph—77, 78
Eagle Spring—51, 177
East, Isaac—152
East Danville—169
East Monroe—165
East Monroe Falls—165
Edgington, John and Asahel—41
Edmiston, Dr.—176
Edward Lee McClain
   High School—71, 72
Edwards, Charles—147
Ellicott, Benjamin—52
Ellicott brothers—67
Ellison, Andrew—26
Elmville—151, 152
Emrie, Jonas R.—229
Etowah—26, 27
Evans, Dan—188
Evans, Richard—49, 188
Eversole, Jacob—187
Eubanks, Joe—154
Eyler, Aaron—197

— F —

Fairfax—159-160
Fairfax View—159
Fairview—198, 199
Fallsville—146
Farm agencies—58
Faris, Elizabeth, David, James—196
Faris, Lillie Ann—208-209
Father Cheynol—81
Father Gacon—81
Finley, James B.—26, 76, 77,
   78, 188, 201
Finley, John—77
Finley, William—50, 83, 84
Firestone, Clark B.—17
Fitzpatrick, James—76, 201
Flax breakings—34
Folsom—200
Folsom, Frances—200, 201
Foraker, Joseph Benson—190, 209, 229
Foreman, Samuel—157
Forest Lawn—62
Forest Lawn sale—62-63
Fort Hill—14, 15, 16, 17
Fort Salem—14, 28
Franklin, Anthony—172

Fullerton, Alexander—51
Fullerton, Hugh—15, 51, 209-210

— G —

Gall, Nancy Washburn—153-155
Gardner, George B.—173
Gardner, Grace—176
Garrett, George L.—59, 69, 191
Georgetown—146
Ghost Towns—145-149
Gibson, Samuel—41
Gilland, Rev. James—202
Gigging fish—34
Gist Settlement (Darktown)—123-126
Glasscock, Noah—190
Glenn, William H.—173
Goldsberry, Rev. William—163
God's Garden—189
Gormon, John—174
Gossett, Charles—197, 221
Gossett, John—188
Grand-Girard, Emily—65, 202
Granger, Dr. Benjamin—199
Greenfield—179-183
Greenfield Seminary—65, 181
Griffith, Anna—160

— H —

Hair, Daniel—42
Harper, William—163
Harps, James A.—182
Harriett—184
Harris, Frank Raymond—221-222
Harris, George—145
Harris, Oliver—47, 48, 80
Hart, Alphonso—229
Harwood (See Pulse)
Hastings, John Sr.—197
Hawk, Ira Gossett—197
Hay, John—165
Haynes, Roy Asa—210-211
Hays, David—49, 51, 172, 187, 189
Head, Bigger—184
Head, William and Sarah—185
Henderson, Charles—162
Herrod, Capt.—21, 184
Herron, Capt. James Boyd—138-143
Hess, Anthony—197
Hetherington, James—161
Hibben, Dr. Frank C.—12
Hibben, Dr. Samuel Galloway—222-223
Hiestand, Jacob—152
Hiestand, Joseph—223-224
Highland—165-166
Highland County's French Settlement—116-122

Highland County Poultry Farm—57
Highland Institute—65
Highland Station—166
Hill, Capt. Billy—51, 172
Hillsboro—171-178
Hillsboro Academy for Boys—65, 67
Hillsboro Band—176
Hillsboro and Cincinnati Railroad—86
Hillsboro High School—72-73
Hillsboro's Mystery Child—114-116
Hiser, Dan T.—154, 155
Hiser, Marion—154, 155
Hoagland Crossing—178
Hogsett, James—51, 52
Hollow, Anthony—158
Hollowtown—158
Holmes, John—147
Honeygrant—29
Hough, Peyton—202
Hoyt, Dr. Maurice—173
Hoyt, Dr. William M.—173
Hope, Edward—194
Howard, John—166
Huggins, Burch D.—62, 63, 64
Huggins, Estelle Huntington—224-225
Huggins, John Newton—158, 159
Huggins, Judge H. M.—173
Hughes, Oliver—186
Hughey, Rev. William—163
Hulitt, John—194
Hull, John Edwin,—74, 175, 225
Hunt, Phineas—52
Hussey, Martha—54
Huston, Robert—147, 187

— I —

Irick, David—172
Irvin, Admiral—182

— J —

Jarnagin, Isaac Wesley—154
Jackson, Jacob—166
Jeans, Dr. Philip C.—225-226
Jenkins, Arthur—174
Jenny, John—164
Jones, John and Mary (Turkey Farm)—57
Jones, Greenbury—162
Johnson, Alfred—199
Johnson, William—170
Johnson, "Whitewash"—147
Jolly, David—25
Jolly, family—25
Jolly, James—25
Jolly, John—25

Jolly, Joseph—25
Jolly, William—25

— K —

Kennipe, Jackson—172
Kenton, Simon—
  18, 19, 20, 26, 41, 50, 83
Kerr, John—50, 51, 188, 189
Kilbreath—164
Kincade, Thomas—49
King Solomon—27, 162, 163
Kinzer, David—196
Knott, Francis—181
Knox, John—53

— L —

Laforges—159, 160
Leaming, Bert—183
Lee, Rev. Ignatius—56
Leesburg—166, 167, 168
Lewis, Daniel—144, 145
Lewises—159
Liggett—164
Lindsley, Robert—157
Little Miami Railroad—86
Logan, Colonel—26
Lucas, Richard—145
Lucas settlement—195
Lupton, Bathsheba—46, 167
Lutteral, Lewis—179
Lynchburg—162-163

— M —

Manary, James—83
Mancher, Zimri—200
March, Daniel P.—168
Marconet, John—158
Marietta and Cincinnati
  Railroad—86, 87
Marshall—184-186
Martin, Isaac Fenton—159
Massie, Benjamin—170
Massie, Henry—46, 47, 187
Massie, Nathaniel—41, 46, 167, 170, 179
Matthews, Rev. J. McDowell—10
Matthews, Maud Butler—153
Mershon, Timothy—46
Miller, Mrs. D. S.—159
Miller, Dusty—51, 79
Miller, Earle V.—174
Miller, William Hampton—79, 80, 186
Milligan, James—179
Moccasin Church—202
Mongor, James—161
Monocue, Chief—27

Morgan David—175
Mooney, Judge—180
Moore, Robert—190
Mount Erie—146
Mowry, Abe—201
Mother Thompson—89-93
Mullenix, Joseph—173
Murphy, Alexander—196, 197
Murphy Temperance Movement—180

— Mc —

McArthur, Duncan—27, 83, 179, 211-212
McCafferty—187
McClain, Edward Lee—182, 183, 212-213
McClain, Rev. John—181
McClure, T. H.—155
McCoppin, Ove—151
McDaniel, George—200
McDowell, Rev. Joseph—65, 229
McIntyre, Alexander—163
McKeehan, Jennie—156
McKimie, Robert—6, 126-136
McMullen, John—65
McNary, John—65
McPherson, Isaac—168
McSurely, William H.—226-227

— N —

Nace, Henry—161
Naces—159
Nevins brothers—168
New Edenborough—146
New Market—47, 49, 187-189
New Market Inn—189
New Petersburg—194-195
Norfolk and Western Railroad—86, 87
North Union—171

— O —

Oakland Female Seminary—65
O'Donoghue, Rev. John B.—181
Ohio Tavern—189
"Old Clarence"—56
"Old College Township Road"—82
"Old Mad River Road"—83
Oldaker, Isaac—199
Osborne, Lydia—197
Ottewill, Ann Quinn—62
Overman, Enoch—194

— P —

Paint Post Office—194

238

Palmyra—146
Parker Hotel—53
Parkinson, George—49, 188
Parmer, Joseph—49, 179
Parshall, Flo—154
Parshall, Dr. Hugh M.—227
Pearne, Thomas Hall—78
Pence, Harry Langley—227-228
Pennington, Abraham—190
Pike, Capt. James—173
Pike, Samuel—173
Polk, James G.—166, 228
Pope, Fred—24
Pope, Gen. J. W.—24
Pope, Mrs. Nathaniel—24
Pope, Nathaniel—23, 41, 166, 167
Pope, William—24
Powell, Robert—170
Prayer for French Travelers—74, 75
Price, Prof. Ralph W.—181
Price's Premier Band—181
Pricetown—196-197
Prospect—201
Pugh, Robert—162
Pugsley, J. J.—173, 229
Pulliam, Benjamin—159, 160
Pulse (Harwood)—197-198
Pummell, A. J.—194
Purcell, Archbishop—181

— Q —

Quinn, James—75, 76, 201

— R —

Radcliffe, Harrison—168
Rains, Aaron—190
Rains, George—190
Rainsboro—190-194
Reece, David—53, 165
Reece, James—165
Reynolds, William—155
Richards, Will—62
Ridings, John Duvall—157
Ridings, Lydia House—157, 158
Ridings, Samuel—144, 157, 158
Roads, John—147
Roads, Miss Katie—7
Roads, Philip—27, 28
Roberds, Susan—160
Roberts, Isaiah—202
Rockingham—146
Rocky Spring Church—78
Roebuck, Aaron—160
Rogers, John—144
Rogers, Col. Thomas—143
Rogers, William—83, 143

Ross, Oliver—47, 187
Ross, Rebecca—47, 187, 188
Ross, St. Clair—161
Rotroff, Jonas—161
Rouse, Edna Grey—159
Ruble, Dr. William K.—33
Russell—199

— S —

Salem Echo, The—197
Samantha—196
Sams, Isaac—66-69
Sams, Oliver Newton—154, 213
Sauer, Mack—168
Saylor, Jacob—4, 57
Schooley, Samuel—179
Scott, Samuel Parsons—213-214
Sergeant, Amos—200
Setty, Anthony—154
Seven Caves, The—5-6
Shackleton—189
Shade, William Henry Taylor—214-215
Shannon Stock Co.—178
Sharpsville—199
Shepherd, Baylis—199
Shetrone, Dr. Henry—13, 16
Sicily—158, 159
Simmons, William—184
Sinking Spring—152-157
Sinton, David—215-216
Sloan—201
Smart, Lavinia—179
Smith, Bruden—200
Smith, John A.—229
Spargur, Henry W.—190
Spargur history—191-194
Spargur Reunion—193-194
Strasburg—158
Stroup, Michael—49, 50, 83-84
Stultz, P. P.—154
Sugargrant—29
Sugar Tree Ridge—160-161
Sunlight Farm—57
Swadley, Mrs. Margaret Spargur—191
Sypherd, Matthew—185

— T —

Taylorsville—202
Tecumseh—20, 23, 162
Terrell, David—166
Timberlake, John—146
Thompson, James Henry—89
Thompson, Mrs. James H. (See Mother Thompson)
Thornton, Abner—194
Traction line—87

Trautman, Milton B.—9
Travelers' Rest, Greenfield—61, 180
Trimble, Allen—41, 53, 55, 89, 146, 216-217
Trimble, Capt. James—41, 146, 172
Trimble, William A.—172, 229
Tumbleson, Moses—145
Turley, Frank—156
Tuttle, Mary McArthur Thompson—217

— U —

Underwood, James—147
Underground Railroad Stations—143-145
Uniontown (See North Union)

— V —

Vance, Minnie—85
VanPelt, Jonathan—144, 198, 199

— W —

Wade—41
Walker—159
Walker, Polly—50, 188
Walters, Rev. Isaac Newton—80
Walters, John—166, 167
Washburn, Joe—154
Washburn, Sanford—154
Washburn, Thomas—154
Washington, George—47, 153
Watts, Joseph M.—30
Watts, Louise Dunlap (Mrs. E. B.)—79, 180, 181

Watts, Olive (Mrs. Joseph M.)—154
Watts, T. M.—151
Waw-wil-a-way, Chief—21, 22, 23, 24, 164, 184-185
Weaver, Jonathan—169
Weaver, Peter—194
Weber—163
Webertown—163, 164
Webster, Daniel—12
Webster, Dan—160
Webster, Aunt Susanna—160
Welty, Abraham—196
West, Enos—200
Whiskey Road—84, 85
Wilcox, Zeno—203-204
Wilcoxon, John—42-46, 199
Wilkin, Rachel—161
Willett, John—199
Willettsville—199, 200
Williams "Charley"—160
Williams, Henry G.—184
Williams, Joseph—41
Wilson, John T.—159, 160, 170, 171
Wilson, John—78
Wilson, William—78
Winkle (See East Danville)
Winkle families—169
Wishart, William—187, 188
Witching water—203
Wood, John—99-114
Woodmansie, Isaac—147
Wool picking—34, 35
Wright, Job—54, 179, 182
Wright, John—180

— Z —

Zane Trace—83
Zink, David—145

www.ingramcontent.com/pod-product-compliance
Lightning Source LLC
Chambersburg PA
CBHW030319100526
44592CB00010B/497